The
First Crusade

Origins and impact

edited by
Jonathan Phillips

D1332696

Manchester University Press
Manchester and New York
distributed exclusively in the USA by St. Martin's Press

Published by Manchester University Press
Oxford Road, Manchester M13 9NR, UK
and Room 400, 175 Fifth Avenue, New York, NY 10010, USA

Distributed exclusively in the USA by
St. Martin's Press, Inc., 175 Fifth Avenue, New York,
NY 10010, USA

Distributed exclusively in Canada by
UBC Press, University of British Columbia, 6344 Memorial Road,
Vancouver, BC, Canada V6T 1Z2

British Library Cataloguing-in-Publication Data
A catalogue record for this book is available from the British Library

Library of Congress Cataloging-in-Publication Data
The first crusade : origins and impact / edited by Jonathan Phillips.
         p.   cm.
    Based on papers presented at the London Centre for the Study of
the Crusades conference "Deus Vult: The Origins and Impact of the
First Crusade", held at the Institute of Historical Research,
London, 11-25-1995.
    Includes bibliographical references and index.
    ISBN 0-7190-4985-7 (cloth).—ISBN 0-7190-5174-6 (pbk.)
    1. Crusades—First, 1096–1099—Congress.   I. Phillips, Jonathan
(Jonathan P.).
D161.2.F54   1997
956'.014—dc21   96-52877

ISBN 0 7190 4985 7 *hardback*
     0 7190 5174 6 *paperback*

First published 1997

01 00 99 98 97   10 9 8 7 6 5 4 3 2 1

Typeset in Great Britain by
Northern Phototypesetting Co. Ltd, Bolton

Printed in Great Britain
by Bell & Bain Ltd, Glasgow

Contents

Acknowledgements

The essays collected here are based upon papers presented at the London Centre for the Study of the Crusades conference, 'Deus Vult: The Origins and Impact of the First Crusade', held at the Institute of Historical Research, London, on 25 November 1995. The conference was only possible through the generous support of the Royal Historical Society, Oxford University Press, Cambridge University Press and the History Department, Royal Holloway University of London. I am pleased to acknowledge the invaluable advice and assistance of Rosemary Bailey, Bridget Taylor, Robert Lyons, Ian Quelch and Suzanne and Martin Phillips. Dr Peter Edbury (Cardiff), Rev. John Cowdrey (Oxford), Dr Peter Jackson (Keele), and Professor James Ryan (City University of New York) kindly chaired the sessions on the day. A grant from the Miss Isabel Thornley Bequest to the University of London helped in the publication of this volume. I would also like to thank Richard Rowley for compiling the index and Richard Purslow, Vanessa Graham and Carolyn Hand of Manchester University Press for their patience and professionalism in bringing this project to fruition.

List of contributors

Dr Thomas Asbridge is an Associate Lecturer in History at Royal Holloway University of London.

Dr Marcus Bull is Lecturer in Medieval History at the University of Bristol.

Dr Susan Edgington is Senior Lecturer in History at Huntingdonshire Regional College.

Dr John France is Senior Lecturer in History at the University of Swansea, Wales.

Dr Carole Hillenbrand is Reader in Arabic and Islamic Studies at the University of Edinburgh.

Professor Colin Morris is Emeritus Professor of Medieval History at the University of Southampton.

Dr Alan Murray is Editor of the International Medieval Bibliography, University of Leeds.

Dr Jonathan Phillips is Lecturer in Medieval History at Royal Holloway University of London.

Professor Jonathan Riley-Smith is Dixie Professor of Ecclesiastical History at the University of Cambridge.

Dr Jonathan Shepard is Lecturer in Russian History at the University of Cambridge.

William G. Zajac is an Associate Lecturer in History at the University of Wales, Swansea.

List of abbreviations

AA	Albert of Aachen. 'Historia Hierosolymi-tana', *RHC Oc*. IV – all references to this work are by book and chapter in order to facilitate the use of the forthcoming edition by Dr Susan Edgington
Anna Comnena	*Alexiad*, ed. and trans. B. Leib, 3 vols (Paris, Société d'édition les belles lettres, 1937–45)
BB	Baldric of Bourgueil, 'Historia Jerosolim-itana', *RHC Oc*. IV
EA	Ekkehard of Aura, 'Hierosolymita', *RHC Oc*. V
EHR	*English Historical Review*
FC	Fulcher of Chartres, *Historia Hierosoly-mitana (1095–1127)*, ed. H. Hagenmayer (Heidelberg, Carl Winters Universtäts-buchhandlung, 1913)
France, *Victory*	J. France, *Victory in the East: A Military History of the First Crusade* (Cambridge, Cambridge University Press, 1994)
GF	*Gesta Francorum et aliorum Hierosoli-mitanorum*, ed. and trans. R.M.T. Hill (Oxford, Clarendon Press, 1962)
GN	Guibert of Nogent, 'Gesta Dei per Fran-cos', *RHC Oc*. IV
Hagenmeyer, *Epistulae*	*Epistulae et chartae ad historiam primi*

	belli sacri spectantes quae supersunt aevo aequales ac genvinae, ed. H. Hagenmayer (Innsbruck, Verlag der Wagner'schen Universitätsbuchhandlung, 1901)
IQ	Ibn al-Qalanisi, *The Damascus Chronicles of the Crusades*, ed. and trans. H.A.R. Gibb (London, Luzac and Co., 1932)
JEH	*Journal of Ecclesiastical History*
JMH	*Journal of Medieval History*
Michael the Syrian	*Chronique de Michel le Syrien, patriarche jacobite d'Antioche (1166–99)*, ed. and trans. J.B. Chabot, 4 vols (Paris, Ernest Leroux, 1899–1924) – all references to volume III
MGHSS	*Monumenta Germaniae Historica, Scriptores*, ed. G.H. Pertz et al., 32 vols (Hannover, Weimar, Stuttgart and Cologne, 1826–1934)
OV	Orderic Vitalis, *The Ecclesiastical History*, ed. and trans. M. Chibnall, 6 vols (Oxford, Clarendon Press, 1969–80)
PL	*Patrologia cursus completus. Series Latina*, publ. J.P. Migne. 217 vols and 4 vols of indexes (Paris, 1844–64)
PT	Peter Tudebode, *Historia de Hierosolymitano itinere*, eds J.H. and L.L. Hill (Paris, Librairie Orientaliste Paul Geuthner, 1977)
RA	Raymond of Aguilers, *Liber*, eds J.H. and L.L. Hill (Paris, Librairie Orientaliste Paul Geuthner, 1969)
RC	Ralph of Caen, 'Gesta Tancredi', *RHC Oc.* III
REB	*Revue des Etudes Byzantines*
RHC Arm.	*Recueil des historiens des croisades: Documents arméniens*, 2 vols (Paris, Imprimerie Nationale, 1869–1906)
RHC Oc.	*Recueil des historiens des croisades: Histo-*

	riens occidentaux. 5 vols (Paris, Imprimerie Nationale, 1844–95)
RHC Or.	*Recueil des historiens des croisades: Historiens orientaux*. 5 vols (Paris, Imprimerie Nationale, 1872–1906)
RM	Robert the Monk, 'Historia Iherosolimitana', *RHC Oc*. III
RS	Rolls Series: *Rerum Britannicarum Medii Aevi Scriptores* (London, HMSO, 1858–96)
Runciman	*A History of the Crusades*, 3 vols (Cambridge, Cambridge University Press, 1951–4)
Sewter, *Alexiad*	Anna Comnena, *Alexiad*, trans. E.R.A. Sewter (Harmondsworth, Penguin, 1969)
TRHS	*Transactions of the Royal Historical Society*
WT	William of Tyre, *Chronicon*, ed. R.B.C. Huygens, Corpus Christianorum, Continuatio Mediaevalis, 63/63A, 2 vols [Continuous pagination] (Turnhout, Belgium, Brepols, 1986)

List of maps

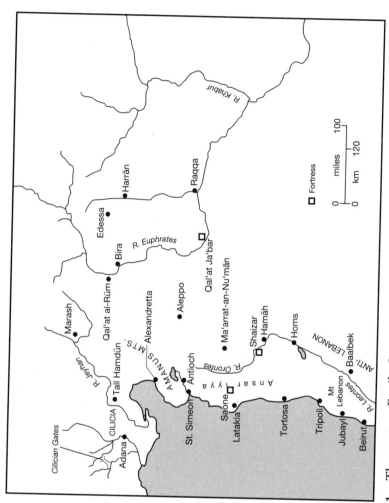

1   The western Fertile Crescent (northern half)

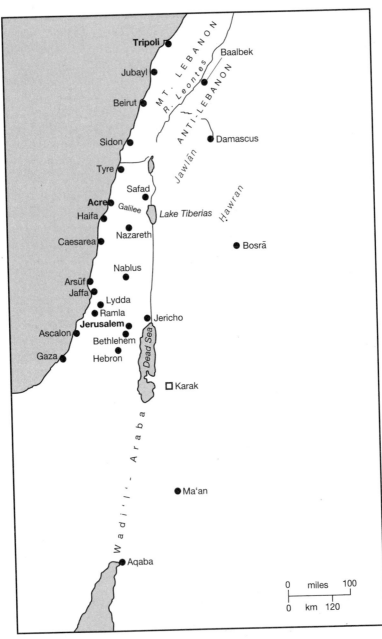

Tripoli

Jubayl

Baalbek

M T . L E B A N O N

R. Leontes

Beirut

A N T I - L E B A N O N

Sidon

Damascus

Jawlān

Tyre

Safad

Acre

Galilee

Lake Tiberias

Ḥawrān

Haifa

Nazareth

Caesarea

Bosrā

Nablus

Arsūf

Jaffa

Lydda

Ramla

Jerusalem

Jericho

Dead Sea

Ascalon

Bethlehem

Gaza

Hebron

Karak

Ma'an

W a d i   ' l -   A r a b a

Aqaba

0   miles   100

0   km   120

2   The western Fertile Crescent (southern half)

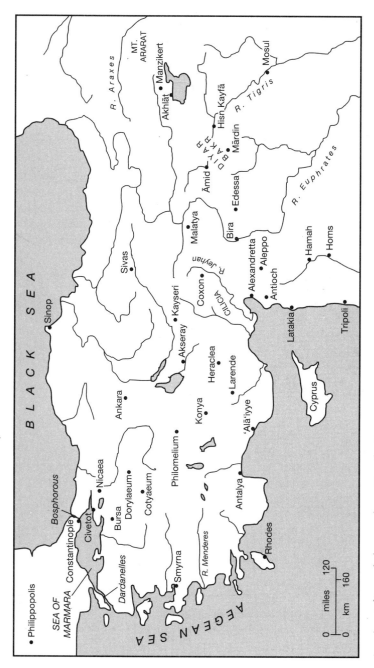

3 Anatolia and the northern Fertile Crescent

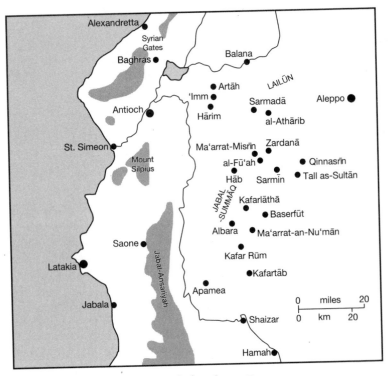

4 Northern Syria and the Jabal as-Summāq

Introduction

Jonathan Riley-Smith

When on 27 November 1095 Pope Urban II called on Christians to fight a penitential war-pilgrimage to recover the Holy Sepulchre, he cannot have known that he was initiating a movement which was to last for seven centuries and was to involve millions of men and women in many theatres of war, as fighters or opponents or victims, and millions of others, who were to pay taxes in support or attend services of intercession or suffer in the absence of fathers, husbands or children. Crusading used to be regarded as something peripheral to the mainstream of history, but there is now a growing realisation that it was of central importance to nearly every country in Europe and the Near East until the Reformation and that it played a significant role in the relations between the Catholic West and the Ottoman empire thereafter.

And it has a bearing on modern politics. What chain of ideas, hatreds and obsessions links the First Holocaust – the pogrom against Jewish communities which was the opening act of the First Crusade – and the 'Final Solution'? What part did the crusades against Greeks and Russians play in the formation of modern Orthodox hostility to Catholicism? Acts of violence have been perpetrated by Christians and Muslims in the Lebanon, Bosnia and parts of the former Soviet Union. There is talk of the re-emergence of holy war and of the lasting effects of the crusades on relations between Christians and Muslims, even if the demonising of the crusaders by Muslims has much more to do with nationalist reactions to the West since the late nineteenth century. Professional historians, therefore, can do the modern world a service by taking a long hard look at the movement and the revival of crusades studies in recent years may well be a response to contemporary imperatives.

The strength of the subject in Britain – and the youthfulness of so many of those involved in it – is demonstrated in these essays. The contributions of Thomas Asbridge – on the importance of geography to the struggles between the crusade leaders – and of William Zajac – on the conventions of engagement that were applicable even in the confusion that prevailed in Syria – reveal how much work still needs to be done on the details of the campaign, but the chief message of this collection is that, although we may have thought we knew what the crusade was about, our knowledge is based on such deficient and inadequate source material that we should pause and think again.

Of the nine essays published here no fewer than six deal directly or indirectly with sources. They make two main points. The first is that we should re-examine some of the better known narrative accounts, which have been the staple of historical writing on the First Crusade. Four of the longer ones are known to have been written by men who took part, but there has been a century's debate about the trustworthiness of a fifth, the *History* of Albert of Aachen. Albert was definitely not a participant, but his narrative is full of circumstantial detail; and Susan Edgington, who is editing it and considers it in her chapter, seems to be close to resolving the discussion in his favour. If she is successful it is likely that Albert's account will join the canon and this will have a knock-on effect on other issues such as the significance of the role of Peter the Hermit in the crusade's origins, a subject to which Colin Morris returns. On the other hand, the strange and late family history of the lords of Herrenzimmern has had far more weight attached to it than it can bear and Alan Murray demonstrates why it should not be used at all.

The second, and potentially even more important, point is that historians have never used all the material to which they could have had access. Nearly all of them have been trained in European history, cannot read Arabic and rely on translations. No Western historian, as far as I can tell, has used the major narrative of Ibn Wāsil when writing about the Fifth Crusade, but Carole Hillenbrand points out that there is also much more in Arabic about the First – in histories, poetry and geography – than has usually been supposed. And Jonathan Shepard shows how the Greek material can be supplemented with references in a corpus of Latin *testimonia minora*, in which can be found evidence for the experiences of westerners in Constantinople and the rest of the Byzantine empire.

Most striking of all is the general ignorance of the documents which can be found in the cartularies of Western religious communities and cathedrals. Many of the charters have been available in print for a century, but they were hardly looked at until Giles Constable drew attention to them. They contain, as Marcus Bull explains, a lot of information about the ideas, decisions and actions of departing and returning crusaders, and even about their experiences on campaign. Few people have even an approximate understanding of the amount of material which needs to be sifted. Some years ago I estimated that there were over 1,500 cartularies or collections of documents relating to eleventh- and early twelfth-century Europe *in print*. Some are fragmentary and for various reasons many contain no references to crusaders at all. But after reading about half of them systematically – I have worked through most of the French and English ones, but have seen only a fraction of those relating to Spain, Italy and Germany – I have some idea of the treasures they contain: even at this stage I know the names of at least 200 first crusaders who do not appear at all in the narrative accounts. No one has yet embarked on the odyssey involved in navigating through all the unpublished material.

The conclusion that has to be drawn from this is inescapable. Since no one has yet looked at all the material for the First Crusade – we do not even know yet know much there is – nothing written so far on the subject can be said to have more than a partial value. We are faced by the paradox that, although the study of crusading is in a particularly exciting phase, in which it has been expanded in space – to encompass theatres of war in Europe as well as in the East – and in time – with fields of study in the sixteenth, seventeenth and even eighteenth centuries opening up – here, right at the start of the movement, an enterprise which has attracted more attention, literary and historical, than anything comparable in the Middle Ages, still needs almost the same intensive treatment as, let us say, the history of the later military orders or the crusading background to the holy leagues of the sixteenth and seventeenth centuries.

It is obviously essential that all the material should become available as soon as possible. A useful start would be the publication of a calendar of the crusaders' charters, which would provide a guide to the evidence for recruitment, for preparations – the raising of cash, the purchase of equipment and animals, the arrangements for the management of estates, the endowments for prayer – and for the settlement of affairs, including the repayment of debts, on return. Studies of the development of ideas of Christian violence would also benefit from a calendar of charters. It is astonishing that the concept of penitential war – unprecedented in Christian thought – came to be preached at all, but until recently the subject was being approached only through the writings of men from the upper echelons of the clergy, whereas just as important as the motives of Pope Urban II and his advisers were those of the men (and women) who answered his call and whose voices can be heard in the preambles to their charters.

The 'new' material, and indeed the old, must be evaluated in the light of all the research undertaken in the last thirty years on the religious, political, social and economic background in western Europe, which has revised the view historians used to have of the context in which the First Crusade was preached and organised. Since the charter material has a particular bearing on motivation, a topic to which John France draws attention in his paper, there should follow a series of regional studies along the lines of Marcus Bull's recent book (*Knightly Piety and the Lay Response to the First Crusade*, Oxford, 1993), because only in that way will variations in response and the reasons for it come to light. The study of motivation is of particular importance, because from the moment the First Crusade was preached nine centuries ago nothing seems to have divided commentators – and the wider public – more than the reasons for recruitment to it. Were men taking the cross for materialistic or ideological reasons, or were they driven by some lemming-like hysteria? Can one generalise about their motives at all?

As in many historical debates sides are often taken more because individual historians have gut reactions to the issues involved than because they have read all the material – patently they have not in this case – or have taken serious account of the contemporary context in which men and women were making their decisions. Some arguments can never be resolved because the evidence is exiguous – one thinks of those over the baptism of Clovis or the coronation of Charlemagne – but where plentiful evidence does exist it is never justifiable to take up positions in advance of reading it.

The message of this book is surely that there are many more sources for us to digest and that we should concentrate on immersing ourselves in them before we allow ourselves to engage too strongly on one side or the other of the debate.

Jonathan Riley-Smith

1

Patronage and the appeal of the First Crusade

John France

The central mystery of the First Crusade has always been why so many people responded to Pope Urban II's appeal for an expedition to the East, launched at Clermont in 1095. Later crusades could draw on an established idea and the notion of a common obligation to maintain and protect distant outposts in a hostile land. Family connections and traditions became established. Once the 'crusading idea' had firmly taken root it created its own piety which could, in the manner of many earlier cults, be spread from family to family by marriage. The very notion of chivalry was shaped by the need to succour the Christians of the East. But it is peculiarly difficult to explain the attraction of the First Crusade because in 1095 there was none of what we may call this crusading infrastructure. Pope Urban introduced, or at least popularised and gave force to, a new idea – salvation by a sustained act of violence. This was a notion so unprecedented that even participants had doubts about it – they performed penance frequently, as if uneasy at entrusting their immortal souls to such a novel exercise. The crusade delivered an astonishing success, the liberation of Jerusalem, and the monastic historians of the early twelfth century had to find a place for this new piety in Christian thought. It is even possible that some French nobles consciously opposed it and preferred the older notion of holy war which was not so clearly governed by ecclesiastical authority.[1] This chapter is concerned with the social context in which men and women responded to Urban's appeal, negatively or positively, and suggests, first, that we have made too little of the social context in which people made decisions about Urban's appeal, partly because of the preconceptions of influential modern writers; second, that the social context suggests quite considerable limitations on what we can know, while at the same time casting some new light on decisions; and, third, that we need to see ideology as being only one of many factors in the decision to go or not to go.

In what numbers people responded to Pope Urban's appeal is itself a matter of debate, but I believe firmly that something like 60,000, including 6–7,000 knights, gathered at Nicaea in Asia Minor in June 1097. Therefore, allowing for the slaughter of the so-called People's Crusade, losses along the way through Italy and eastern Europe, and desertions, something approaching 100,000 people must have stirred from their homes.[2] It is worth noting that the figure of 100,000 can be measured against a total population for France, Italy, Germany and England, the main contributing areas, of about twenty millions. The total modern population of these areas is of the order of 264 millions, so an equivalent movement nowadays would involve participation in the order of 1,320,000 persons.[3] In the early 1980s there were occasions when the Peace Movement mobilised 500,000 in a single day across the face of Europe and such manifestations dominated our news. Any parallel can be objected to, and of course eleventh-century society had no mass media, but I doubt whether many people in these parts of western Europe in 1096–7 would have been unaware that something was going on, though participation was not evenly spread. It is often said that England was barely touched, but William Rufus's tax of four shillings on the hide to raise the 10,000-mark mortgage needed by his brother, Duke Robert of Normandy, for the crusade must have affected almost everyone in the kingdom. Moreover the two substantial English fleets which journeyed to the East represented a huge investment which must have involved whole communities along the south coast – the sheer ramifications of naval organisations have, I think, been underestimated. Elsewhere outside the supposed crusading mainstream it is striking that Saxony made some contribution.[4] Chroniclers of the early twelfth century were undoubtedly anxious to stress the variety of peoples taking part in the crusade in order to emphasise its common 'ownership' by all of Christian Europe; but this was a huge movement which seems to have impressed itself on contemporaries even before the capture of Jerusalem – though it is interesting that a writer as eminent and prolific as Herbert Losinga, bishop of Norwich (1091–1119), never mentions it in his surviving works.[5]

The numbers who travelled to the Levant were indeed large by contemporary standards, but nothing of the scale suggested by Anna Comnena's 'whole of the West and all the barbarians'. Moreover Anna introduced into the discussion of motives a very simple dichotomy which, along with other factors, has had a very powerful influence on all our discussions of crusader motivation. This is a quotation from an A-level candidate discussing the reasons why people went on the First Crusade: 'the rich, the knights *[sic]*, went to get richer, while the poor wanted to save their souls'. What is this but a reflection of Comnena's highly charged and politically motivated distinction? In her words: 'The simpler folk [were] ... led on by a desire to worship at Our Lord's tomb ... but the more villainous characters ... had an ulterior purpose ... To seize the capital [Constantinople] itself'.[6] But this dichotomy is far from confined to A-level candidates. It actually underlies much scholarly discussion about crusader motivation. In part this is because Anna makes so much of it, and Steven Runciman's generally pro-Byzantine attitude amplied it. But more generally this chimes in with other modern conceptions. The separateness of the poor – in Marxist dialectic, their alienation from political structures – is an idea that pervades the writings of, for example, Georges Duby, who, in his *The Three Orders: Feudal Society Imagined*, makes the clearest distinction possible between the 'toiling classes' or 'popular rabble' and the rest of society. One of the most influential books on medieval history in the English language is Norman Cohn's *Pursuit of the Millennium* where the 'Crusade of the Poor' (and that notion needs to be dealt with) is sharply distinguished from that of the knights, is alone guilty of persecuting the Jews (palpably incorrect) and develops its own organisation and structure. This last point refers to the so-called *Tafurs* whom Cohn characterises as an association of poor, although such sources as there are suggest that their 'king' was a knight. It may be added that rather a lot has been made of these people on the basis of very little firm evidence.[7] The analysis of the motives of the first crusaders based on the notion of a simple stratified society has been peculiarly unhelpful, because in most of the countries of the West vertical ties of patronage were at least as important and probably had more bearing on individual decisions about Urban's appeal.

For it was the nature of contemporary society that almost every important man and woman lived in the *mouvance*, the patronage, of another. Only those the crusader sources refer to as 'princes' stood above the *mouvances*, and had different constraints upon their actions. The power of these princes even in the very difficult and novel circumstances of the crusade was remarkable – the various armies which gathered around them were not perfectly stable, but then no medieval army was. Godfrey of Bouillon's army has been investigated in some depth by Alan Murray, revealing an inner core of close associates to which substantial numbers from other areas were added at various times; and there is evidence, which is at least suggestive, that this fluidity was characteristic of the other armies of the First Crusade which formed and reformed about the princes.[8] The positive and powerful influence such princes wielded even in the conditions of the crusade emphasises that, for those who received the call for the crusade and were moved to consider taking the cross, the attitude of a head of *mouvance* must have been critical. The power of monastic houses to influence the ideas and attitudes of noble families has recently been closely studied in the south-west of France by Marcus Bull whose important book will, I suspect, lead the way to many other regional surveys. His work points to the interaction between the religious community on the one hand and, on the other, family ideas and policy in the aristocratic lay community within its sphere of influence.

George Beech has recently pointed out that no participants in the First Crusade came from amongst the *mouvance* of William, abbot of Saint-Florent de Saumur, who appears to have been on bad terms with Urban II at the time of his visit to the Loire after the Council of Clermont. It should be noted that Saint-Florent was a monastic lordship, but, as I have suggested elsewhere, the links between monks and leading laymen were not merely, or even necessarily mainly, religious.[9] It is a mark of the limitations of our knowledge that the material just now considered is drawn from ecclesiastical sources which may provide a special view of the operations of patronage. Moreover, we need to remember the prevalence of multiple homage in eleventh-century society, and the lack of rules to govern its operation. Any given landed knight of Saint-Florent may also have been the vassal of somebody else far more friendly to Urban's appeal, perhaps another monastic house, or perhaps a layman. The complexity of patronage ties and the prevalence, at least in France, of multiple homage at the time of the First Crusade is very notable and these complicated influences have to be weighed against others. For example, the kinship ties which bound Peter of

Dampierre and Rainald of Toul to Godfrey of Bouillon may have outweighed their obligations to Theoderic, bishop of Verdun, and influenced their decision to join the crusade.[10] The complicated ramifications of patronage structures in medieval society and the lack of clear evidence should warn us about the limitations of what we can know of the reasons for any individual's decision to join the crusade. But what we are able to say is that very few of those who owned land, or their dependants, could have ignored ties of patronage. All too often there is little evidence which bears upon such matters. Furthermore, where evidence exists it is sometimes misleading. Cartularies have about them an apparent and appealing simplicity as objective administrative records of the organisation which produced them. Recent work suggests that the Cluniac scribes of the later eleventh century who produced their famous cartulary were engaged in a multi-faceted literary construction designed to create as well as to record history – to the extent that one authority has not hesitated to speak of the 'confection' of the cartularies.[11]

If we try to look at those to whom the appeal of 1095 was addressed, in their social context, we can see that for most the decision to go or or not to go must have been a complex one. That Urban's message created an ideological pressure is undoubted, but the general behaviour of the landowning classes shows precisely what we would expect – that ideology influenced behaviour only spasmodically. Hence the long gestation of land disputes revealed in the cartularies, and the notable tendency for settlements with the Church to occur at moments of crisis – William Rufus's acceptance of Anselm as archbishop of Canterbury when severely ill is a case in point. Urban's appeal at Clermont and subsequent journey through France in 1095–6 provoked just such a crisis for those in any way receptive to his message. For Urban's appeal had enormous force: he offered an escape from the burden of sin by a single penitential act of violence. Neither he nor his contemporaries could have foreseen that this would create a crusading movement – his message must have appeared to open a narrow and once-only escape from the burden of sin and the fear of hell. Even so, some very notable people refused to respond. Fulk IV Le Réchin, count of Anjou, seems by his own account to have been the subject of intense pressure, while we can suppose that Duke William IX of Aquitaine was treated in a similar manner.[12] Presumably Fulk wanted to consolidate his precarious political situation, while the departure on crusade of Raymond of St Gilles, count of Toulouse, could well have opened up opportunities for William.

At a slightly less exalted level, a particularly interesting case is the house of Roucy. In terms of our picture of the perfect crusader, it would be interesting to know why apparently no leading member of this notable family joined the First Crusade. They had a strong tradition of participation in Holy War: Hilduin of Roucy died at Barbastro in 1063 and his son Ebles fought in Spain at the behest of Pope Gregory VII and later in Italy against Robert Guiscard. Their support for the papacy was remarkable: after 1073 Ebles was the leading secular champion of the reform movement and Gregory VII in the complex struggles over the see of Rheims to which his family contributed no less than three archbishops in the course of the eleventh century. The family were great patrons of the new monasticism, supporting the abbey of Marmoutiers and later the Cistercians of Valroy. Ebles married a daughter of Robert Guiscard and his sister was the queen of King Sancho I Ramirez of Aragon. The family were related to Count Stephen of Blois, who did join the First Crusade, and Count Hugh of Champagne, later famous in the Levant.[13] It is certainly possible to speculate why the Roucy apparently did not join the crusade – and one has to say apparently, for our documentation is incomplete even for a notable family as important as this. When we consider who did not go, we can only be reminded of the complexities which must have lain behind the decisions of those who went.

For, in facing the decision whether to respond to Urban's appeal or not, or to allow a family member to respond, no responsible person – and we are here speaking of any landholder with family obligations – would wish to anger his head or heads of *mouvance*. Much would depend on how much pressure was brought in favour of taking the cross – and that seems to have been most frequent and intense in areas visited by Urban II. But the landowning family was anchored in its locality, or rather its localities, and had to live with its masters and neighbours. Princes and magnates, the leaders of society, ruled scattered lands, each of which formed the focus for a local *mouvance*, families who were relied upon to provide, for example, manpower for defence, especially the garrisoning of castles or the exercise of political clout; any kind of defection from this structure would have to be carefully calculated. Many have commented on the small sizes of medieval armies and the nature of their warfare, characterised by ravaging and skirmishes. But there was a clear relationship between this and the fragmented pattern of land tenure. As a result even a powerful prince might only maintain his pre-eminence in a particular zone by a hair's breadth. Moreover, if there is one factor which the charters of the late eleventh century shriek out to us, it is the need of the landed family to preserve its domain – and the interdependence of all its members in that enterprise. Many modern historians have been addicted to the footloose younger son, but he too was caught in this web of obligation and was by no means free to make his own decision, certainly not one that would involve the provision of arms and armour, food, money, at least two horses and a servant. Through those simple necessities he was forced into the calculations of his head of household with all their ramifications. And our sources were not written by the people we are interested in – they speak of them but not through them, so all too often we make the mistake of seeing the 'knights' in rather simple terms as landowners, people charged with a particular social status, and this too is erroneous. Furthermore the sources contain one massive distortion: they speak by and large of those who were landed, people such as Duby's noble knights of the Mâconnais, to the exclusion of others.

The knights were not a class – the very word, with its Marxist overtones, is unhelpful – and the word *milites* does not designate status, rather it refers to function. In a military context the opposition *milites et pedites* is a commonplace often noted.[14] But *milites* in the literary sources can often mean no more than cavalry and some writers, notably Albert of Aachen, prefer other terms, such as *eques/equites*. Even the term *caballarius* goes on through the eleventh century into the twelfth while in the East Frankish lands free knights, *milites*, were much less common and the term *ministeriales* is preferred for those who were definitely unfree. When we speak of *milites* we are referring to a large and highly disparate group. Many of them were landowners, sometimes substantial, as for example in the area of Mâcon where their noble origins have been stressed. A lively debate in English academic circles has revealed enormous differences of status amongst those who were called knights.[15]

It is quite evident that there were enormous numbers of horsed military men, often describing themselves as *milites*, who were not landed or only nominally so. In Spain *caballeros villanos* subsisted with *caballaros hidalgos* and in France there are references to *milites ignobiles*. These last could often be classified with the *ministeriales*, petty officers of the seigneural household and demesne. Lambert, a *prévot* of the count of Champagne at the end of the eleventh century, is described in a charter as a knight, but he may originally have been a merchant (a title which I suspect might be better rendered procurator or agent). The insistence of Anglo-Saxon law at this time that a merchant who made three voyages abroad should take on the status of thegn is well-known.[16] On the First Crusade, Albert of Aachen refers to Peter the Hermit's captain of infantry, Godfrey Burel, and portrays him as the equal in council of men who were knights, though it is possible, as Matthew Bennett has remarked, that he lacked proper armour. In 1103 King Baldwin I of Jerusalem employed Reinoldus, a *miles regis* as *magister sagittariorum*.[17] The only thing a count or the lord of a castle had in common with such people was military function and, to a degree at least, probably equipment. But even here there were differences: our main sources for the armour and equipment of knights at the end of the eleventh and beginning of the twelfth centuries are artistic representations and they appear to show considerable variations in armour which presumably reflect wealth and status.

How can we understand the term *miles*? A modern parallel would be the title of Manager – for what does the General Manager of ICI have in common with the manager of a subdepartment of a food store? Only the function of spending time organising the work of others, but so different is the scale and substance of what they do that it would be a nonsense to suggest that they belonged to a 'class'. No wonder our top managers spend so much time inventing distinctive titles for themselves – Director is the obvious one. Yet so did eleventh-century nobles who often used the title of *miles* but qualified it by such epithets as *noblissimus* or *optimus*, or even harked back to terms like *procer*.[18] This underlines the point that we need to be very careful indeed about ascribing motives and ideas to 'knightly persons' on the basis of what we suppose about their social status. Amongst those whom we rather casually call knights there were enormous differences. These become more apparent as our sources improve. By the end of the twelfth century the mounted sergeant is an established figure and in the thirteenth the knight banneret emerges – both clearly a rather inferior kind of cavalryman compared to the knight. By about the same time, distinctions are evident even amongst the infantry, especially between those mounted and those not. Now it is not suggested that all these distinctions existed at the time of the First Crusade but parallel distinctions were then probably pretty apparent; and I would repeat that, in the art of the period, it is very difficult to trace the development of military equipment and that inequalities of wealth probably go some way to explaining this. 'Knight' is not a clear status designation in the age of the First Crusade and we should not imagine that those who are so referred to in the sources for that expedition were all like those at the battle of Bouvines in the early thirteenth century who jeered when confronted by mere mounted sergeants.

It is clear that the knightly milieu was one of quite extraordinary fluidity. At the lowest level, the *milites* jostle with superior peasants who have become the servants of the seigneurie, competing with them for jobs and seeking to raise their own aspirations.[19] At the highest level, men of considerable status and entire *mouvances* of their own use the description, though usually in a context which allows a general estimate of their standing. The term *miles* was a convenience, and its application to men of the highest status made it highly desirable in a milieu which was characterised by social mobility. William of Jumièges tells the story of a smith of Beauvais whose sons became 'knights' of Duke William of Normandy. Orderic Vitalis underlines their greed and brutality, and by implication their limited background, when he tells us of a young man who, once made a knight, went out and robbed a monk – a story with numerous parallels.[20] In his masterly analysis of the Capetian charters of the eleventh century, Jean-François Lemarignier remarked upon the humbleness of the testors as evidence of the declining importance of the royal dynasty, but this could be interpreted differently – as evidence of the kings being in touch with new and developing forces in a realm where social mobility was powerful.[21] Even in the early eleventh century writers had bemoaned the new fluidity of society and the ambition which inspired men, appealing to the notion of the 'Three Orders' as a defensive concept which would justify keeping people in general, and not merely the poor, in their appointed places. It is interesting that when Glaber, writing in the 1020s, believed the invading Normans of the ninth century had been led by an apostate Frank, he was at pains to stress that the man 'rejected the station of his poor parents'.[22] Most of us are familiar with the Church as a milieu for social mobility, but this was true also

of secular service and specifically military service – the story of
William Marshal is a very well known example from a later age, but
the mercenary captains of King Stephen and the members of the
militarised household of Henry I are earlier examples of the same
phenomenon which bring us back to the very beginning of the crusading age. The second half of the eleventh century was an age of
great social mobility, for by then the new wealth of Europe was
opening up new horizons and providing new opportunities. We
should not think of Urban's appeal falling upon a closely defined
and well-delineated group, still less a social class – rather it fell on a
society in which there was social movement and, at the level which
concerns us just below the nobility, less social definition.

By and large the theatre of ambitions in which this new game was
played out was the noble *mouvance*, and, occasionally, the structure
of the monarchical state. Henry I was known for his 'new men' but
the very archetype of them was Ranulf Flambard who was in a position of great power before the First Crusade. The Emperor Henry
IV of Germany caused intense anger by promoting men of low
status, his creatures, to great office within the German Church. If
such people were mainly clerics they had their secular counterparts
who were often soldiers, the much-hated royal *ministeriales* of the
German monarchy whom we can compare to Henry I of England's
Odo Borleng, the victor at the battle of Bourgthéroulde in 1124.[23]
It was in fact the structure of the *mouvances* which fostered social
mobility. They were designed to tap the growing wealth of the age
and it was to them that the ambitious and the aspiring were drawn.
We are accustomed to the view that the city and its wealth were the
focus of social change, but many small cities (and there were very
few big ones) were effectively created by lordships: Bury St
Edmunds is an example which springs to mind. Many merchants
were little more than the purchasing agents of the lords. We owe the
myth of the liberating force of merchant wealth to Marx and his
obsession with the ever-rising bourgeois.

Duby chose to end his *Three Orders: Feudal Society Imagined*
with his interpretation of William the Breton's report of Philip
Augustus's triumph after Bouvines in 1214. In this view the triumph
is that of the three orders whose guarantor is the glorious monarch;
strangely, one may think, the bourgeois are portrayed as having a
place within this structure but we have already noted their ever-
rising quality. The vision of the three orders here is of a great and

elaborate structure whose very weight crushes society – and there may be some truth in that view and its exposition may well have been the purpose of William's writing.[24] But there is no need for us to swallow it as reality, for the *mouvances* were the theatre of ambition for the competing *mediocres*, some military, some not, who sought entry, favour and promotion within these structures. Far from being merely a dead weight, the masters of society fostered a new and more mobile society by their patronage.

But these *mouvances* were not stable. Europe at the end of the eleventh century was a place of intense mobility. In the simple geographic sense men moved about a great deal, and this was above all characteristic of soldiers. Young knights sustained local wars in Beugy and the Vexin through their search for ransoms. Anglo-Saxons served the emperor at Byzantium alongside Scandinavian cousins who had come across the vast steppe of Rus. Normans and French founded a new dominion in South Italy, Flemings fought for pretty well anyone and European mercenaries were favoured in the armies of North African potentates. William the Conqueror hired large numbers of troops for his army of conquest in 1066, and many of them 'could not afford to wait' for their rewards. In 1101 Henry I concluded the Treaty of Dover with Count Robert II of Flanders, which provided that the latter would raise, if required, 1,000 *milites*, each with three horses, and ship them over to England within a month – it was almost certainly a repeat of a treaty of 1093 between William Rufus and Count Robert I.[25] Where did such huge numbers come from? The earliest code for the German *ministeriales*, that of Bishop Gunther of Bamberg, can be dated around 1060 and it reveals that *ministeriales* could move around and change masters.[26]

It was into this milieu that in 1095 Pope Urban directed his appeal for the First Crusade to the leaders of Christian society in the West. The vital importance of chiefs of *mouvances* and, therefore, of our need to understand their world, is evident. But their ideas and attitudes come to us through filters and even when we know a lot about them there are deep ambiguities and uncertainties. Perhaps Godfrey was a religious man; he clearly respected his pious mother. Perhaps he despaired of a future in imperial service, for he faced considerable problems in 1095; but then again he had faced and overcome similar ones before. We cannot know why even one so eminent decided to take the cross. Many of those in the *mouvances* could have had little choice but to follow the decisions of their masterss, and certainly their servants did not have much choice. But for many, whatever they thought of their religious obligations, the appeal of Urban must have opened new worlds to conquer, away from the ferocious competition of the *mouvances*. It was from this particular milieu that the crusade needed to draw the backbone of its military strength.

The influence of the masters of *mouvance* was clearly great, but the sheer looseness of what we call feudal society in its lower reaches meant that these followers needed to be appealed to and inspired. The message was not to a class or any very homogenous group – rather to an area of social mobility within which there were great differences of wealth and status. Large numbers of those in the knightly milieu would have recognised the hardships of the journey and known of its risks from pilgrims. The chance of escape from the burden of sin must have appealed as much to these people as to any other. But they were a grasping, aspirant group who must have seized upon Urban's references to the material wealth of the East which contemporary opinion would not have interpreted as at odds with Canon 2 of the Council of Clermont.[27] With hindsight we may think that there were few gainers from the crusade, but they did not possess hindsight and it is in the nature of things that humankind travels hopefully – otherwise nobody would play the National Lottery. And in fact there was money to be made. England raised the 10,000 marks for Normandy only with difficulty; in January 1099 when the crusade was in difficulties Raymond of St Gilles met with the other princes at Rugia and offered a total of at least 31,000 gold *solidi*, a coin worth about ten per cent more than the mark, to a number of them to persuade them to enter his service. It is no wonder with this kind of money sloshing around that at Easter 1098 Stephen of Blois could write to his wife boasting about how much richer he had become.[28] And the eagerness with which crusaders took over properties in north Syria and even rushed ahead in the search for them as they approached Jerusalem is a revelation of attitudes. This is hardly surprising: we see pilgrimage as a religious act, but half a century before the crusade Glaber could remark of a pious pilgrim: 'Truly he was free from that vanity which inspires so many to undertake the journey simply to gain the prestige of having been to Jerusalem.'[29]

The crusade offered a welcome outlet for at least some of those who lived in the highly competitive world of the knightly milieu of western Europe. This new social fluidity, which had been growing since the millennium, created the conditions which made possible strong support from military society for the First Crusade. Urban made an enormous missionary effort in 1095 – we often forget that it was half a century since a pope had been north of the Alps. On that previous occasion the scale of Leo IX's impact can be measured by the enormous trail of charters which he left behind. Urban's effort was much greater and it is a sign of his influence that much of the army which went on the journey was from southern France, which he toured after Clermont. The vigour of his recruiting effort was remarkable, and his message fell on a fluid society to whose ambition he catered. The crusade was like any other successful movement – it offered something for everyone – salvation, cash, land, status. That some of these appear contradictory to us really matters little – human behaviour is little disturbed by paradox if somewhere the right message is delivered. We hear what we wish to hear, and to the aspirant knightly milieu Urban's message offered salvation, certainly, but much else more mundane beside. We hear little from them directly, but one comment we all know; it does appear to come from the people who formed the fighting backbone of the army, and it expresses the most mixed of motives, precisely what one would expect from those whose drive and ambition was at least as strong as their religious conviction: 'Stand fast all together, trusting in Christ and in the victory of the Holy Cross. Today, please God, you will all gain much booty.'[30]

Notes

1 J. Flori, 'Pur eshalcier sainte crestiëte. Croisade, guerre sainte et guerre juste dans les anciennes chanson de geste françaises', *Le Moyen Age*, 5 (1991), 171–87.

2 For a discussion of numbers see France, *Victory*, pp. 122–42.

3 J.C. Russell, 'Population in Europe 500–1500', in B. Jaques, *Trade and Finance in the Middle Ages*, Fontana Economic History of Europe (London, 1971), p. 19, suggests 17 millions in these countries about the year 1000 and speaks of it growing subsequently. Modern figures are in the current *Whitaker's Almanac*.

4 On the English contribution, see C.J. Tyerman, *England and the Crusades 1095–1588* (London and Chicago, University of Chicago Press, 1988), pp. 15–21, who stresses the enormous financial burden; on

fleets, see France, *Victory*, pp. 209–20; Cosmas of Prague, *Chronicon*, in *MGHSS* 9.103; p. 112; RA, pp. 46–7.

5 I owe this observation to Dr S.B. Edgington.

6 Sewter, *Alexiad*, pp. 308–11.

7 G. Duby, *The Three Orders: Feudal Society Imagined*, trans. A. Goldhammer (Chicago and London, University of Chicago Press, 1978), pp. 355–6; N. Cohn, *The Pursuit of the Millennium* (London, Temple Smith, 1957), pp. 42–7, 49; AA, IV.54; GN, p. 242; *La Chanson D'Antioche*, ed. S. Duparc-Quioc, 2 vols (Paris, Librairie Orientaliste Paul Geuthner, 1977–8), 1.169–70, 218–21, 228, 318, 407, 438–9, 475–6. J.S.C. Riley-Smith, *The First Crusade and the Idea of Crusading* (London, Athlone Press, 1986), p. 189 comments that literature on the *Tafurs* tends to 'make the evidence ... carry more weight than it can bear'.

8 A.V. Murray, 'The origins of the Frankish nobility of the Kingdom of Jerusalem, 1100–1118', *Mediterranean Historical Review*, 4 (1989), 281–95; *idem*, 'The army of Godfrey of Bouillon: structure and dynamics of a contingent on the First Crusade', *Revue Belge de Philologie et d'Histoire*, 70 (1992), 301–29.

9 M. G. Bull, *Knightly Piety and the Lay Response to the First Crusade: The Limousin and Gascony, c. 970–c. 1130* (Oxford, Clarendon Press, 1993); G. Beech, 'Urban II, the abbey of Saint-Florent de Saumur, and the First Crusade', paper given at the Clermont Conference of the Society for the Study of the Crusades in June 1995. The author has kindly consented to my citing this. J. France, 'Les origines de la première croisade révisitées', given on the same occasion. Both these papers will appear in the Proceedings, ed. M. Balard.

10 Murray, 'Army of Godfrey of Bouillon', 313.

11 D. Iogna-Prat, 'La geste des origines dans l'historiographie clunisienne des xi–xii siècles', *Revue Bénédictine*, 102 (1992), 135–91, 'La confection des cartulaires', O. Guyotjeannin *et al.* (eds), *Les Cartulaires* (Turnhout, Belgium, Brepols, 1993), 27–44; M. Hillebrandt, 'Les cartulaires de l'abbaye de Cluny'. *Mémoires de la Société pour l'Histoire du Droit*, 50 (1993), 7–18; there is an English discussion in P.J. Geary, *Phantoms of Remembrance: Memory of Oblivion at the End of the First Millenium* (Princeton, New Jersey, Princeton University Press, 1994), pp. 100–14.

12 *Fragmentum Historiae Andegavensis auctore Fulcone Rechin*, in *Chroniques des Comtes d'Anjou*, ed. P. Marchegay and A. Salmon (Paris, Société de l'Histoire de France, 1856–1871), p. 373.

13 M. Bur, *La formation du comté de Champagne, v. 950–v. 1150* (Nancy, France, Université de Nancy, 1977), pp. 253–7.

14 See, for example, the forthcoming paper by M. Bennett, 'Milites et pedites: military status and military roles on the early crusades', which the author has been kind enough to allow me to see.

15 G. Duby, La société aux xi et xii siècles dans la région mâconnaise (Paris, Librarie Armand Colin, 1953), pp. 411–26. On the English controversy, see S. Harvey, 'The knight and the knight's fee in medieval England', Past and Present, 49 (1970), 3–43; the reassertion of the substantial nature of the knight in R.A. Brown, 'The status of the Norman knight', in J. Gillingham and J.C. Holts (eds), War and Government in the Middle Ages: Essays in Honour of J.O. Prestwich (Woodbridge, Suffolk, Boydell and Brewer, 1984), pp. 18–32. For a survey of the literature, see T.H. Hunt, 'Emergence of the knight in England', in W.H. Jackson (ed.), Knighthood in Medieval Literature (Woodbridge, Suffolk, Boydell and Brewer, 1981).

16 F.M. Stenton, Anglo-Saxon England (Oxford, Clarendon Press, 1971), p. 530.

17 E. Lourie, 'A society organised for war – medieval Spain, Past and Present, 35 (1966), 55–6; J.P. Poly and E. Bournazel, The Feudal Transformation, 900–1200, trans. C. Higgitt (New York, Holmes and Meier, 1991), pp. 99–101; Bur, Comté de Champagne, p. 441; AA, I.19; IX.20.

18 A. Murray, Reason and Society in the Middle Ages (Oxford, Oxford University Press, 1978), p. 94; Poly and Bournazel, Feudal Transformation, p. 99.

19 Bur, Comté de Champagne, pp. 427–42, 459–60.

20 William of Jumièges, Gesta Normannorum Ducum, ed. J. Marx (Rouen, Société de l'histoire de Normandie, 1914), pp. 106–8.

21 J.F. Lemarignier, Le Gouvernement Royal aux Premiers Temps Capétiens (987–1108) (Paris, J. Picard, 1956), pp. 67–140.

22 Murray, Reason and Society, pp. 81–109; Rodulfus Glaber, Opera, ed. J. France (Oxford, Oxford University Press, 1989), pp. 32–5.

23 A.L. Poole, From Domesday Book to Magna Carta (Oxford, Oxford University Press, 1955), pp. 170–1,388; OV, 6. 350–1; Murray, Reason and Society, p. 90.

24 Duby, Three Orders, pp. 346–53.

25 OV, 4.49; 5.217; M. Bennett, 'Wace and warfare', Battle, 11 (1988), 37–58; Diplomatic Documents Preserved in the Public Record Office 1. (1101–1272), ed. P. Chaplais (London, HMSO, 1964), no. 1; F. Barlow, William Rufus (London, Methuen, 1983), p. 325.

26 B. Arnold, German Knighthood, 1050–1300 (Oxford, Oxford University Press, 1985), pp. 27, 80–1.

27 J.D. Mansi, Sacrorum Concili nova et amplissima collectio (Venice, 1757–98) 20.815.

28 RA, p. 102; J. Porteous, 'Crusader coinage with Greek and Latin inscriptions', in *A History of the Crusades*, eds K.M. Setton and M.W. Baldwin (Madison, University of Wisconsin Press, 1969–89), 6. 360; Hagenmeyer, *Epistulae*, p. 149.
29 Glaber, *Opera*, pp. 200–1.
30 GF, pp. 19–20.

2

Peter the Hermit and the chroniclers

Colin Morris

Peter the Hermit was a distinctive figure among the leaders of the First Crusade. For one thing, his part in it was largely over before the rest began: the armies which had gathered around him had been destroyed by the Turks while most contingents were still on the way to the East. Thereafter, Peter appears occasionally in the records as an odd-job man, who is sometimes charged with important tasks. Most of these posed questions for the historians of the crusade. He acted as ambassador to the unbeliever; he was treasurer of the poor; he organised prayers in the mixed Christian communities at Jerusalem; and on one occasion he also ran away. In presenting these episodes, the chroniclers were trying to describe what had happened in terms which they and their readers would understand, and the information sometimes left them puzzled or offended.

The primary interest of subsequent historians has naturally been to use the chroniclers' reports to reach the facts which lay before him. This approach is particularly marked in Heinrich Hagenmeyer's book on Peter the Hermit, which is still the classic discussion, even though it is more than a century old.[1] It is necessary for us to perform this exercise, if we are to have any sort of history of the First Crusade, but modern studies of the art of narrative have shown how difficult it often is to extract a common factual layer from divergent accounts. The First Crusade chronicles pose special problems, because the writers were having to adjust their traditional Western assumptions to an unfamiliar, indeed a unique, situation. It was inevitable that they would shape verbal reports to correspond with their underlying view of the expedition, and even direct dependence on a written account was no guarantee of objectivity. When they re-shaped the style, they were liable to re-fashion the contents, which in many cases they may have been recalling in their memory rather than revising from the text.[2] Recent scholarship has given more attention to exploring the presuppositions of the writers, which are central for instance to some of Jonathan Riley-Smith's work.[3]

Peter the Hermit's unique career made him a controversial figure. There were marked differences in the way the various chroniclers understood his part in the expedition, and some of his activities posed questions which challenged their basic assumptions. Within the framework of a story of God-given success Peter had led the first crusading army to abject failure: why did this happen? He was also the envoy involved in the only negotiation with the unbeliever which was reported in detail in the West; and, as we shall see, this again raised difficult questions for the chroniclers of the crusade. This chapter will discuss the way the defeat of Peter's expedition and his embassy at Antioch were handled by Western writers, as a basis for some closing remarks on the historiographical tradition.

The most dramatic divergence within the tradition is that between Albert of Aachen's story of Peter as the messenger who brought the appeal from Jerusalem, and the accounts of other writers, who either provided no explanation of the decision to launch the crusade, or found no place in it for Peter. Albert's story of Peter's vision and embassy to Pope Urban II was for centuries accepted as the definitive origin of the crusade, and it earned Peter a censorious comment in no less a place than the Adams–Jefferson correspondence:

> I could not help wishing that ... all the prophets at least from Peter the Hermit to Nimrod Hess inclusively, had been confined in the stocks and prevented from spreading so many delusions and shedding so much blood.[4]

German scholars in the nineteenth century, culminating in Heinrich Hagenmeyer, were generally sceptical about Albert's authority, and in particular they dismissed the story of Peter's first pilgrimage to Jerusalem as a legend. About ten years ago, Ernest Blake and I argued that Albert's account incorporated early and reliable information about the expedition, and that the story of Peter and the patriarch was already current at the time of the crusade.[5] It is not my intention to return to this topic now, especially as research by Susan Edgington on Albert has substantially altered the terms of the debate.[6] The discussion of sources in this present volume suggests that Albert has now returned to favour as a major authority on the history of the crusade.

The first stage in the crusade proper covered the recruitment of the earliest armies, their march across the Balkans and their destruction at Xerigordo and Kibotos in Asia Minor.[7] Peter the Hermit was prominent in this whole process, although he was never the sole effective commander of this 'People's Crusade', as it has been rather dubiously called by modern historians. It was all over before the chroniclers who travelled on the crusade (Raymond of Aguilers, Fulcher of Chartres and the anonymous author of the *Gesta Francorum*) had arrived. Undoubtedly, they could have gathered a good deal of information, had they so chosen. Apart from other survivors, Peter himself was with the host as it assembled in the region of Constantinople. Fulcher of Chartres, however, almost brushed the episode aside. In the course of reporting the assembly of the armies, he noted the fate of Peter's expedition, but his brief summary gave the larger place to Walter Sans-Avoir.[8] Raymond of Aguilers similarly devoted only a few lines to the disaster, which for him was significant as a further example of the treasonable conduct of the Greek Emperor Alexius, proved by his deception of the crusaders at Nicaea. He points out that it was then that 'we learned that the emperor had betrayed Peter the Hermit, who had come to Constantinople with a great multitude far in advance of our armies'. Presumably because of the role for which Raymond had in his imagination cast these unfortunates, as victims of Greek treachery, he gives much the most exaggerated description of them as an unmilitary bunch: Peter was *ignarus ... tocius milicie* and his army an *imbellis multitudo*.[9]

The author of the *Gesta Francorum*, like Fulcher, included his account in the section devoted to the gathering of the armies, and he told us little about the crossing of the Balkans. Where the *Gesta* is different from the others is in the careful reporting of events in and around Constantinople. There is no indication that this army was not a proper fighting force, even if it was shamefully undisciplined. The Emperor Alexius was not to blame: he advised them not to cross to Asia Minor, and subsequently ordered them to do so only because they were sacking houses, palaces and churches. Peter went with them, but eventually returned to Constantinople, because (we are told) 'he could not control such a mixed company of people'.

Although I think that written sources, like entities, should not be multiplied beyond necessity, there are some signs that a pre-existing account was being edited for inclusion in the *Gesta*, without being made to accord adequately with the author's overall views. The section ends with the comment that 'when the emperor heard that the Turks had inflicted such a defeat on our men he rejoiced greatly'. That seems a gratuitous insult, which does not fit with the earlier passages, but comes naturally from the pen of a writer who is shortly going to be talking about the *iniquus* and the *infelix imperator*.[10]

The major French histories composed during the decade after the crusade depended primarily on the *Gesta Francorum* for information. Baldric of Bourgueil and Robert the Monk offered little that was not in the *Gesta*, beyond a more flowery style.[11] The Western writer who did rewrite the *Gesta*'s history into something new and wider was Guibert of Nogent.[12] Guibert prefaced the departure of Peter's army with an account of Peter himself: he was born at Amiens and had been a monk in 'upper Gaul'. He then provided a description of Peter's preaching. It would be marvellous to think this was a detailed account of crusade recruiting, and some historians have treated it as such; but it is clear that Guibert was telling his readers about Peter's previous activity within the poverty and preaching movement. It fits the crusade setting very inadequately. The remark that Peter left his monastery 'with what intention I do not know' is a polished sneer from a Benedictine monk to an itinerant preacher, which would be pointless if Peter had left in order to preach the crusade. Similarly, his generosity in bestowing funds on prostitutes to provide them with dowries hardly suggests that he was engaged in collecting financial support for the expedition. Guibert ends with a semi-satirical account of the veneration in which Peter was held, with hairs from his mule treated as relics – a cult which reminds one of the career of Tanchelm of Antwerp and other radical or heretical preachers of the time.[13] As this description stands, it seems to be an eye-witness account by Guibert: 'we have seen him going around cities and towns'. It forms part of the report of the departure of the armies, and is not designed to provide information about the origins of the expedition; there is no indication of where Peter preached, or whether his activity had been authorised at Clermont. Still less, of course, does it go back before the Council to suggest the Peter had any earlier commitment to Jerusalem. In the same way, the information provided by Orderic Vitalis, who knew the date of Peter's arrival at Cologne, is set within context of the assembly of the armies.[14] It would seem that memories of Peter were circulating in the West, but they were not part of any nucleus of reports about the cause of the crusade.

Guibert then proceeded to provide some new information which he had collected, about the march of Peter's army across Hungary and the Balkans. However, his sources seem to have confused the progress of Peter with that of the other armies which set off in advance of the princes' contingents. The chronicle of Solomon bar Simson, which describes at length the persecution of the Rhineland Jews, also reports savage fighting between Peter's army and the Hungarians.[15] It is most unlikely that the anti-semitic Guibert was drawing his information from Jewish sources, and one must presume that Solomon bar Simson and Guibert had heard similar reports circulating in northern France and the Rhineland. Almost certainly, they are not accurate. In all probability he believed the account, which would have been difficult for him to check, but he would have been happy to receive stories which were to the discredit of Peter. Even when he is using material from this section of the *Gesta Francorum*, which was certainly not designed as a criticism of the Hermit, Guibert does his best to discredit him. The account ends with a damning conclusion: 'This was the end of the company of Peter the Hermit. We have followed his story to this point without inserting other material, to show that he provided no assistance to the others, but added to the confidence of the Turks.'[16]

Effectively, we know nothing about Peter's crossing of the Balkans except what Albert of Aachen tells us.[17] On the events around Constantinople also he provided a lot of detail, some of which makes comprehensible for us references obscured by the brevity of other writers, and he included material which was unknown to them, including an amicable interview between Peter and the Emperor Alexius. His account of the background to the disaster at Kibotos is rather different: according to Albert, Peter agreed to cross the Hellespont, but accepted Alexius' advice not to march on Nicaea until the main group of armies arrived. When his followers did in fact attack because Peter could not restrain them, he went back to Constantinople – according to Albert, specifically to secure supplies. The emperor refused to allow him to return to the army, until the news of the disaster arrived, when Peter successfully pleaded for the Greeks to rescue what was left of his companions. All of this gives more credit to Peter than the *Gesta Francorum* had done. There is no way of checking it, but it is consistent within itself and full of solid-sounding information.

Inevitably, there are some queries. The summary of the imperial embassy which arrived at Sofia is highly questionable. The ambassadors allegedly knew about the fighting at Nish, only four days before, and their language was very unlike that of the court at Constantinople. They offered to allow Peter free passage 'because you are a Christian, and your companions Christians'. This is such a favourite concept of Albert's that it seems reasonably sure that these are his own words, not those of the ambassadors, nor even of an earlier Latin version. Messages from ambassadors constituted an invitation to any self-respecting chronicler to replace them with a version of his own, and this should not lead us to doubt the general accuracy and reliability of Albert's account.[18] The descriptions of Peter's expedition thus span the whole range of possibilities from the briefest of mentions (Fulcher, Raymond) through a solid summary of the events in Asia Minor (*Gesta Francorum*) and a confused and misinformed amplification (Guibert) to a remarkably full, and probably accurate, description of the disaster which overtook this, the first of the crusading expeditions (Albert).

The report of the embassy to Kerbogha (or Corbaran as most chroniclers called him) in June 1098 raises a different range of issues. This time, we are as close to news from the horse's mouth as we can ever hope to be. After the Christian army had been enclosed in Antioch by the advance of the Turkish force, and after their morale had been raised by the discovery of the Holy Lance, a council of the princes decided to send an embassy to Kerbogha. We have an account of it in the letter from Anselm of Ribemont to Archbishop Manasses of Rheims.[19] The ambassadors, whom Anselm did not name, delivered their message in the name of 'the army of God', saying, 'withdraw from us and the inheritance of Saint Peter, or else you will be put to flight by arms'. Kerbogha drew his sword (probably an oath-taking gesture rather than a threat) and swore that he would always possess the land 'justly or unjustly' and that he would not rest until they had left Antioch, denied Christ and professed the law of the Persians. The ambassadors must have reported back to the princes in some form, although we do not have the details; and the Christian army was ordered to prepare for battle. This is all fairly close to the source of the report, but there are problems. Kerbogha's defiance is reported in thoroughly Western style. It is hard to think that he said that he intended to hold the land whether justly or not, and professing the law of the Persians sounds an odd concept in the mouth of a Muslim ruler – it suggests a reminiscence of the 'law of the Medes and Persians' in Daniel 6:15. It is impossible to be sure where these distortions entered the tradition. Perhaps this is merely the ambassadors' attempt to translate what they had heard, or Anselm or his scribe had put the message in terms more familiar to the Frankish mind. Anselm may well have been present at the council of the princes; other writers would only have heard of events at second hand, or even conceivably by camp-fire rumour.[20]

Nevertheless, much of their reporting is quite plausible. Raymond of Aguilers and Fulcher both provide the name of Peter the Hermit as the ambassador.[21] The *Gesta Francorum* has further information: the author knows that Herluin went as translator ('dragoman' as Tudebode has it). Robert the Monk, on the other hand, whose regular source was the *Gesta*, elaborated the story in the direction of legend. Although Robert in general is not an admirer of Peter, he thought that he was a volunteer, perhaps because of a clumsy phrase in the *Gesta Francorum*: 'inuenerunt quosdam uiros, Petrum scilicet et Herluinum'. He also though that Herluin was a second ambassador, who went along with an unnamed interpreter. This is probably more than a misunderstanding of the text of the *Gesta*: Robert, as we shall shortly see, had got hold of a story that Herluin insulted Kerbogha, speaking (one supposes) more like an ambassador than a translator. Most writers insist at some length on the ambassadors' assertion that Antioch belongs to Saint Peter. In fact, the *Gesta Francorum*, in a short account, insists three times that it is 'the land of Christians and ours' and 'the land which Saint Peter the apostle long ago converted by preaching to the worship of Christ'. Fulcher, too, had Peter remind Kerbogha that Antioch 'had belonged to the Christians in former times'. There is a good evidence that the leaders of the First Crusade were strongly attached to the importance of Saint Peter's role as first bishop of Antioch, and it is likely that they did in fact brief Peter the Hermit to claim the city as Saint Peter's by right. There is some concern to justify their claims by precedent, rather than to send a mere defiance, with threats of vengeance upon the persecutors of Christ.[22]

Raymond of Aguilers reports another proposal by the princes, which is not mentioned by Anselm: an offer of representative combat by a small group. Raymond did not include this in his account of the embassy: it apparently came to him separately, as part of the report of the battle:

> Kerbogha also informed our princes that he was now ready to do what he had previously refused, namely that five or ten Turks should fight with the same number of Franks, and the party whose knights were defeated should peacefully withdraw before the others. Our people answered: 'You would not do so when we wanted it. Now that we have prepared ourselves for battle, let each side fight for its right.'[23]

Albert of Aachen and Fulcher of Chartres, on the other hand, have integrated this offer into their account of Peter's challenge to the Turks. Albert presents it very much as a second stage of the negotiations: after Kerbogha's expression of contempt for Christianity, Peter, he says, disclosed the rest of his message to him:

> It seemed best to the Christian princes that at the point you rejected the offer of such renowned men to subject themselves to you and that you refused to become a Christian, that you should choose twenty recruits from your force, and the Christians likewise from theirs ...[24]

Fulcher differs only as to the number: 'five or ten or even a hundred knights'. The occurrence of this offer in three independent early accounts makes it clear that it was widely known in the host at the time. We can be reasonably sure, then, of the contents of the offer to Kerbogha: an assertion of the justice of the Christian cause, since Antioch properly belongs to Saint Peter, followed by a proposal for a representative combat to avoid unnecessary bloodshed.

The chroniclers, however, were not solely concerned with reporting the content of the negotiations: they had other fish to fry. To deal with unbelievers was to open a range of unfamiliar issues, some of which were very worrying to the Western self-consciousness. It could appear as supping with the devil, and it was made worse by the fact that diplomatic niceties required a representative to do honour to the prince with whom he was negotiating. They seem to have been troubled about this already on the crusade: Raymond of Aguilers noted, in technical language, that Kerbogha 'forced Peter the Hermit, who did not want to bow (*inclinare*), to supplicate to him'. Such a gesture was gravely disturbing, because in Western society 'lords were not only addressed deferentially, they were also entreated with language and gestures that assimilated their authority to God's'.[25]

Further away from the realities of the 1098 campaign, Western writers elaborated floridly on this issue. Robert the Monk, who was perhaps of all these chroniclers the least inclined to inter-faith dialogue, put a hair-raisingly insulting speech into the mouth of Herluin, whom he took to be a joint ambassador, beginning 'O prince of no chivalry and all malice' – O princeps nullius militiae set totius malitiae.[26] An insertion into the Blois manuscript of Baldric, which was apparently written in the late twelfth century, illustrates how by then perceptions had changed, and in a sense been normalised: 'Then Peter the Hermit arose and put round his neck the stole which he was carrying in his hand, and by the authority given to him by God and the pope of Rome cursed and excommunicated them.' As a result, he was given a powerful blow by one of the Turks, but Kerbogha was upset by this and ordered the Turk to be executed, while the interpreter explained to Peter that envoys were regarded as sacrosanct.

The chroniclers were also concerned about what religious content there was in the negotiations. This worry presumably explains one of the Gesta Francorum's more tortured and obscure sentences: 'we think and believe that perhaps you have come here because you want above all to be made Christians, or have come here above all to injure Christians.'[27] Conversely, Kerbogha makes the offer that if the crusaders will all 'become Turks', none of them will any longer be a footman (pedes), but all will be knights (milites) like the Turks. This clearly reflects the crusaders' awareness of the great numbers of horsemen in the Turkish host, and more speculatively it may be the product of a situation in which few horses were left to the Franks. In Albert of Aachen, the same sort of concern produces a clearer and more radical proposal:

> The leaders of the Christian army have decreed that, if you should concede to believe in Christ the Lord, who is the true God and Son of God, and if you renounce the filth of the Gentiles, they will become your knights (milites), and, restoring the city of Antioch into your hands, are ready to serve you as lord and prince.[28]

This is an essentially Albertian concept: as we saw earlier, he has a strong sense of Christian identity and brotherhood. It is rather hard to see Bohemond voting for the proposal in the council of princes.

If we make an exception for Albert's account of the crossing of the Balkans, all the material about Peter the Hermit came to the chroniclers in fragmentary form. There is no distinctive 'Hermit' source. The difficulty in handling the material was increased by the diversity of the episodes: Peter as the brave ambassador to the Turks, and as the organiser of prayers at Jerusalem, compelled admiration, even while his dealings with unbelievers and heretics raised some queries in the writers' minds. It was, however, difficult to praise his failure to keep discipline in the first contingents, and even more his later flight from Antioch. Given that some of these writers were producing very long books, and were processing material which posed a variety of special problems, one might expect that they would fail to shape it into any coherent judgement about Peter. Sometimes, indeed, an episode does escape control, but in general the striking feature is the extent to which each writer draws his own conclusion and maintains it throughout many of the separate episodes.

For many of the crusaders, Peter was evidently a very secondary figure. He was never mentioned by name in their letters to the West. In Fulcher, he occurs only twice: there is a brief record of his initial defeat (although even then Walter Sans-Avoir is perhaps more important) and his embassy is described. There is a little more in Raymond, but not a lot. Apart from the great princes, who dominate all the chronicles, he gives more time among clergy and religious to the Holy Lance visionaries and even to Peter of Narbonne, the bishop of Albara. The *Gesta Francorum*, as we have seen, does have a great deal more about the fate of Peter's army and the embassy. The author is characteristically reserved in his judgements of the Latin leaders, but on the whole Peter appears in his pages as brave, devoted and committed to the cause.

It is the more surprising to find the existence in the West of a strong tradition of hostility to Peter. This appears already in the earliest version of the Frutolf/Ekkehard account of the crusade, where the report of Peter's preaching is qualified by the comment that 'many afterwards said that he had been a hypocrite'. Since Ekkehard removed this comment in later versions, it is natural to suppose that this was a first, angry reaction to the news of the destruction of the armies which the preachers had raised on Germany.[29] The real champion of the anti-Peter cause, however, was Guibert of Nogent.

As we saw earlier, Guibert's accounts of Peter's preaching, although they gave him credit for some things, had a bitter edge to them. He then subsequently went out of his way to dismiss Peter's unsuccessful military leadership as totally useless, and as providing no assistance to the others.[30]

He was most expansive, however, on Peter's flight from Antioch. None of the chroniclers seem to have known much about this, and they did not say much. Guibert had no new information of his own, but made it the basis for a full-scale satire:

> Upon this, like the star which was seen falling from heaven in the Apocalypse, Peter, that famous hermit about whom we have written already, also turned to folly and transgressed.
>> Why, Peter, did you fail at Antioch?
>> Why were you so forgetful of your name?
>> For 'Peter' has its origin in rock,
>> So both mean 'solid'; both should be the same,
>> Not liable to slip when there's a shock.
>> So why did you forget it, to your shame?[31]

Guibert had no liking for an itinerant monk, a failed general and a coward who had run away from God's army. The criticism of Peter apparently continued within French tradition until the time of the Second Crusade. A recruiting letter of Bernard of Clairvaux warned those who 'love the pre-eminence' not to leave early on the expedition, as Peter had done.[32]

For Albert of Aachen, on the contrary, Peter the Hermit has a status among the crusaders different from, but almost as great as, that of Godfrey of Bouillon, his hero. He was the *primus auctor*. He received the crucial vision, bore the essential appeal to the churches of the West, and 'with all the natural power at his command, in every admonition and sermon, first urged the constancy of this way'.[33] Albert, of course, has a mass of material about the march of the armies to Asia Minor, but after that he does not know enormously more about the Hermit than did the other chroniclers. There is no mention of the flight, perhaps because it would spoil the picture, but perhaps because he genuinely did not know; it is not in all the chronicles.

Albert, however, likes to remind us of Peter's merits, as in his account of the embassy:

They found no one with courage to speak to so ferocious and proud a man, until Peter, tiny in stature but great in merit, braving his way through the midst of the Gentiles, under God's protection, arrived alone at Kerbogha's tent.[34]

In this whole subject, there is little personal description and not much emotion, but (just as we cannot miss the venom in Guibert), so there is an unmistakable affection in Albert, as we read for example how, into the awe-inspiring presence of the Greek emperor, there came this little man, God's agent in the delivery of the Holy Sepulchre, 'tiny in stature' (we are told again), 'but great in heart and speech'.[35]

Notes

1   H. Hagenmeyer, *Peter der Eremite* (Leipzig, O. Harrassowitz, 1879).
2   For the general issues posed by the use of memory in the study of medieval texts, see M.J. Carruthers, *The Book of Memory* (Cambridge, Cambridge University Press, 1990).
3   See, for example, *The First Crusade and the Idea of Crusading* (London, Athlone Press, 1986).
4   Cited by J.Z. Smith, *Drudgery Divine* (Chicago, University of Chicago Press, 1990), p. 2 from L.J. Cappon (ed.), *The Adams–Jefferson Letters* (Chapel Hill, University of North Carolina Press, 1959), vol. 2, p. 302. Adams was writing in 1813.
5   E.O. Blake and C. Morris, 'A hermit goes to war: Peter and the origins of the First Crusade', in *Monks, Hermits and the Ascetic Tradition*, ed. W. J. Shields, Studies in Church History, 22 (1985), 79–109. Our conclusions are discussed by M.D. Coupe, 'Peter the Hermit – a reassessment', *Nottingham Medieval Studies*, 31 (1987), 37–46, and by France, *Victory*, esp. pp. 88–9. The article by J. Flori, 'Faut-il réhabiliter Pierre l'Ermite? Une réévaluation des sources de la première croisade', *Cahiers de Civilisation Médiéval*, 38 (1995), 35–54, contains a valuable survey of the historiographical tradition, which was not available to me at the time of preparing this chapter.
6   S.B. Edgington, 'The *Historia Iherosolimitana* of Albert of Aix: a critical edition', Ph.D. thesis, London, 1991.
7   The sources are discussed by Hagenmeyer, *Peter der Eremite*, ch. 4 and France, *Victory*, ch. 4.
8   FC, pp. 158–9. Fulcher's prologue had laid a great stress on recording the glorious martyrdom of the participants in the crusade, but it apparently did not occur to him (as it did to the author of the *Gesta Francorum*) that these men could be listed as the first martyrs.

9   RA, pp. 44–5. The Provençal contingent had arrived in Constantinople later than the rest, and that was no doubt the reason why they only learned at Nicaea about the fate of Peter's force.

10   GF, pp. 3–5. A further indication of editing is the insertion of the comment that 'these men were the first to endure blessed martyrdom', which in the context refers to the prisoners, not to those who were killed.

11   BB, p. 732; RM, p. 731.

12   GN, pp. 142ff.

13   M. Lambert, *Medieval Heresy* (Oxford, Blackwell, 1992), pp. 50–2.

14   Peter's arrival at Cologne was dated to Easter Saturday (12 April 1096): OV, 5. 28–9.

15   See S. Eidelberg (trans.), *The Jews and the Crusaders* (Madison, Wisconsin University Press, 1977), pp. 68–71.

16   GN, p. 174.

17   AA, I.6–22.

18   On this aspect of Albert's thought, see C. Morris, 'The aims and spirituality of the First Crusade as seen through the eyes of Albert of Aix', *Reading Medieval Studies*, 16 (1990), esp. 108–10.

19   Hagenmeyer, *Epistulae*, XV.18 (p. 160). The letter does not seem to have been known to Western chroniclers, unless (as suggested below) Raymond's account contains echoes of it.

20   The accounts of the embassy are to be found in GF, pp. 65–7; PT, pp. 108–10; RA, p. 79; FC, pp. 274–50; GN, pp. 203–4; BB, pp. 74–5; RM, pp. 825–7; AA, IV.44–6. The sources are discussed by Hagenmeyer, *Peter der Eremite*, pp. 229–42, and France, *Victory* p. 280.

21   Raymond appears to echo one distinctive phrase in Anselm when he says that Kerbogha will defend his land *iure iniuria*. He also is close to him when he says that Antioch is the *iuris ... Beati Petri et Christianorum*. Perhaps he had seen Anselm's letter, or heard its contents.

22   Their thinking about Antioch as the see of Saint Peter is examined by J.S.C. Riley-Smith, *First Crusade and the Idea of Crusading*, (London, Athlone Press 1986) pp. 104–5, and 'The First Crusade and Saint Peter' in B.Z. Kedar, H.E. Mayer and R.C. Smail (eds), *Outremer: Studies in the History of the Crusading Kingdom of Jerusalem Presented to Joshua Prawer* (Jerusalem, Yad Izhak Ben-Zvi Institute, 1982), pp. 41–63.

23   RA, p. 81.

24   AA, IV.45.

25   The great social importance of such ceremonies is underlined in G. Koziol, *Begging Pardon and Favour* (Ithaca, New York, Cornell University Press, 1992). The quotation is from pp. 8–9.

26 The episode was enthusiastically adopted in vernacular epic: *La Chanson d'Antioche* ed. S. Duparc-Quioc, (Paris, Librairie Orientaliste Paul Geuthner, 1977–8), l. 368–9, line 7382ff.

27 *Putamus forsitan et credimus, quia ideo huc venistis, quoniam per omnia uultis effici Christiani; aut propterea igitur huc venistis, ut per omnia Christianos afficiatis.* (GF, p. 66). I am not sure of the exact force of the phrase *per omnia*.

28 AA, IX.44–6.

29 *MGHSS*, 6.208, *s.a.* 1096. See, however, Blake and Morris, 'A hermit goes to war', esp. 95–6, on the persistence of criticism in later versions of Ekkehard.

30 GN, pp. 142, 146. Guibert contradicts himself on p. 163, where he acknowledges that the hermit's defeat misled the sultan into over-confidence.

31 GN, p. 174. I confess to taking liberties in the translation of the verse.

32 J. Leclercq, 'L'encyclique de St Bernard en faveur de la croisade', *Revue Bénédictine*, 81 (1971), 298.

33 AA, I.2.

34 AA, IV.44.

35 AA, I.15.

3

The diplomatic of the First Crusade

Marcus Bull

The value of charters for the study of the First Crusade has been highlighted in studies by John Cowdrey and Giles Constable, and confirmed by the exhaustive researches of Jonathan Riley-Smith, who has used documentary sources extensively in his compilation of a database of early crusaders, their families and connections.[1] The work of these scholars demonstrates that charters are an invaluable complement to the information which can be gained from narrative sources. They add to the overall picture by supplying evidence about the preaching, organisation and financing of the crusade. They are able to throw light on the sort of commonplace details which would not normally have been within a chronicler's scope. They reveal a good deal about perceptions as well as actions: the fact that many documents written independently of each other contain similar language and ideas is important evidence for how the crusade message was communicated and understood. And the numbers of surviving documents enable us to identify trends in thought and practice which might have eluded an individual contemporary observer.

The question must therefore be asked why charters are a rich source of information about the First Crusade. This is a problem which may be tackled on two levels. First, crusade diplomatic needs to be set against the background of changes in documentary practice which created the raw potential for references to the crusade and crusaders to enter the written record. Second, it is useful to examine the particular aspects of the crusade which enabled scribes to realise that potential. For the purposes of this chapter, attention will be focused on documents from the kingdom of France and Romance-speaking parts of the Empire. These areas offer the student of the First Crusade the greatest scope for research. In part this is simply because the francophone world accounted for the majority of first crusaders. But it is also a reflection of the fact that French diplomatic practices in the eleventh century enable us to draw on a particularly extensive, informative and variegated body of material.[2]

The historian using eleventh-century charters benefits from two important and connected trends. In the first place, far more documents survive, as originals or copies, than from the Carolingian period. In large measure this reflects the growth of economic activity from around 1000, and an increase in the number of religious institutions generating records. It is also a consequence of greater systemisation and care in the production and preservation of documents. Heightened sensitivity towards creating written evidence was a corollary of growing interest in ecclesiastical reform, for writing was an invaluable tool in constructing versions of the past which could be mobilised to influence the future.

Second, between the tenth and twelfth centuries the social range of those regularly featuring in charters expanded considerably: the great ecclesiastical and secular princes who dominate the surviving diplomatic record in the late Carolingian era are increasingly joined by lesser lords, castellans and *milites*.[3] In so far as writing was something done by or on behalf of the powerful as a function of their power, the social broadening of active participation in the written record (peasants appear, of course, but mostly as passive objects of property) is rooted in changes in the distribution and perception of authority in France. The result is that the First Crusade took place at an optimal time for the documentary record to embrace a broad cross-section of those military classes to which Pope Urban II's appeal was principally directed.[4]

The greater number of charters and the broadening of their social range are important considerations, but in and of themselves they cannot fully explain why charters are useful to students of the First Crusade. A further significant development is rooted in changes in the composition and utility of documents in the eleventh century. In a recent, very impressive, study of the form and content of documents from the Vendômois, Dominique Barthélemy has detected the appearance from *c.*1060 of a diplomatic style which he labels *narrativité*.[5] This is characterised by a relaxation of the diplomatic conventions inherited from the Romano-Frankish legal formulism of earlier centuries, and by greater attention on the part of scribes to the overall context within which the particular transaction being recorded was situated. Documents conditioned by *narrativité* did not encapsulate a single moment, abstracted from the events which led up to or flowed from it. However selective a scribe had to be in his choice of background detail because of the constraints of space, and however stylised the idioms which were available to him when he wanted to describe ideas and actions, he was able to depict the men and women who entered into property transactions with churches as moving in space and time, and in relation to one another. The documentary record became more dynamic as the people featuring in it could now be presented reacting to events and the initiatives of others (such as Urban II's launching of the First Crusade).

It should be noted that the use of contextualisation in documents was not invented in the eleventh century. It had antecedents in the expositive clauses of charters drawn up by or on behalf of secular and ecclesiastical rulers. For example, a prince or bishop, when confirming a predecessor's grants to a church, could refer to the circumstances in which he was approached, acquainted with past transactions, and persuaded to give his consent.[6] Here, clearly, the act communicates a sense of movement through time. Yet, compared to the possibilities open to a scribe influenced by *narrativité*, the perspectives which could be offered by older-style expositives were limited. Greater contextualisation was a liberating force. It equipped scribes to treat events as parts of longer processes and to consider the relationship between individual and group action – both perspectives which bore on crusading. Of course, some caution is necessary in assessing the significance of *narrativité*. Barthélemy's observations, which are the result of minute researches into one area, should not be applied generally without making allowance for regional variations in the pace and chronology of diplomatic change. In addition, it is important to note that within a single region diplomatic practice could vary considerably between different scriptoria: this is apparent, for example, from Emily Zack Tabuteau's study of eleventh-century property law in Normandy, a duchy which is commonly held up as precociously centralised and possessed of a highly developed sense of its distinctiveness.[7] On the other hand, Barthélemy's study is very important as a methodological exemplar, and because its analysis breaks free from the constrictive terminology of old diplomatic manuals, as well as from some of the orthodoxies which have grown up to explain changes in the nature of documents in the eleventh century.

What, then, brought about the relaxation and accelerated variegation of eleventh-century diplomatic? The customary answer focuses upon what is now the orthodox interpretation of change in French society in the central medieval period: the *mutation féodale* (feudal transformation).[8] Developments in diplomatic practice are explained by reference to the breakdown in the tenth and eleventh centuries of the public court system which had been inherited from the Carolingian period. As private justice became more prevalent, the growth of seigneurial courts brought with it an atomisation of juridical norms and traditions. This resulted in the production of documents which were less responsive to the homogenising force of whatever central direction survived, and increasingly varied as legal procedures became more imprecise and *ad hoc*. Thus a scribe recording a grant to a church would no longer feel obliged to create a heavily formulaic document, obedient to traditional models, because he knew that any future dispute about the grant would most likely be resolved by a process of informal bargaining and compromise.

There is much to commend this view. But it is reasonable to ask whether it is a sufficient explanation of why documents changed. If this argument is applied in isolation it can easily lead to a picture of eleventh-century society which is too negative and value-laden: attention is focused only on dysfunction and failure to keep to legal and documentary norms which other centuries, so it seems, contrived to follow better. The eleventh century can be made to appear as nothing more than a hiatus between periods when government was more assertive and legal procedures were closer to the (supposed) ideal of consistency. The problem is more complex than this. If documents became more homogenised and decontextualised in the twelfth and thirteenth centuries because of the growth of effective public authority and greater interest in written law, it does not follow that the relative relaxation of documentary conventions in the eleventh century was simply the result of the same processes in reverse.[9]

Other factors may be suggested which help to explain the characteristics of diplomatic in our period: the accelerating pace of economic activity outstripping the capacity of old diplomatic forms to keep pace; greater sensitivity on the part of churches and their scribes to the tenurial and dynastic complexities of the lay world, now that a wider social range of people was being encouraged to involve itself in pious benefactions; and, linked to this, the need to be alive to the motivations and life patterns of the sort of lay persons who could both support and harm the Church's material interests. Thus it can be argued that references to first crusaders do not appear in charters simply as a by-product of social and judicial fragmentation; they are also a consequence of the fact that the religious institutions responsible for almost all the surviving documents were busily engaging with the lives of lords and knights. In other words, the diplomatic is not a passive witness to the events and processes it records; it is part of the dynamic of the interaction between churches and the dominant elements of lay society. Consequently, there is a direct link between the technical diplomatic reasons why crusaders appear in documents and the underlying circumstantial reasons why they do so, for example as vendors or mortgagors of property, or because they were concerned to secure intercession before their perilous undertaking.

What potential does *narrativité* create for the student of the crusade? A useful starting point is to examine the variety of forms which eleventh-century documents could take. Old diplomatic manuals draw a neat distinction between two basic documentary types. First there is the charter proper, typically in the first person and present tense. This type of document has a distinct quality as an artefact: it often contains a solemn preamble and malediction, and it is usually subscribed by the author (the person who 'speaks' through the text) and other interested parties. Second, there is the notice; this is in the third person and uses the past tense to refer back to an earlier episode or episodes. It is less likely to contain an elaborate preamble, and it usually refers to the presence of witnesses rather than concluding with subscriptions, with the result that those mentioned are more detached from participation in the production of the document itself.[10] The customary explanation of these contrasting forms is that the charter proper was dispositive, the document sufficing in itself to establish and transfer title, whereas the notice was merely probative, bearing witness to an event in a similar manner to the role of the human *testes* recorded as present.[11] In essence the difference between the two types is that between a title-deed and a memorandum.

This distinction is useful, but only if it is treated as a convenient set of categories which does not accurately correspond to actual practice or the looser terminology of the time: *carta* and *notitia* were not clearly differentiated terms in the eleventh century.[12] Moreover, however conclusively dispositive a charter might outwardly appear, it too could serve as a witness to actions: few disputes were resolved simply by the production of a deed. Charters and notices, as narrowly defined in the terms used above, are best seen as the extreme points of a continuum along which there were many intermediate and hybrid forms. References to the crusade and to crusaders occur throughout the length of this continuum. It is noteworthy that documents in the first person – the supposedly 'pure' dispositive form – account for a substantial number of mentions of the crusade. In many cases a mini-expositive, in the form of a statement of intent expressed by a subjunctive or participle, was inserted into the dispositive clause. Usually placed between the subject and the verb or verbs expressing the nature of the transaction, the expositive clause served to encapsulate the actor's decision-making processes and the important influences acting on him or her: for example, *Ego N ... Hierosolimam pergens ... dono; Ego N ... cum vellem ire in Jerusalem ... dedi.*[13] Mention of participation in the crusade was also made at the other extreme, in those parts of notices which recalled the circumstances leading up to the transaction at issue.[14]

It is important, however, to recognise the limitations of *narrativité* and the nature of the information it is able to preserve. At first glance, the greater attention to context and the interplay of actors and events through time might seem to result in documents which resemble short chronicles. It is worth noting that the drawing up of a charter could have a creative, interpretative and commemorative quality when recording, for example, the foundation legend of a church, the grant of important properties and rights, or the resolution of a dispute. The same applies to the process of preserving a church's documentary memory by means of pancartes and cartularies, compilations which often shaded into *gesta abbatum* and other forms of narrative.[15] 'Documentary' and 'narrative' are useful labels for historians to apply to different types of sources, but they are not wholly distinct categories. Furthermore, it is reasonable to suppose that there was a general connection between the emergence of narrative-type documents and contemporary interest in the writing of history: both were products of the same learned, predominantly

Benedictine, cultural milieu focused upon the scriptorium. But it does not follow that all documents – especially the more 'routine' ones, which account for most of those that survive – were produced in precisely the same spirit as chronicles. The two forms required different approaches to the interpretation and contextualisation of events, different ideas about the didactic value of texts, and different assumptions about the use which future generations would make of written records.

These differences are apparent from a consideration of the types of contextual or descriptive material which could find their way into documents. Often charters contain what appear to be extraneous details which do not directly bear on the nature of the transaction being recorded or on how it might conceivably be disputed at a later date. No doubt some scribes enjoyed the opportunity of putting pen to parchment to indulge in adding a touch of colour to their texts. But a closer examination of many of these apparently incidental details reveals that they served an important function, well beyond the decorative, which was germane to the transaction as a whole. The cardinal goal in drawing up a document was to make it as difficult as possible for its subject matter to be contested in the future.[16] It was therefore useful to record details which could jog memories.[17] For example, in 1096, the year in which he set out on the First Crusade, Arnulf of Hesdin, a noble from north-eastern France, stopped off at the abbey of Fécamp during a pilgrimage to Mont-Saint-Michel. There he happened to witness a sale of some property to the monks. He was not a party to the sale, which featured a layman with whom he had no connection, but it is recorded that he became formally involved by handing the vendor a foxskin as the transaction was being made.[18]

The same impulse – to make transactions memorable and distinctive – accounts for the inclusion in documents of details such as that a woman consented to a gift made by her brother as she lay ill in bed,[19] that a benefactor had been mortally wounded at the time he made over property to a church,[20] or that a young boy, when asked to consent to a grant made by his father, was handed a bright red tunic.[21] There is an interesting paradox here: details were recorded in writing for the future benefit of people who themselves seldom reconstructed their pasts directly from written sources. References to colour, gesture and location, and particular emphasis on the unusual (such as Arnulf's foxskin), all exploited a developed visual sense. A good example is a document from Molesme which records that a benefactress's nephew, about to set out for Jerusalem, consented to grants she had made as he sat near the abbey church's west door in the company of Abbot Robert.[22] The act of sitting was not a superfluous detail, for it helped to recreate the scene for anyone who had been present, and it lent the all-important giving of the consent an identifiable, personalised quality for future generations.

The potential importance of seemingly incidental detail is also evident in the fact that it was often supplied when it was necessary to explain that the normal procedures and rituals which attended property transactions had not been followed. For example, a Norman knight who died in England made a gift to Jumièges by entrusting his hauberk to his companions, who took the armour to the abbey to corroborate their story.[23] A mid-eleventh-century charter from Marmoutier records that a mortally wounded knight, lying near the banks of the Loire outside a castle, made a gift of land to a monk who was passing by: once again the unusual circumstances created the risk that the donation could be contested, so it was important to give the episode a precise and readily visualised locus.[24] In 1080 a noble from the Bourbonnais called Arno of Veauce fell ill on the return leg of a pilgrimage to Santiago de Compostela. As he lay dying in the Gascon monastery of Saint-Sever he made over properties to the monks of Ebreuil in the presence of three *milites* who had accompanied him on pilgrimage. The value of recording this detail is revealed by the statement in the document concerned that the grants were later confirmed in Ebreuil's chapterhouse by Arno's wife and son, who clearly had not been with him when he died. The verb used to express their consent – *testificaverunt* – is interesting. They too were bearing witness to the donation, much as they would have been expected to do had Arno been there in person. But the nature of that witness was changed by the circumstances of Arno's death, and it was therefore wise to record that fact for posterity.[25] It is noteworthy that notices featuring crusaders who found themselves in the same sort of predicament as Arno account for a small but richly informative number of First Crusade documents.[26]

Details could not only serve as a reminder of the fact that a transaction had taken place; they could also relate to the nature of that transaction. Thus many references to crusaders in documents can be explained by the functional value of the information. Clearly, if someone pledged property to a church or made a conditional grant, it would be useful to record that he was leaving on crusade, because the anticipated length of his absence and the possibility of his failing to return bore directly on the circumstances in which property rights would change hands.[27] On the other hand, the desire to set the transaction in its broad context, and thus to locate the individual in a recognisable situation, was at least as important as the narrower consideration of setting out the exact terms of conditional transfers of property. If this had not been so, one would expect that references to crusading would only occur in acts recording pledges and conditional gifts. Donations and sales taking immediate effect would not, strictly speaking, have needed to mention the crusade, because there was no causal link between the passage of title and future events. Yet many documents of this sort also make mention of a departure on the crusade.[28] Similarly, some documents presented the crusade as the background circumstance which explained why a transaction took place. A Norman woman, for example, cited her husband's absence on crusade, and the difficulties this caused her, as the reasons why she had arranged to lease some property for a term of years to the abbey of Troarn.[29]

One reason, therefore, why crusaders appear in charters and notices is the simple fact that the First Crusade was a memorable event which made a wide impact.[30] In this connection it is significant that mention of the crusade is made in a substantial number of dating clauses, usually as an addendum to the customary reference points such as indiction, year of the Incarnation, and regnal year.[31] Here a precedent was well established, for before the crusade many charters were dated by reference to noteworthy or exceptional episodes.[32] Yet it is noteworthy that this usually involved events which were of local interest or directly touched the lives of one of the parties to the document. It was recorded, for example, in a charter from Saint-Evroult that the transaction took place in the same year that one of the monks returned to the abbey from Apulia.[33] If dating clauses opened up their perspective away from the local and immediate, they tended to do so by focusing on the actions of prominent individuals.[34] For instance, a pilgrimage which Count Fulk Nerra of Anjou (987–1040) made to Jerusalem served as a reference point for an Angevin scribe.[35] Some Aquitanian documents referred to Duke William VIII's campaigning in Spain in 1064.[36] A serious illness which befell Duke William II in or shortly after 1063 was recorded in a Norman charter.[37] Some instances of a broader perspective can be found. For example, a charter from the Poitevin abbey of Nouaillé mentions the Almoravid invasion of Spain in 1086. It is noteworthy, however, that in this instance the observation was immediately relevant to the subject matter of the act, a transaction involving someone who was leaving to fight in the peninsula.[38]

In contrast, many of the dating clauses which referred to the First Crusade emphasised the size and communal nature of the crusading enterprise.[39] Moreover, the crusade was often mentioned in documents even though none of the parties was, as far as we can tell, directly involved in the expedition. The crusade's great impact made it a universal reference point, the memory of which could help people to locate their own past actions with greater precision.[40] It is interesting that the language of the dating clauses often resembles those expositives in dispositive clauses in which an individual's actions were placed in the context of a large collective enterprise. Thus the dispositive of a charter from Cluny dated April 1096 includes the following: 'I, Achard, knight, from the castle called Montmerle ... excited by the same intention as this vast and great upheaval and expedition of Christian people wanting to go to Jerusalem to fight for God against the pagans and the Saracens.'[41] This is very similar in emphasis to a dating clause in a document from Marcigny which is otherwise not expressly about crusading: 'in the year that Pope Urban II came to Aquitaine and stirred up an army of Christians to restrain the savagery of the eastern pagans'.[42]

A further reason why crusading influenced diplomatic practice was the tendency of monastic and clerical scribes to focus particular attention on what were, from their point of view, the extremes of lay behaviour in relation to the Church's institutions, teachings and material resources. Lay people were commonly portrayed in stark terms as either well-disposed and praiseworthy supporters or as hostile aggressors.[43] This is particularly clear in the many instances in which the two types are juxtaposed: an individual is introduced in a document as an opponent and then transforms into a benefactor.[44] It is noteworthy that the transition from the one state to the other was routinely expressed very tersely by means of short adjectival constructions referring to the actor's state of mind (for example, *penitentia tactus*), or by simple adverbs as abrupt and unnuanced as *tandem* or *postea*.[45] Scribes seldom concerned themselves with the precise and delicate stages by which people revised their ideas. Actions with long-term consequences, the stuff of written memory, were seen to flow from well defined and discrete sets of attitudes. Consequently, certain types of activity tended to be prominent in documents because they sat neatly within the prevailing dichromatic view of lay behaviour.[46]

It follows that an important reason why crusaders appear in the documentary record is that the crusade fitted easily within the existing categories of noteworthy behaviour. This was so because crusading could be treated as an extension of pilgrimage, both in terms of its motivational underpinning and because of its harsh physical realities. In charters from before the First Crusade, pilgrimage is the most frequently mentioned contextual reference point apart from situations in which the institution producing the document was directly involved, for example when a lay person made an entry gift on taking the habit, when children were handed over as oblates, or when a lay person's family made a request for his or her burial.[47]

Monks and canons were accustomed to taking note of the pilgrimage practices of their neighbours. Departure on pilgrimage, like going on crusade, was seen as a suitable opportunity to resolve outstanding disputes about past transactions.[48] A long absence on pilgrimage or crusade, and the demands made on family resources, posed a serious threat to a kindred's equilibrium. A family in disequilibrium was a potentially litigious and disruptive force. Some crusade charters therefore originated in monks and clerics making it their business to anticipate trouble.[49] Departing pilgrims and crusaders also made their way into the documentary record because they sought intercessory services; knowing that prayers were being offered on one's behalf could be very comforting.[50] On a more practical level, pilgrims and crusaders used property transactions to obtain money and supplies for their journeys.[51] The two benefits, spiritual and material, were not mutually exclusive: many pilgrims' charters mention both, as do documents featuring departing crusaders.[52] An intending pilgrim or crusader stood to gain a great deal. For example, the large number of references in eleventh-century charters to the giving of horses or mules as counter-gifts is a good illustration of the potential usefulness of dealings with a religious community.[53]

It is important, however, to distinguish between the motives which might lead pilgrims or crusaders to enter into a property transaction with a religious institution, and thus create the possibility of their entering the diplomatic record, and the reasons why scribes should have felt it appropriate to record their intentions. It is not difficult to think of many different circumstances in which an eleventh-century lord or knight might have wanted to be prayed for, or raise cash, or obtain something useful such as a horse, by realising assets in land. For the most part charters and notices did not expatiate on what these circumstances were.[54] These were generally, though not invariably, beyond the purview of the scribe. But pilgrimage, and by extension crusading, represented important exceptions to the general rule of scribal reticence.[55] They were activities which many charters reveal were treated as closely related to conversion to the religious life; they were therefore within the charmed circle of positive categorisation.[56]

In conclusion, it is important to remember that the documentary record of crusaders is very fragmentary. Neglect, moths, fire, parchment's usefulness as wrapping for gunpowder, the Wars of Religion, and the French Revolution have all taken their toll. It is also important to note that the mention of the First Crusade in contemporary documents was an option, not an imperative. The very diplomatic freedom which makes research into these documents so fruitful can also cut the other way. There are charters dated 1096 or shortly after in which a lord or knight sells or pledges land in return for cash, horses, mules or supplies, but which make no mention at all of the crusade. It is reasonable to suppose that some of these men were intending crusaders, but without independent evidence there is no way of knowing.[57] There also survive documents featuring known crusaders in the performance of the sort of actions which were characteristic of those planning their departures, but which do not mention the crusade.[58]

Yet if one makes allowance for the survival rate of eleventh-century documents and for the chances against the crusade being mentioned in any one charter or notice, the number of surviving references is striking. The documents provide hundreds of names. This is still a small fraction of the total, of course, and by no means a representative sample in terms of the social range of those who left for the East. But it is a significant advance on the sort of picture painted by older histories which drew almost exclusively on the narrative evidence to portray the First Crusade as a quasi-Homeric feat dominated by a handful of great leaders. Crusading can be studied through charters for a number of reasons. Contextualisation created the potential for the crusade to make an impact on the documentary record. The need to locate transactions by reference to the memorable supplemented the more immediately practical reasons why documents mentioned departure on, or death during, the crusade. Scribes communicated their understanding of crusading by developing its analogies with pilgrimage and conversion, actions which already sat comfortably in their expanding, increasingly *narrativité*-coloured, diplomatic vision of the world. Charters therefore serve as important evidence in two ways: for what they reveal about names and details; and because they are a direct link between the people who went on crusade and, in the religious communities which created the documents, one of the mainsprings of the idealism which substantially contributed to their going.

Notes

1 H.E.J. Cowdrey, 'Pope Urban II's preaching of the First Crusade', *History*, 55 (1970), 181–3; *idem*, 'Cluny and the First Crusade', *Revue Bénédictine*, 83 (1973), 302–3; G. Constable, 'Medieval charters as a source for the history of the crusades', in P.W. Edbury (ed.), *Crusade and Settlement: Papers read at the First Conference of the Society for the Study of the Crusades and the Latin East and Presented to R.C. Smail* (Cardiff, University College Cardiff Press, 1985), pp. 73–89; J.S.C. Riley-Smith, *The First Crusade and the Idea of Crusading* (London, Athlone Press, 1986), pp. 23–4, 27–8, 36–9, 44–7, 126–8. See also M.G. Bull, *Knightly Piety and the Lay Response to the First Crusade: The Limousin and Gascony c. 970–c. 1130* (Oxford, Clarendon Press, 1993), pp. 259–61, 267–80. Professor Riley-Smith is preparing a monograph study of early crusaders.

2 The essential guide to the study of diplomatic, particularly useful with regard to France, is now O. Guyotjeannin, J. Pycke and B-M. Tock, *Diplomatique Médiévale*, L'Atelier du Médiéviste, 2 (Turnhout, Belgium, Brepols, 1993). For many useful points of comparison see M.T. Clanchy, *From Memory to Written Record: England 1066–1307*, 2nd edn (Oxford, Blackwell, 1993).

3 See for example, P.D. Johnson, *Prayer, Patronage, and Power: The Abbey of la Trinité, Vendôme, 1032–1187* (New York, New York University Press, 1981), pp. 85–98; A. Debord, *La Société Laïque dans les Pays de la Charente Xᵉ–XIIᵉ s.* (Paris, Picard, 1984), pp. 196–207.

4 For Urban II's requirement that *milites* should go on the crusade see *Die Kreuzzugsbriefe aus den Jahren 1088–1100*, ed. H. Hagenmeyer

(Innsbruck, Verlag der Wagner 'schen Universitäts–Buchhandlung, 1901), pp. 137–8; 'Papsturkunden in Florenz', ed. W. Wiederhold, *Nachrichten der K. Gesellschaft der Wissenschaften zu Göttingen, Phil.–hist. Kl.* (1901), 313–14.

5 D. Barthélemy, *La Société dans le Comté de Vendôme de l'An Mil au xive Siècle* (Paris, Fayard, 1993), pp. 11, 14–15, 19, 28–69, 91–101.

6 For example *Cartulaire de l'Abbaye de Saint-Aubin d'Angers*, ed. B. de Broussillon, 3 vols (Paris, Alphonse Picard, 1903), I, no. 23, an episcopal act referring to an earlier pilgrimage by the abbot of Saint-Aubin; *Recueil des Documents Relatifs à l'Abbaye de Montierneuf de Poitiers (1076–1319)*, ed. F. Villard, Archives historiques du Poitou, 59 (Poitiers, Société des archives historiques du Poitou, 1973), no. 4, in which Duke William VIII of Aquitaine refers back to a pilgrimage he had made to Rome. See also *Cartulaire du Prieuré de Saint-Flour*, ed. M. Boudet (Monaco, Imprimerie de Monaco, 1910), no. 5.

7 E. Zack Tabuteau, *Transfers of Property in Eleventh-Century Norman Law* (Chapel Hill, University of North Carolina Press, 1988), pp. 10–12, 28, 37–9, 142–63.

8 A useful introduction, which offers an overview of the many regional studies, is J-P. Poly and E. Bournazel, *The Feudal Transformation 900–1200*, trans. C. Higgitt (New York, Holmes and Meier, 1991).

9 See the comments of Barthélemy, *Société*, pp. 14–15, 61–4.

10 A. Giry, *Manuel de Diplomatique* (Paris, Librarie Hachette, 1894), pp. 816–18, 826; A. de Boüard, *Manuel de Diplomatique Française et Pontificale*, 2 vols (Paris, Editions Auguste Picard, 1929–48), I, pp. 47–50, 253–4, 321–9; II, pp. 67–107, 117–24. For a useful discussion of subscribers and witnesses, see O. Guillot, *Le Comte d'Anjou et son Entourage au XIe Siècle*, 2 vols (Paris, Editions A. et J. Picard, 1972), II, pp. 5–20.

11 See the useful discussion, with illustrative material referring to a pilgrim or crusader, in Guyotjeannin, Pycke and Tock, *Diplomatique Médiévale*, pp. 272–7. See also Guillot, *Comte d'Anjou*, II, pp. 2–3.

12 Barthélemy, *Société*, pp. 35, 91–2.

13 *Cartulaires des Abbayes d'Aniane et de Gellone*, ed. P. Alaus, abbé Cassan and E. Meynial, 2 vols (Montpellier, Société archéologique de Montpellier, 1898–1900), I, no. 299; *Cartulaire de l'Abbaye de Savigny suivi du Petit Cartulaire de l'Abbaye d'Ainay*, ed. A. Bernard, 1 vol. in 2 (Paris, Imprimerie impériale, 1853), I, no. 867; *Actes des Comtes de Flandre 1071–1128*, ed. F. Vercauteren (Brussels, Académie royale des sciences, des lettres, et des beaux-arts de Belgique, 1938), no. 20; *Cartulaire Manceau de Marmoutier*, ed. E. Laurain, 2 vols (Laval, Imprimerie–librarie Goupil, 1911–45), II, nos. 13–15; *Cartulaire Roussillonnais*, ed. B. Alart (Perpignan, France, Charles Latrobe,

1880), no. 78.

14 *Recueil des Chartes de l'Abbaye de Cluny*, ed. A. Bernard and A. Bruel, 6 vols (Paris, Imprimerie nationale, 1876–1903), V, no. 3755; *Cartulaire de Saint-Vincent de Mâcon*, ed. M-C. Ragut (Mâcon, Emile Protat, 1864), no. 537; *Cartulare Monasterii Beatorum Petri et Pauli de Domina Cluniacensis Ordinis Gratianopolitanae Dioecesis*, ed. C. de Monteynard (Lyons, Louis Perrin, 1859), no. 237 [1]; *Le Cartulaire de Marcigny-sur-Loire (1045–1144): Essai de Reconstitution d'un Manuscrit Disparu*, ed. J. Richard (Dijon, Société des Analecta Burgundica, 1957), no. 286; *Cartulaire de Marmoutier pour le Dunois*, ed. E. Mabille (Châteaudun, France, H. Lecesne, 1874), no. 156.

15 See P.J. Geary, *Phantoms of Remembrance: Memory and Oblivion at the End of the First Millennium* (Princeton, Princeton University Press, 1994), esp. pp. 100–7; A.G. Remensnyder, *Remembering Kings Past: Monastic Foundation Legends in Medieval Southern France* (Ithaca, Cornell University Press, 1995), pp. 19–22, 110–12, 190–1, 274–5.

16 Ignorance that a property transaction had taken place was often used as a basis for subsequent litigation: see for example *Cartulaire de Marmoutier pour le Dunois*, no. 132.

17 For an interesting example see *Chartes de Saint-Julien de Tours (1002–1227)*, ed. L.-J. Denis, 2 vols, Archives historiques du Maine, 12 (Le Mans, France, Société des archives historiques du Maine, 1912–13), I, no. 26, which explains the unusual circumstances in which a vassal of Duke William II of Normandy became a benefactor of the abbey. For a similar case see Tabuteau, *Transfers*, pp. 124–5.

18 Tabuteau, *Transfers*, p. 116 and n. 16.

19 *Cartulaires de l'Abbaye de Molesme, Ancien Diocèse de Langres, 916–1250*, ed. J. Laurent, 2 vols (Paris, A. Picard, 1907–11), 'Premier cartulaire', no. 110.

20 *Cartulaire de Marmoutier pour le Dunois*, no. 25; Cf. *The Cartulary of Flavigny 717–1113*, ed. C.B. Bouchard, Medieval Academy Books, 99 (Cambridge, Mass., Medieval Academy of America, 1991), no. 37; *Cartulaires de l'Abbaye de Molesme*, 'Premier cartulaire', no. 238; Barthélemy, *Société*, p. 92; Tabuteau, *Transfers*, pp. 121–2.

21 *Cartulaire de Marmoutier pour le Dunois*, no. 64.

22 *Cartulaires de l'Abbaye de Molesme*, 'Premier cartulaire', no. 74.

23 *Chartes de l'Abbaye de Jumièges (v. 825 à 1204)*, ed. J-J. Vernier, 2 vols (Rouen, A. Lestringant, 1916), I, no. 32 [v].

24 *Marmoutier: Cartulaire Blésois*, ed. C. Métais (Blois, France, E. Moreau, 1889–91), no. 11.

25 *Chartes du Bourbonnais, 918–1522*, ed. J. Monicat and B. de Fournoux (Moulins, France, Crépin–Leblond, 1952), no. 7. Cf. *Cartulaire de l'Abbaye de Savigny*, I, no. 868; *Recueil des Chartes de l'Ab-*

baye de Cluny, IV, no. 3577; *Cartulaires de l'Abbaye de Molesme*, 'Premier cartulaire', no. 101. See also *Cartulaire de l'Abbaye de Saint Jean de Sorde*, ed. P. Raymond (Paris, Librarie archéologique de Dumoulin, 1873), no. 39, in which an ailing pilgrim struggles home and dies after making a gift to the abbey.

26 *Cartulaire de l'Abbaye de Vigeois en Limousin (954–1167)*, ed. M. de Montégut (Limoges, France, H. Ducourtieux, 1907), no. 113; *Cartulaires de l'Abbaye de Molesme*, 'Premier cartulaire', no. 101. See *Cartulaire de l'Abbaye de Saint-Etienne de Baigne (en Saintonge)*, ed. P-F-E. Cholet (Niort, France, L. Clouzot, 1868), no. 26, which possibly refers back to events on the First Crusade.

27 *Cartulaire de l'Abbaye de Savigny*, I, no. 867; *Recueil des Chartes de l'Abbaye de Cluny*, V, nos. 3703, 3712; *Cartulaire Roussillonnais*, no. 78; *Cartulaire de Marcigny*, nos. 109, 286; *Cartulaires de l'Abbaye de Molesme*, 'Premier cartulaire', no. 245; *Cartulaire de Marmoutier pour le Dunois*, no. 152; 'Cartulaire du prieuré de Saint-Pierre de la Réole', ed. C. Grellet-Balguerie, *Archives Historiques du Département de la Gironde*, 5 (1863), no. 100 [93–7]; *Cartulaire des Abbayes de Tulle et de Roc-Amadour*, ed. J.-B. Champeval (Brive, France, Roche, 1903), no. 644; *Cartulaire de Saint-Jean d'Angély*, ed. G. Musset, 2 vols, Archives historiques de la Saintonge et de l'Aunis, 30 and 33 (Paris, A. Picard, 1901–3), I, nos. 319, 326; *Chartes et documents de Saint-Bénigne de Dijon*, II *(990–1124)*, ed. G. Chevrier and M. Chaume (Dijon, Bernigaud & Privat, 1943), no. 394.

28 For example *Chartes et Documents pour Servir à l'Histoire de l'Abbaye de Saint-Maixent*, ed. A. Richard, 2 vols, Archives historiques du Poitou, 16 and 18 (Poitiers, France, Oudin, 1886), I, no. 183; *Cartulare Monasterii Beatorum Petri et Pauli de Domina*, no. 103; *Cartulaire de Marmoutier pour le Dunois*, no. 151.

29 R. N. Sauvage, *L'Abbaye de Saint-Martin de Troarn au Diocèse de Bayeux des Origines au Seizième Siècle*, Mémoires de la Société des Antiquaires de Normandie, 4th ser., 4 (Caen, France, Henri Delesques, 1911), pp. 304–5.

30 See M.G. Bull, 'The roots of lay enthusiasm for the First Crusade', *History*, 78 (1993), 360.

31 Dating clauses are a subject which would repay further study. For a stimulating demonstration of their potential, see M. Zimmermann, 'La datation des documents catalans du IXe au XIIe siècle: un itinéraire politique', *Annales du Midi*, 93 (1981), 345–75.

32 Giry, *Manuel de Diplomatique*, pp. 579–81. The document in *Recueil des Actes des Ducs de Normandie (911–1066)*, ed. M. Fauroux, Mémoires de la Société des Antiquaires de Normandie, 36 (Caen, France, Caron, 1961), no. 229 mentions the comet of 1066. For an

example of a more prosaic but politically noteworthy event, see the dating of a document from Saint-Evroult referring to William Rufus: *ipso anno quo rex Vuillelmus ... una cum fratre suo Rotberto comite ultra mare profectus est*: Orderic Vitalis, *Historiae Ecclesiasticae*, ed. A. Le Prévost and A. Delisle, 5 vols (Paris, J. Renouard, 1838–55), V, p. 189. Cf. F. Barlow, *William Rufus* (London, Methuen, 1983), pp. 283–4.

33 Orderic Vitalis, *Historiae Ecclesiasticae*, ed. Le Prévost and Delisle, V, p. 185 (part of an appendix of documents not present in Marjorie Chibnall's modern edition of Orderic's *Ecclesiastical History*). Dating by the consecration of churches was a common point of local reference: see for example *ibid.*, V, p. 196.

34 For a notable instance see the early twelfth-century Poitevin charter in *Chartes et Documents pour Servir à l'Histoire de l'Abbaye de Saint-Maixent*, I, no. 238: *quando Guillelmus comes et Ugo Brunus habuerunt guerram, et illa terra et alie multe combuste sunt et destructe.*

35 *Cartulaire de l'Abbaye de Saint-Aubin d'Angers*, I, no. 130. See also *Cartulaire Noir de la Cathédrale d'Angers*, ed. C. Urseau (Paris, A. Picard, 1908), no. 28. For Fulk's pilgrimages see B.S. Bachrach, 'The pilgrimages of Fulk Nerra, count of the Angevins, 987–1040', in T.F.X. Noble and J.J. Contreni (eds), *Religion, Culture, and Society in the Early Middle Ages: Studies in Honor of Richard E. Sullivan*, Studies in Medieval Culture, 23 (Kalamazoo, Michigan, Medieval Institute Publications, 1987), pp. 205–17. Cf. *Chartes et Documents pour Servir à l'Histoire de l'Abbaye de Saint-Maixent*, I, no. 118, which refers to a pilgrimage to Rome by Duke William VIII of Aquitaine.

36 *Cartulaire de l'Abbaye Royale de Notre-Dame de Saintes*, ed. T. Grasilier, Cartulaires inédits de la Saintonge, 2 (Niort, France, L. Clouzot, 1871), no. 229; *Cartulaire de l'Abbaye de Saint-Cyprien de Poitiers*, ed. L. Rédet, Archives historiques du Poitou, 3 (Poitiers, France, Oudin, 1874), no. 569. Cf. *Recueil des Documents Relatifs à l'Abbaye de Montierneuf*, no. 62.

37 *Recueil des Actes des Ducs de Normandie*, no. 224.

38 *Chartes de l'Abbaye de Nouaillé de 678 à 1200*, ed. P. de Monsabert, Archives historiques du Poitou, 49 (Poitiers, France, Société des archives historiques du Poitou, 1936), no. 158; cf. no. 157. See Bull, *Knightly Piety*, pp. 83–4.

39 *Cartulaire de Marmoutier pour le Dunois*, no. 64: *tempore quo exercitus Christianorum ibat in Jerusalem contra paganos*; *Chartes et Documents pour Servir à l'Histoire de l'Abbaye de Charroux*, ed. P. de Monsabert, Archives historiques du Poitou, 39 (Poitiers, Société française d'imprimerie et de librairie, 1910), no. 22: *anno secundo*

postquam fortissimi milites ac pedites Christi ... prefatam sanctamque urbem [Jerusalem] *divina potentique virtute ceperunt non minima Turcorum atque paganorum multitudine interempta, ipso etiam sanctissimo loco ab illorum spurciciis emundato*; *Recueil des Documents Relatifs à l'Abbaye de Montierneuf*, no. 36: *tempore Willelmi* [WIlliam IX of Aquitaine] *qui Jherosolimam exercitum conduxit*; *Cartulaires de l'Église Cathédrale de Grenoble dits Cartulaires de Saint-Hugues*, ed. J. Marion (Paris, Imprimerie impériale, 1869), B no. 2: *quando Jherusalem obsessa fuit et capta a christianis nostris*; *Chartes de Saint-Julien de Tours*, I, no. 51: *tempore profectionis communis Aquilonensium et Occidentalium*; *Cartulaire de l'Abbaye de Lézat*, ed. P. Ourliac and A-M. Magnou, 2 vols, Collection de documents inédits sur l'histoire de France, 17–18 (Paris, Comité des travaux historiques et scientifiques, 1984–7), I, no. 649: *anno .III°. quo sancta civitas Jherusalem a christianis capta est*; *Cartulaire de l'Abbaye de Saint-Aubin d'Angers*, I, no. 354: *quando Urbanus papa primum commovit orbem ire Jerusalem*; *Cartulaire Noir de la Cathédrale d'Angers*, no. 65: *anno quo innumerabilis populus ibat in Hierusalem ad depellendam pincenatorum perfidiae persecutionem*. See also *Chartes et Documents de Saint-Bénigne de Dijon*, no. 394: *cum, post captam a Xpristianis sanctam civitatem Jherusalem, innumerabilis omnium hominum multitudo illuc pergeret ardenti amore et desiderio*.

40 A substantial number of dating clauses were inspired by Pope Urban II's presence in France in 1095–6: see for example *Cartulare Monasterii Beatorum Petri et Pauli de Domina*, no. 126: *Marmoutier: Cartulaire Blésois*, nos. 69, 73–4; *Cartulaire de Marmoutier pour le Dunois*, nos. 64, 151–3; *Cartulaire de Marcigny*, no. 119; *Cartulaire de l'Abbaye de Saint-Chaffre du Monastier, Ordre de Saint Benoît, suivi de la Chronique de Saint-Pierre du Puy et d'un Appendice de Chartes*, ed. C.U.J. Chevalier (Paris, Picard, 1884), p. 139.

41 *Recueil des Chartes de l'Abbaye de Cluny*, V, no. 3703. See also *Cartulaires de l'Abbaye de Molesme*, 'Premier cartulaire', no. 10; *Chartes de Saint-Julien de Tours*, I, no. 57; *Cartulaire de l'Abbaye de Saint-Chaffre*, p. 88.

42 *Cartulaire de Marcigny*, no. 119.

43 See for example *Cartulaire de Marmoutier pour le Dunois*, no. 57, in which the story of the theft of a prior's horses is used to establish the enmity towards the abbey of the layman who is the main subject of the notice.

44 See *Cartulaire de l'Abbaye de Saint-Chaffre*, pp. 88, 139–41.

45 *Marmoutier: Cartulaire Blésois*, no. 73; *Cartulaire de Marmoutier pour le Dunois*, no. 57; *Cartulaires de l'Église Cathédrale de Grenoble*, B no. 71; *Cartulare Monasterii Beatorum Petri et Pauli de Domina*, no. 126.

46 For a good example, involving first crusaders, see *Cartulaire de l'Abbaye de Saint-Chaffre*, pp. 139–41.

47 For example, *Recueil des Chartes de l'Abbaye de Cluny*, IV, no. 2867; *Chartes de Saint-Julien de Tours*, I, no. 9. See Bull, *Knightly Piety*, pp. 210–17.

48 *Cartulaire des Abbayes de Tulle et de Roc-Amadour*, no. 119; *Cartulaire de l'Abbaye de Saint-Aubin*, II, no. 826; *Cartulare Monasterii Beatorum Petri et Pauli de Domina*, no. 233 [107]; *Cartulaire de l'Évêché du Mans (936–1790)*, ed. B. de Broussillon, Archives historiques du Maine, 1 (Le Mans, France, Société des archives historiques du Maine, 1900), no. 7. For crusaders resolving disputes before departure see *Cartulaire de Saint-Jean d'Angély*, II, no. 448; *Cartulaire de Marmoutier pour le Dunois*, no. 152; *Chartes et Documents de Saint-Bénigne de Dijon*, no. 398; *Cartulaire de l'Abbaye de Saint-Chaffre*, pp. 88, 140.

49 For example *Cartulaire de Marmoutier pour le Dunois*, no. 85; *Chartes Normandes de l'Abbaye de Saint-Florent près Saumur*, ed. P. Marchegay (Les Roches-Baritaud, Société des Antiquaires de Normandie, 1879), no. 20.

50 *Chartes et Documents de Saint-Bénigne de Dijon*, no. 398; *Cartulaire de Marmoutier pour le Dunois*, no. 92; *Cartulaire Manceau de Marmoutier*, II, no. 15; *Cartulaire de l'Abbaye de Beaulieu (en Limousin)*, ed. M. Deloche (Paris, Imprimerie impériale, 1859), no. 84; *Cartulaire de Saint-Jean d'Angély*, II, no. 416; *Cartulaires de l'Abbaye de Molesme*, 'Premier cartulaire', nos. 7, 146.

51 *Cartulare Monasterii Beatorum Petri et Pauli de Domina*, no. 103; *Cartulaire du Prieuré de Saint-Mont*, ed. J. de Jaurgain, Archives Historiques de la Gascogne, 2nd ser., 7 (Paris, Honoré Champion, 1904), no. 26; *Chartes et Documents pour Servir à l'Histoire de l'Abbaye de Saint-Maixent*, I, no. 183; *Recueil des Chartes de l'Abbaye de Cluny*, IV, no. 3071; V, nos. 3840, 3850; *Cartulaire de Saint-Jean d'Angély*, II, no. 450; *Cartulaire de l'Abbaye de Saint-Aubin d'Angers*, I, no. 166; *Cartulaire de l'Abbaye de Saint-Chaffre*, pp. 88–9, 141; *Cartulaires de l'Abbaye de Molesme*, 'Premier cartulaire', nos. 111, 238; A. Sohn, *Der Abbatiat Ademars von Saint-Martial de Limoges (1063–1114): Ein Beitrag zur Geschichte des Cluniacensischen Klösterverbandes*, Beiträge zur Geschichte des älten Möchtums und des Benediktinertums, 37 (Münster, Aschendorff Verlag, 1989), p. 347.

52 For example *Cartulare Monasterii Beatorum Petri et Pauli de Domina*, no. 237 [1].

53 For example *Marmoutier: Cartulaire Blésois*, no. 76; Sauvage, *L'Abbaye de Saint-Martin de Troarn*, p. 131; *Cartulaire de l'Abbaye de Saint-Chaffre*, p. 50; *Cartulaire de l'Abbaye de Savigny*, I, no. 748.

54 For an unusual case, see the document in Orderic Vitalis, *Historiae Ecclesiasticae*, ed. Le Prévost and Delisle, V, p. 190, in which a man confirms grants made by relatives and receives 5s with which to buy a psalter for his son, who has been sent off to school. See also *ibid.*, V, p. 184, in which two brothers receive a horse from the abbot of St-Evroult, when confirming predecessors' gifts, because the older brother wishes to train the younger as a knight.

55 See *Chartes de Saint-Julien de Tours*, I, nos. 9, 10; *Recueil des Chartes de l'Abbaye de Cluny*, IV, no. 2867. For praise of a pilgrim going to Jerusalem, see *Cartulaire Noir de la Cathédrale d'Angers*, no. 109.

56 See *Chartes de l'Abbaye de Jumièges*, I, no. 39; *Cartulaire de Cormery précédé de l'Histoire de l'Abbaye et de la Ville de Cormery d'après les Chartes*, ed. J-J. Bourassé, Mémoires de la société archéologique de Touraine, 12 (Tours, France, Guilland–Verger, 1861), no. 51. Departing pilgrims/crusaders sometimes negotiated the option of taking the habit on their return: see *Cartulaire de Saint-Jean d'Angély*, I, no. 319; II, no. 416; *Cartulaire de l'Abbaye de Lézat*, I, no. 240. In *Cartulaire de Marmoutier pour le Dunois*, no. 133, an ill layman decides to convert, recovers his health, and journeys to Jerusalem. See also *Cartulaires de l'Abbaye de Molesme*, 'Premier cartulaire', no. 107, in which dying, the taking of the habit, and travelling to Jerusalem are treated as equivalent forms of *discessus*.

57 For example Sauvage, *L'Abbaye de Saint-Martin de Troarn*, pp. 131–2, 220–1; *Cartulaire Noir de la Cathédrale d'Angers*, no. 66; *Cartulaire de Saint-Jean d'Angély*, I, no. 321; *Cartulaire de l'Abbaye de Saint-Aubin*, II, no. 742; *Cartulaires de l'Église Cathédrale de Grenoble*, B no. 95.

58 For example *Cartulaire de Marmoutier pour le Dunois*, no. 64, which features the crusader Nivelo of Fréteval.

4

The First Crusade: reviewing the evidence

Susan Edgington

There is a legendary moment in the historiography of the First Crusade: in 1837 Leopold von Ranke held a seminar in Berlin at which he overturned all previous ideas about the relative value of the sources.[1] His pupil Heinrich von Sybel took up the challenge and in 1841 produced a history of the First Crusade which stressed the primacy of the eye-witness accounts and set the agenda for a century and a half of crusade historiography.[2] This survey of the sources for the First Crusade does not reveal any dramatic new finds in the field, but it proposes a re-evaluation which perhaps – ironically – brings us closer to the ideal of Ranke himself, who believed it was the task of the historian to 'tell it as it really was': *wie es eigentlich gewesen.*[3] Nowadays three of the Latin narrative accounts are generally accepted to be the work of eye-witnesses.

The narrative entitled *Gesta Francorum* is the shortest and most direct. An English translation, by Rosalind Hill, has been available since 1962.[4] It was accepted by Professor Hill, as by previous commentators since Heinrich Hagenmeyer in 1890, that the anonymous author was a knight, but Colin Morris has recently argued cogently, using stylistic evidence, that he was a cleric.[5] He was certainly a pilgrim who had started as an adherent of Bohemond of Taranto but left him after Antioch to continue with the main army to Jerusalem. The greater part of the text was completed soon after the capture of Jerusalem, but as long ago as 1928 August Krey drew attention to the possibility that Bohemond used the *Gesta* for propaganda purposes during his campaign against the Byzantine Empire in 1105–6, and that he was responsible for at least one interpolation, namely a passage where the emperor is said to have granted Bohemond lands around Antioch.[6] Nonetheless, the immediacy of the *Gesta*'s narrative soon attracted interest in the West, as we shall see, and it retains a high reputation today, even though Professor Morris has exposed it as less ingenuous than its artless style suggests, and John France has challenged its value to the military historian of the First Crusade.[7] It should be noted here that Professor Hill's readable version does have one idiosyncracy, important in view of the historiographical argument below, which is the use of 'Franks' to translate both *Galli* and *Franci*. This gives the impression that in this earlier work the expedition was already viewed as an exclusively 'Frankish' enterprise.

Like the *Gesta* author, Raymond of Aguilers ended his account with the battle of Ascalon. Raymond wrote in the early 1100s and had access to the *Gesta Francorum*. His style is certainly more 'clerical' than the *Gesta*'s, as befits a chaplain of Raymond of St Gilles, count of Toulouse. An English translation was published in 1968 by J.H. and L.L. Hill; their edition appeared in 1969.[8] The same duo later translated (1974) and edited (1977) Peter Tudebode's *Historia de Hierosolymitano Itinere*, and in their introduction they posited that these three histories (Raymond's, Tudebode's and the *Gesta*) all drew on a common source, which Tudebode represented most closely.[9] The more usual position is that Peter Tudebode, though a participant in the First Crusade (on which his two brothers died), used the *Gesta* extensively, and his work is therefore chiefly of ancillary value, adding convincing and circumstantial detail particularly about the sieges of Antioch and Jerusalem.

Raymond, in contrast, added a great deal to the *Gesta*. He certainly used the anonymous account, especially for the period of the siege of Antioch, but after that his work may be treated as an independent source. As history, Raymond's account has the strengths and weaknesses of his position as chaplain to the count of Toulouse: he was privy to the councils of the princes and has a clearer idea about policy than other writers, but he was more interested in religion and politics than in military matters or the day-to-day experience of crusading. He is, of course, blatantly partisan, but his Provençal bias is in itself a valuable corrective to other sources.

The third important eye-witness, Fulcher of Chartres, was also a cleric. He had been present at the Council of Clermont in November 1095 and travelled east with the army of Duke Robert of Normandy, Court Stephen of Blois and Count Robert II of Flanders. He joined Count Baldwin of Boulogne, Godfrey of Bouillon's brother, when he captured Edessa and remained there with him rather than participating in the sieges of Antioch and Jerusalem. Fulcher wrote at some length and, unlike the other two primary narratives, he continued after the establishment of the Latin kingdom, when his chronicle, as the work of one of Baldwin's own household, becomes invaluable. The most accessible translation of Fulcher's first book is perhaps the one in Edward Peters (ed.), *The First Crusade* (1971), and in his preface Peters claims high importance for him:

> Fulcher's presence throughout most of the expedition, his close connection with the princes of northern France and later with Baldwin, and his ability to organize a maze of complex experiences and motives, make his chronicle perhaps the most reliable of all sources for the First Crusade.[10]

This judgment does not stand up to critical assessment: Fulcher provided an excellent description of the battle of Dorylaeum, but after early 1098 he was not an eye-witness of the events he described and was reliant on the accounts of others, including the *Gesta Francorum*.[11] His partiality for Baldwin is a matter of slanted perspective rather than a basis for reliable reporting and anyway, rather disappointingly, he is very discreet about controversial matters, and reluctant to commit himself on the quarrels of the leaders. As for any tendency to 'organize' his material: this immediately renders his account suspect by today's standards of historiography.

Crusade historians are, of course, immensely fortunate that three independent eye-witness accounts of such quality have survived. That the writers travelled with different leaders and therefore wrote from different viewpoints makes them even more valuable. Yet there is a danger of complacency. Historians have examined exhaustively how the three authors confirm and complement each other; they have looked less readily at the gaps and shortcomings they have in common. First, these accounts were all written after the event. They were composed in the light of the successful outcome of the expedition, and this imparts an air of historical inevitability to the narratives. This, of course, may be taken into account and allowed for. It is easier to forget other ways in which later developments may have coloured attitudes to earlier events. An example is the crusaders' dealings with the Byzantines, where reciprocal accusations of treachery over events at Antioch heavily influenced the way in which the writers depicted the crusaders' reception in Constantinople and subsequent relationships. The historiographical consequences of this are discussed in more detail below.

The most readily available redress to the imbalance which hindsight imports to the sources is to look at the crusaders' letters. One or two of these are comparatively well known and widely reproduced, but there are in all about twenty, which were collected by Hagenmeyer at the turn of the century, and provided with his usual detailed commentary.[12] In the letters we read the views of the crusaders unmediated by their subsequent experiences. To touch again on the example of relations with the Byzantines, the first surviving letter of Stephen of Blois to his wife Adela gives a completely different picture of the Emperor Alexius from the three narrative accounts ('he received me like his own son, with all kindness and honour'): Stephen had his own reasons for glamorising his role to his wife, but he may not have been alone among the leaders in being flattered by Alexius, though the others were quick to disown such feelings later. In the same letter Stephen communicates the optimism felt by the crusaders after the capture of Nicaea: 'I tell you, my beloved, we shall reach Jerusalem from Nicaea in five weeks, unless Antioch stands in our way,' a prophecy which reads poignantly in view of his later desertion, but gives a true glimpse of the moment in which it was written.[13] Stephen's letters are outstanding and often quoted, but those of the nobleman Anselm of Ribemont to Archbishop Manasses of Rheims, and from the leaders of the crusade to the pope also provide snapshots of thoughts and attitudes at different stages during the expedition.[14] A critical translation of the letters would be a useful adjunct to the narrative sources.

There is another type of evidence which shares the immediacy of the letters. This is the information provided by charters, mainly in France. Giles Constable drew attention to this source,[15] but it is Jonathan Riley-Smith who has led the systematic examination of the cartularies. Some of the results may be seen in his work, *The First Crusade and the Idea of Crusading*, but the most perfect elaboration to date is Marcus Bull's *Knightly Piety and the Lay Response to the First Crusade*.[16] These specialised pieces of research have begun to address fundamental questions, such as, 'Why did people go on crusade?' and 'Did they expect to come home again?' Like the letters, contemporary charter evidence, where it exists and is used critically, disentangles people's thoughts and actions at the time from later reflection and justification. Unfortunately, charter evidence does not exist for all groups of people who went on crusade, and it is important not to misconstrue a lack of charters as meaning an absence of crusaders from areas where charter evidence has never existed or has been destroyed, and where other arrangements may have been made for the safeguard of property and the provision of funds. There is, for example, evidence in other sources for substantial contingents of pilgrims from Germany and Scandinavia who made the journey by sea.[17] Details of their financial arrangements do not survive.

This reflection introduces another criticism of the evidence reviewed so far. All of it shares an inherent bias which is more insidious, because less easily recognised, than the gloss which hindsight has lent to proceedings. All of it was written by people who lived in or came from territories in France and Italy (as they are today) which adhered to the papal line. For these writers there was no room for doubt: Pope Urban II was the instigator of the expedition, and its participants, if not called 'pilgrims' or 'soldiers of Christ', were collectively referred to as 'Franks'. But all the participants were not Frankish: for example, there was a large and influential contingent of Lotharingians led by Godfrey of Bouillon, who had actively fought *against* the pope in the Investiture Contest. The role of these people has been consistently understated in the historical record. It is certainly true that many of the leaders and participants were broadly speaking French or Norman, but nonetheless the 'Frankish' sympathies of the eye-witness narrators began a distortion that has been magnified by time.

This progressive bias may be seen developing in the group of historians who reworked the *Gesta Francorum* in the first decade of the twelfth century: Guibert of Nogent, Baldric of Bourgueil and Robert the Monk.[18] Guibert, a prominent theologian, actually called his history *Gesta Dei per Francos* and the theme of the French as chosen people was taken up by Robert too, quite explicitly, in the words he put into Urban's mouth at Clermont: 'Race of the French, race living beyond the Alps, race chosen and beloved by God, as is radiantly shown by your many deeds ....' Robert's *History* survives today in over 120 manuscripts, which is a phenomenal index of popularity for a twelfth-century work and far eclipses any other narrative of the First Crusade. He was evidently telling the story as people wanted to hear it, and his version quickly became established as the standard narrative of events – and the accepted interpretation, too. The crusades, first proclaimed by a Frenchman on French territory (to use again anachronistic political–geographical terms) became viewed as an almost exclusively French activity. Later, when times were bad for the French, they took comfort from their glorious crusading history, notably in the nineteenth century.[19] Twentieth-century historians have scarcely questioned this perception. For example, in his commentary on the works of Guibert, Baldric and Robert in *The First Crusade and the Idea of Crusading*, Jonathan Riley-Smith analysed the term *Gesta Dei* and commented on the phrase *per Francos*, but he did not perceive the incipient nationalism of the latter term to be as remarkable as the theological implications of the former expression.[20]

There are three other Latin historians of the First Crusade, all of whom were in the Holy Land soon after the kingdom of Jerusalem was established. Caffaro, the Genoese civil servant, wrote that rare thing, a totally secular chronicle, very short but valuable for its different perspective.[21] Ekkehard of Aura participated in the 1101 expedition and also wrote a brief account, drawing on chronicles by Frutolf of Michelsberg and on his own experience.[22] Ralph of Caen went out to the East in 1108 and there wrote a panegyric of his lord, the *Gesta Tancredi*, which, despite its pretentious style and its rabid anti-Provençal tone, contains some fascinating and valuable detail.[23] None of these exists in a complete English translation, and all of them merit a wider readership.

Beyond this handful of Latin writers, together with the *Historia* of Albert of Aachen, which is discussed below, and the Old French *Chanson d'Antioche* (if we accept its attribution to Richard the Pilgrim), surviving contemporary evidence from the West concerning the First Crusade is either indirect or fragmentary, frequently both. Among the indirect sources of information may be classed such materials as hagiography and vernacular epic, which provide insight into the mentality of the crusaders. Likewise, the iconography of eleventh-century churches highlights some of the ideas of popular religion, as Malcolm Barber has shown.[24] Monastic annals, crusader songs and liturgical fragments rarely add anything of factual importance to our knowledge, although they do, again, bear testimony to attitude, to motivation and – importantly – to theological interpretation.[25]

The first six books of the *Historia* attributed to Albert of Aachen comprise the most complete, the most detailed and the most colourful narrative of the First Crusade.[26] Yet his work is comparatively little used, largely because there has been no consensus as to the reliability of the text, or, indeed, other aspects of it, even the author's name. There is one certainty, which has coloured historians' opinions of the work perhaps unduly: we know that the author never went to the East.

Within the constraints of this essay it is possible to do no more than offer a résumé of the author's credentials before examining what his work contributes to the panel of evidence. There is very little intrinsic or extrinsic information about the writer. He was probably called Albert and almost certainly a cleric at Aachen in the Rhineland. From the way he wrote his preface it would appear that his initial intention was to write about the great expedition of 1096 and the liberation of the Holy Places, an aim he achieved in six books, probably completed in the early 1100s, though not before 1102. He subsequently carried the narrative forward to 1119, perhaps inspired by the knowledge that the kingdom of Jerusalem was established by his local noble family, the lords of Bouillon. These second six books are of prime importance for their period, when far fewer other sources survive, but they are not our current concern.

The reason Albert's evidence is crucial is that it is fully independent of the Latin sources enumerated above. Hagenmeyer suggested that Albert knew both Fulcher of Chartres' work and the *Gesta Francorum*, but his claim cannot be substantiated: it would require Albert to have used tiny fragments of these narratives and to have ignored vast amounts of tempting material, and it may be said with some certainty that Albert was not a selective writer.[27] Modern historians are uncomfortable with an independent source with no known written antecedents, and this led Bernhard Kugler, over a hundred years ago, to hypothesise a 'lost Lotharingian chronicle', that is to say a written prose source, now lost, which Albert augmented with other records, both oral and written, some in prose but some in verse.[28] It was a seductive theory because, firstly, it accounted for the uneven quality of Albert's information, which combines prosaic detail with poetic flights of fancy; secondly, it licensed an eclectic use of the *Historia* (not unknown today) whereby details could be attributed to the Lotharingian eye-witness if they supported one's case; consigned to the realm of epic romance when they did not.

Referring to 'epic romance', there is one extant source which shares a relationship with Albert's *Historia*, though the nature of the relationship is contentious. This is the *Chanson d'Antioche*, an epic poem in Old French which now exists only in a late-twelfth-century form, as reworked by Graindor of Douai from, he claimed, an earlier *chanson* by an eye-witness, Richard the Pilgrim. The *Chanson*'s twentieth-century editor, Suzanne Duparc-Quioc, undertook a rigorous analysis of the *Chanson d'Antioche* which separated the material she believed Graindor had taken from Richard the Pilgrim's original *chanson* (which she claimed Albert used) from that which Graindor added in his reworking, largely from Robert the Monk.[29] She found some support for her reconstruction of Richard's *chanson* in a 'Provençal fragment'.[30] Mme Duparc-Quoic was sufficiently confident of her case to claim that Albert could be used to 'reconstitute' Richard the Pilgrim's *chanson*.[31]

This interpretation of the relationship between Albert's *Historia* and the *Chanson d'Antioche* was unchallenged until 1980 when Robert Cook published a new study of the *Chanson*, in which he offered a revisionist thesis.[32] He argued at considerable length that the *Chanson* was written entirely in the late twelfth century and according to the rules of epic prevailing at that time, which included the fabrication of the eye-witness, Richard the Pilgrim. Professor Cook pointed out that the 'historical' content of the *Chanson d'Antioche* was to be found in different chronicles, a circumstance which was most easily explained by the writer's drawing on several of them, including Albert. However, Cook's theory does not meet in full the old, but valid, point that the poet, if he had at his disposal all the riches of Albert's *Historia*, was most eccentric in his selection of certain incidents for inclusion and his ignoring of others equally exciting and colourful. Because Albert's is the fuller account the most likely relationship remains the one assumed by Duparc-Quoic, that Albert used an earlier version of the *Chanson*. Thus the primitive *Chanson* might be added to the select group of eye-witness sources.

As far as Albert is concerned, and assuming he used the *Chanson*, it seems unlikely that there was a written copy of it in front of him: there are differences which he might then have avoided. The assumption which would best explain the relationship between the text of the *Historia* and the putative primitive *Chanson d'Antioche* is that Albert wrote his own detailed notes after hearing a recitation or recitations. This would fit in with what Albert himself tells us about his sources: in his preface he says he had his information *ex auditu et relatione ab his qui presentes affuissent* – 'from listening to those who had been there, and from their reports' (AA, I.1). This implies a mixture of oral and written information, gathered from returning crusaders, which he wove into a coherent narrative. As well as factual information, his work contains anecdotes and travellers' tales, invented speeches and exaggerated numbers. All of these things make it difficult to use as historical evidence and have contributed to its neglect, but it is arguable that Albert's very lack of selectivity enhances his value as a source, or resource, today. He gives a picture of the *experience* of crusading which is unparalleled: he assumed that his audience would be as interested in the Turks' use of carrier pigeons or the Syrians' manufacture of sugar as they were in battles and sieges; he recounted the privations of pregnant women as well as the councils of princes. The result is a synthesis rather than an analysis of information, which leaves the historian to make value judgments instead of imposing them on him.

Used critically, then, what light does Albert's history throw upon the First Crusade? Albert focused his account on Godfrey of Bouillon and on the house of Lorraine. This is not extraordinary if – as all the evidence suggests – he lived in Godfrey's home territory and gained his information largely from Godfrey's followers as they returned from the East. Book II of the *Historia* is a detailed account of Godfrey's expedition across Europe; most of the information is found only in the *Historia*. In Book III and later books, his brother Baldwin's career in Edessa is related, again with much circumstantial detail found nowhere else.

Albert is also responsible for the story that Peter the Hermit was the prime mover of the crusade, a story which was adopted and disseminated by William of Tyre and was virtually unchallenged for seven hundred years. The best discussion of this tale is in 'A Hermit Goes to War' by Ernest Blake and Colin Morris.[33] This focus in Albert's *Historia* away from the pope as instigator of the crusade and from Adhémar as spiritual leader is in contrast to the eye-witness accounts and there has been a tendency to confuse two separate issues: that is to say, Raymond, Fulcher and the *Gesta* author have been given credence because of their eye-witness status, while

Albert has been accused of distortion because he did not go on crusade. But Albert *was* an eye-witness of the preaching of the crusade, and whether he was genuinely unaware of the magnitude of the pope's role or he deliberately suppressed it, he has to be taken seriously as representing perceptions and opinion in the Rhineland.

In reality the difference of emphasis, here as elsewhere, has less to do with participation in the crusade and much more to do with the politics of Christendom: Godfrey had fought on the side of the emperor in the Investiture Contest and Albert continued to be a strong supporter of Henry IV. It is notable that Albert does not describe the crusaders as Franks; his preferred term is 'Gauls'.[34] The question whether Albert consciously exaggerated the extent of 'German' participation in the crusade was examined in detail by Peter Knoch in his 1966 study.[35] That Albert should have done so is no more surprising than that Robert, Guibert and Baldric stressed the 'Frenchness' of the enterprise. Papal/imperial bias is a factor to consider in reading any history of this period.

Albert also has a distinctively ecumenical concept of Christianity, which Colin Morris has explored in a paper on the 'Aims and spirituality of the First Crusade'.[36] Throughout Albert's narrative he portrays a strong sense of Christian fellowship, transcending different traditions of worship, which again sets him apart from the 'French monastic' writers. Notably, his view of eastern Christians, and especially of the Byzantines, is relatively impartial. This different perspective, with its implications for understanding the internal and external politics of the crusade, is examined in detail below. For centuries perceptions of the part played by the Greeks in the First Crusade were formed by the consistently anti-Byzantine narratives of the Latin eye-witness accounts. Historians of the post-war generation were brought up on Runciman's history, which redressed the balance in a heavily pro-Byzantine direction.[37] Recently Ralph-Johannes Lilie's study, *Byzantium and the Crusader States, 1096–1204*, has appeared in English.[38] This provides a wealth of detail, and it is particularly welcome for its critical appraisal of Anna Comnena's work,[39] but Lilie also adopts a conflict model to examine the relationship from the earliest days of the crusade.

Throughout Albert's work, and in contrast to the eye-witness narratives, his treatment of the Byzantines is outstanding for its lack of prejudice. Bunna Ebels-Hoving, who dealt with this in her doctoral thesis, referred to Albert's 'simple and objective' rendering of the facts and his 'exceptionally independent and impartial mind-set'.[40] As evidence she cited the way in which Albert described the Emperor Alexius: not only did he refrain from negative qualifications, he frequently valued him very positively; he used admiring adjectives (*magnificus, nominatissimus* AA, I.13; *Christianissimus* AA, I.15), and he emphasised details of the emperor's conduct, including his generosity and forbearance towards a stream of Latin leaders. The worst epithet Albert applied to the Greeks as a people is *effeminati*, in a speech by Qilij Arslan, the sultan of Rūm (AA, IV.6). When he censured treason towards Swein of Denmark (AA, III.54), he made it clear that it was the act of a defined group of people – 'their presence was betrayed by certain wicked Christians, that is to say Greeks' (*quorundam Christianorum, Grecorum scilicet*). On two occasions Albert recorded unfavourable opinions of the emperor: where Godfrey was warned against him by some Franks (AA, II.10), and where Bohemond hesitated to take the oath *eo quod imperator uir callidus et subdolus haberetur* (AA, II.18). In both cases Albert was quoting the opinion of others, not necessarily concurring with it.

The first leader to arrive in Byzantine territory in 1096 was, of course, Peter the Hermit, whose followers had caused trouble *en route*. News of this reached the emperor – whose amazement at the nature of the West's response to his appeal echoes even forty years later in his daughter's account – by way of a message from the governor of Nish, Nicetas.[41] Alexius' response was to admonish Peter rather paternally and to furnish him with an escort to ensure that he would move quickly and peaceably through Byzantine territories (AA, I.13). According to Albert, the emperor directed that Peter was to be treated well as a fellow-Christian. When the nature of Peter's company became clear to him Alexius did not abandon the pilgrims, but continued to look after them by ensuring an abundance of supplies for as long as two months, and he warned them explicitly about the dangers from the Turks in the area around Nicaea (AA, I.15). Albert makes it absolutely clear that the Turkish attack, and the massacre of pilgrims which ensued, resulted from their disobeying both Peter and the emperor. Peter was in Constantinople at the time, negotiating for more supplies. Albert's Book I is the sole Latin source for all this.

He also gives the fullest description by far of Godfrey's journey across Europe and his reception in Constantinople; since it is so uniquely detailed it has, of necessity, formed the basis of all subsequent accounts, from William of Tyre to Steven Runciman. However, Runciman, as will be seen, employs selectivity and subtle distortion to throw an unfavourable light upon the crusaders and, where Anna Comnena's account differs from Albert's, Runciman invariably prefers hers. This may be seen in the description of Godfrey's reception.[42] Albert records that Godfrey was welcomed with entire goodwill and sumptuous gifts in every major city of the empire. More importantly – in order to ensure there was no looting – licences to buy food were granted. The crusaders' response (according to Albert) has the ring of truth: 'Therefore it was proclaimed to all that they should not seize anything at all by unjust force, except fodder for the horses.'

All went on in an orderly fashion until the army reached Philippopolis (Plovdiv). Albert's account of the sequence of events there differs significantly from Runciman's, although this section of Runciman's history is based entirely on Albert:[43]

> Messages were brought to him there that the emperor held Hugh the Great, the king of France's brother, Drogo and Clarebold in prison and in chains. … When the duke heard this he sent an embassy to the emperor, requesting him to restore to freedom these princes of his land whom the emperor was holding prisoner, otherwise he would not be able to keep the duke's trust and friendship. … [When] the duke's messengers came back from the emperor, they reported that he had not given up the captive princes at all. This made the duke and all his company furiously angry, and they refused to give the emperor trust and friendship any longer. And at once on the duke's instructions all that land was handed over to the pilgrims and foreign soldiers for plundering; they delayed there for eight days and devastated all this region. (AA, II.7–8)

The emperor's response was to invite Godfrey to make haste with his army to Constantinople, where he camped outside the city. An early messenger was Count Hugh of Vermandois; Runciman claims: 'Hugh, so far from resenting his treatment at the emperor's hands, willingly undertook the mission.' This goes rather beyond the evidence: Albert merely says Hugh was delighted to see Godfrey and that imperial envoys arrived at the same time with an invitation to visit the emperor, which Godfrey declined.

Runciman says, 'He felt out of his depth.' Albert explains it more logically:

> Hardly had the duke received this legation when certain strangers from the land of the Franks arrived secretly in the duke's camp, and they warned him very seriously to beware the tricks and poisoned garments of the emperor, and his deceitful words, and under no circumstances to go into his presence, no matter what coaxing promises he gave, but to sit outside the walls and, in safety, mistrust everything he offered to them. The duke, therefore, warned in this way by the strangers and well schooled in the Greeks' deceptions, did not go into the emperor's presence at all. On this account the emperor felt a violent indignation against the duke and all his army, and forbade them a licence to buy and sell.

Baldwin responded by looting the suburbs; the emperor lifted the blockade. A four-month stand-off ensued (AA, II.10).

There is then in Albert's account a curious incident which Runciman ignores. Godfrey received messengers from Bohemond:

> 'Bohemond, the most wealthy prince of Sicily and Calabria, asks you in no way to return to friendship with the emperor, but to withdraw into the Bulgarian cities of Edirne and Plovdiv and to spend the winter months there, confident because at the beginning of March Bohemond himself will be there with all his forces to help you overcome this emperor and invade his domain.'
>
> When he had heard this legation from Bohemond, the duke put off making any reply to it until the next sunrise when, after taking counsel of his men, he replied that he had not left his homeland and family for the sake of profit or for the destruction of Christians, but had embarked on the journey to Jerusalem in the name of Christ, and he wished to complete the journey and to fulfil the intentions of the emperor, if he could recover and keep his favour and goodwill.
>
> After Bohemond's messengers understood the duke's meaning and his reply, and they were courteously commended by him, they returned to the land of Apulia to report everything just as they had learnt it from the lips of the duke. (AA, II.14)

Of course, we have only hearsay evidence that it happened thus – but such a message is very much in character for Bohemond.

Far from Godfrey's realising 'he was no match for the emperor' (as Runciman would have it), the Lotharingians who reported their experiences to Albert did not feel that their duke had been over-awed and manipulated; they reported his actions as those of a man of honour who negotiated on something like equal terms with Alexius:

> Now, the emperor found out about this new legation from Bohemond and his suggestion, and he urged the duke and his comrades the more concerning a peace, saying that if he wished to please him and cross his land peacefully the duke should indeed present himself face to face in discussions; he, the emperor, would give his own very beloved son, John by name, as hostage, and would grant to the duke and his men all necessary supplies, with the permit to buy. (AA, II.15)

The long-delayed meeting was a splendid affair, but though Albert stresses the magnificent dress of the crusaders, he is alive to the significance of the protocol, and reports that Alexius remained seated while Godfrey and his men were expected to bow. While this is disagreeable enough to be true, the description of the vow made has the air of wishful thinking and was probably invented by Albert or his informant:

> Then when everyone had been kissed according to rank he spoke to the duke in these words: 'I have heard about you that you are a very powerful knight and prince in your land, and a very wise man and completely honest. Because of this I am taking you as my adopted son, and I am putting everything I possess in your power, so that my empire and land can be freed and saved through you from the present and future multitudes.'
>
> The duke was pleased and beguiled by the emperor's peaceful and affectionate words, and he not only gave himself to him as a son, as is the custom of this land, but even as a vassal with hands joined, along with all the nobles who were there then, and those who followed afterwards. (AA, II.16)

Alexius' reception of Godfrey has been reported in detail because it is on this episode that Albert is most likely to be well informed. His account of the arrival (or in Tancred's case, non-arrival) of the other leaders agrees with the established sources, including the 'special relationship' formed between the emperor and Raymond.[44] It is important to recognise that there is no evidence in the Lotharingian source that Godfrey arrived in Alexius' territory with anti-Byzantine prejudices in his baggage, so to speak. When suspicion and antagonism did arise, logical explanations are offered, and the resultant discord seems to have been resolved without residual bitterness. Above all, Albert does not read back into the reception at Constantinople the division which arose after Antioch.

At Nicaea, Albert's account makes clear the co-operation between Byzantines and Latins, and the nature of the agreement as he understood it:

> On imperial orders sailing merchants were striving to race across the sea with ships full of rations, corn, meat, wine and barley and oil; they dropped anchor at the port of Civitos where crowds of the faithful procured all sorts of provisions to revive bodies formerly oppressed by hunger. As they enjoyed and rejoiced in this abundance of food they agreed and confirmed that they would not depart until the city was overcome and taken and might be restored into the emperor's power. For of course they had promised with an oath not to keep any part of the emperor's kingdom, no fortresses, no cities, unless by his wish or gift. (AA, II.28)

Albert's portrayal of the emperor's behaviour at Nicaea contrasts with the *Gesta Francorum*, where it is depicted as devious and calculating.[45]

The *Historia*'s treatment of the pivotal event during the siege of Antioch when the renegades, who included Stephen of Blois, dissuaded the emperor from coming to the crusaders' assistance also shows Alexius in a different light from that cast by the *Gesta*:[46]

> William and the other William, Stephen and their fearful and fleeing comrades prepared ships, both rowing- and sailing-vessels, and embarked on the high seas, planning to travel to Constantinople, leaving their brothers besieged, and thinking they would never be rescued from Kerbogha's hands ....
>
> At length ... they heard that the Christian emperor of the Greeks had arrived at the city of Philomelium with a great company of men and much equipment to assist the pilgrims, as he had promised faithfully when they were joined to him in friendship by an oath and agreed treaty. He had brought together some four hundred thousand Turcopoles, Pechenegs, Cumans, Bulgars, and Greeks skilled with bow and arrow, Danes excellent at fighting with the battle-axe, Gaulish exiles, also an army of mercenaries ... from all his very extensive kingdom. The princes mentioned above found the emperor with this

strength of weapons, men and horses, and with supplies of food, tents, mules and camels, and found with him a new army of Gauls, around forty thousand, which had been assembled through the long winter, also Tatikios with the cut-off nose who, like them terror-stricken, had withdrawn in false faith from the allies to that same emperor, to carry a message because of the promised relief, which he had not done faithfully at all, having not returned to Antioch again.

As the emperor recognised the princes coming into his presence he wondered greatly how they came to be there without their allies, and he questioned them closely about the situation of their faithful fellow-soldiers of Christ, about the health of Duke Godfrey, Count Raymond, the bishop of Le Puy, whether things were going well or badly for them. The princes replied that they were not at all in a state of well-being or safety, but were besieged by Kerbogha prince of Khorazan and the gentile nations in such a way that not a single way in or out of the great city was open, and no one could ever escape Kerbogha's hands unless by stealth. They also reported the great famine by which the pilgrims were distressed, and how the Turks had destroyed merchants and ships from hatred of them. They declared that no one at all from the army could live in face of so great a multitude, that they themselves had only just escaped by their own wits, suggesting to the emperor that he turned back and did not put his army through torment to no purpose.

When the emperor heard about these dangers to the Christians and was informed about the gentiles' forces he took counsel with his nobility then, trembling and terrified, he ordered the entire army to turn back immediately. ... Therefore the terrible news of the emperor turning back and his army dispersing sped across the ramparts of Antioch and afflicted the pilgrims' hearts with great grief and shook much of the boldness from their spirits. (AA, IV.40)

This agrees very well with Anna Comnena's account, although Albert is unable to add her clinching argument, concerning the reinforcements being brought up by Kerbogha's son.[47] The *Gesta* depicts Alexius as mean as well as cowardly.[48] And in spite of the emperor's failure to relieve the crusaders at Antioch, Albert reports that Godfrey still considered himself bound by the oath:

It is true that Raymond, count of the aforesaid region of Provence, always insatiable in his acquisitiveness, attacked that tower which was close to the bridge on the Ferna in the direction of the port of St

Simeon and garrisoned it with his followers, and forced this part of the city to submit to his authority. The rest of the princes, Duke Godfrey, Robert of Flanders, Robert prince of Normandy and all those who had laboured no less hard about the city, did not seek at all to rule the city or to bestow on themselves its revenues or tribute, not wanting to violate the treaty and solemn promise they had made to the emperor of Constantinople. For they had vowed to him that if Antioch were taken they would keep it for him with all the castles and cities belonging to his kingdom, because it was part of his kingdom like Nicaea, and they would restore it to his sovereign power. (AA, V.2)

However, in the very next chapter:

Shortly after the victory God granted to them, the above princes, those whose concern was to keep the treaty and oath, sent Baldwin count of Hainault together with Hugh the Great, the king of Francia's brother, in a legation to that same emperor of the Greeks, to find out from him the reason why he had acted so wickedly towards the people of God, and why when they were in so great difficulty he had failed to produce the assistance he had promised, since he could not find the princes deceitful or misleading in anything so far. They were also instructed to point out to that same emperor that the princes of the army considered themselves released from any promise or oath because at the prompting of fearful and fugitive men he lied about all the things he had promised. (AA, V.3)

This passage is quoted *verbatim* because Runciman is selective about his use of Albert's account.[49] In particular he says that the princes could not know at this point that Alexius had turned back, and so he claims that the princes absolved themselves from the oath only because he had not turned up to help them. But according to Runciman's own chronology there was a fortnight between the meeting with Stephen (mid-June) and the battle of Antioch (28 June); while Stephen had only left Antioch, 'with a large body of the Northern French', on 2 June. It is fair to assume that bad news would travel faster than a large body of men. The contradiction between the two passages above is explained if the news of the emperor's withdrawal arrived and Godfrey changed his position on the oath as a result.

That the oath was not a dead issue, even after Antioch and Jerusalem were captured, is shown in Albert's discussion of events at Latakia:[50]

After the capture of Antioch, Count Raymond, having decided to journey with the others to Jerusalem, restored to the emperor of Constantinople the town of Lattakieh which had been seized from the Turks and gentiles, so that he would in this way keep his oath to him unbroken. For Raymond had vowed and made a treaty with him, along with Duke Godfrey and the other princes, that they would not keep any at all of the cities, lands and castles belonging to his kingdom, nor would they deceive him. For this reason, when the princes returned from Jerusalem and were quartered in the territory of the town of Jubay, and they realized Bohemond had unfairly besieged Latakia, and had wronged the emperor and Count Raymond, they appointed messengers who addressed Bohemond in friendly and peaceful fashion on the instruction and request of the Christian brothers returning victoriously from Jerusalem, and asked him to withdraw from the siege of the city and not to inflict any further injustice on Christians. (AA, VI.55)

As before, Albert does not seek to absolve either party from blame, but he seeks a rational explanation for their actions. Of all the contemporary historians he gives the clearest idea of the Constantinople discussions forming a contract. He is, of course, eager to exonerate Godfrey from the blame of breaking it, but he does not assume that there has been an irretrievable breakdown in diplomatic relations even after the conquest of Jerusalem. His later chapters show Godfrey and his brother Baldwin maintaining a relationship of mutual respect with the Emperor Alexius, in spite of Bohemond's efforts to disrupt it.

Thus Albert of Aachen shows impressive independence of mind with regard to the Byzantines. It might be argued that this is a function of his geographical distance from the events he describes, but equally it may represent an attitude shared by his countrymen who went on crusade and whose views, usually under-reported and under-valued, Albert conveys. It has been usual to disregard his evidence, whether it relates to fact or to attitude, if it conflicts with the other sources. This does no service to the political complexity of the First Crusade. To maintain that the Lotharingian contingent did not demonise the Greeks, and that their leaders sought to maintain a reasonable working relationship with them, is not to undermine the different views put forward by other chroniclers, but to add a new dimension of understanding to them.

At the very least Albert's account of the First Crusade should be given weight as that of an intelligent and well informed Western observer; more usefully it should be treated as a serious counter-balance to the three eye-witness accounts of the crusade and those derived from them, who shared a 'Frankish' tendentiousness. If Albert of Aachen's *Historia* is given its due weight, then the contribution to the First Crusade of the Rhinelanders and other forces from the Empire must be re-assessed.

Two Christian writers in the East wrote important, though very different, works in which the crusades are prominent. Anna Comnena's *Alexiad* is well known and is available in two English translations. Sometimes, however, the terms used differ quite significantly. For example, in reference to the crusading leaders' vow to Alexius, it is described by one as an oath of fidelity, by the other as an oath of allegiance; later, one calls it an oath and the other a treaty.[51] This underlines the point that translation is interpretation and hence must be treated with caution. The *Alexiad* has been called 'the most mendacious of the sources',[52] but this is to take it seriously as history, which, to give Anna her due, was never her intention. Read as a panegyric of the Emperor Alexius, and in the knowledge that it was written some forty years after events, with all the selectivity of memory that implies, it may be used, cautiously, to understand the impact the arrival of the Western armies had on the court at Constantinople and how the motives of the leaders were perceived, if not at the time, then by a later generation.

The chronicle of Matthew of Edessa has recently been published in English for the first time, translated by Ara Dostourian as *Armenia and the Crusades*.[53] In fact only ten pages are devoted to the First Crusade, but these are as anti-Byzantine as Anna's are pro-Byzantine. The reporting of events frequently disagrees not only with Anna, but also with the Western accounts; however, the importance of the chronicle lies in its explication of near-eastern politics rather than its factual content. It still awaits a full historical commentary. Also translated from Armenian (into French by Claude Cahen) is a unique fragment written by an inhabitant of Antioch during the siege in 1098.[54] Another Eastern source, the chronicle of Michael the Syrian, is not yet available in English, and its information about the First Crusade is anyway slight.[55] The anonymous Syriac chronicle translated by Arthur Tritton adds convincing detail.[56]

There were two points at which the crusade impacted on Jewish communities. The massacres of the Rhineland Jews in 1096 were commemorated in two Hebrew accounts which have been the subject of an important study by Robert Chazan.[57] These corroborate as well as supplement the fullest Latin account of the pogroms, by Albert of Aachen. The fate of the Jews of Jerusalem after its capture in 1099 is illuminated by the discovery of two letters in the Cairo Genizah: these were published by Solomon Goitein in 1952.[58]

Lastly, a little about the Arabic sources for the First Crusade: those available in translation are few and brief.[59] Of them, the only surviving contemporary account is Ibn al-Qalānisī's *Damascus Chronicle*, of which Hamilton Gibb published some translated extracts in 1932.[60] Ibn al-Athīr and Kamāl āl Dīn wrote in the thirteenth century, incorporating earlier materials now lost, but they contain little of interest for this early period. Some translated extracts from Ibn al-Athīr are available in Francesco Gabrieli's anthology of Arab historians.[61] The paucity of Arabic sources is in itself a salutary reminder that the First Crusade was of peripheral significance to the Islamic East, while the comparative richness and complexity of the Western sources underlines the movement's central importance to the consciousness of Western Christendom.

Notes

1 P. Knoch, *Studien zu Albert von Aachen* (Stuttgart, Ernst Klett Verlag, 1966), p. 10.

2 H. von Sybel, *Geschichte des Ersten Kreuzzugs* (Düsseldorf, Schreiner, 1841).

3 Quoted in A. Marwick, *The Nature of History* (London, Macmillan, 1970) from the preface to Ranke's first book, *Geschichten der Romanischen und Germanischen Volker von 1494 bis 1514* (Leipzig, Duncker und Humblot, 1824), p. vii.

4 GF.

5 *Anonymi Gesta Francorum et Aliorum Hierosolymitanorum*, ed. H. Hagenmeyer (Heidelberg, Carl Winters Universitätsbuchhandlung, 1890); C. Morris, 'The *Gesta Francorum* as narrative history', *Reading Medieval Studies*, 19 (1993), 55–71.

6 A.C. Krey, 'A neglected passage in the *Gesta* and its bearing on the literature of the First Crusade', in L.J. Paetow (ed.), *The Crusades and Other Historical Essays presented to Dana C. Munro* (New York, Crofts, 1928), pp. 57–78.

7   France, *Victory*, pp. 377–9.

8   *Raymundus de Aguilers, Historia Francorum qui ceperunt Iherusalem*, trans. J.H. and L.L. Hill, (Philadelphia, American Philosophical Society, 1968); RA.

9   *Historia de Hierosolymitano Itinere [de] Peter Tudebode*, trans. J.H. and L.L. Hill, (Philadelphia, American Philosophical Society, 1974); PT.

10   E. Peters (ed.), *The First Crusade: The Chronicle of Fulcher of Chartres and Other Source Materials*, (Philadelphia, University of Pennsylvania Press, 1971), p. 23. For a most thorough examination of Fulcher and his work, see V. Epp, *Fulcher von Chartres Studien Zur Geschichtsschreibung des Ersten Kreuzzugs* (Düsseldorf, Droste, 1990).

11   France, *Victory*, pp. 175–80.

12   Hagenmeyer, *Epistulae*.

13   *Ibid.*, pp. 138–40.

14   *Ibid.*, pp. 144–6 (Anselm); 149–52 (Stephen); 153–5 (princes); 156–60 (Anselm); 161–5 (leaders).

15   G. Constable, 'Medieval charters as a source for the history of the crusades', in P.W. Edbury (ed.), *Crusade and Settlement: Papers read at the first conference of the Society of the Crusaders and the Latin East and presented to R. C. Smail* (Cardiff, University College Cardiff Press, 1985), pp. 73–89.

16   J. Riley-Smith, *The First Crusade and the Idea of Crusading* (London, Athlone Press, 1986); M. Bull, *Knightly Piety and the Lay Response to the First Crusade: The Limousin and Gascony, c. 970–c. 1130* (Oxford, Clarendon Press, 1993).

17   The best summary of this evidence is in the introduction to C.W. David, *De Expugnatione Lyxbonensi*, Columbia University Records of Civilization, 24 (New York, Columbia University Press, 1936), pp. 5–26.

18   Latin texts of the three accounts are to be found in *RHC Oc.* as follows: Robert, III.717–880; Baldric, IV.1–110; Guibert, IV.113–262.

19   See, for example, J.S.C. Riley-Smith, 'The crusading movement and historians', *The Oxford Illustrated History of the Crusades*, ed. J.S.C. Riley-Smith (Oxford, Oxford University Press, 1995), photograph and caption, p. 7.

20   Riley-Smith, *First Crusade*, pp. 135–52, and especially pp. 147–8.

21   Caffaro, *De liberatione civitatum Orientis*, in *RHC Oc.* V.41–72. See also R.D. Face, 'Secular history in twelfth-century Italy: Caffaro of Genoa', *JMH* 6 (1980), 169–84.

22   Ekkehard of Aura, *Hierosolymita*, in *RHC Oc.* V.11–38; *Frutolfi et Ekkehardi Chronica*, ed. F.-J. Schmale and I. Schmale-Ott. Ausgewählte Quellen zur deutschen Geschichte des Mittelalters 15 (Darmstadt, Germany, Wissenschaftliche Buchgesellschaft, 1972).

23   RC.

24   M. Barber, *The Two Cities: Medieval Europe 1050–1320* (London, Routledge, 1992), p. 124 and plate 2.

25   See, for example, J. France, 'The text of the account of the capture of Jerusalem in the Ripoll manuscript, Bibliothèque Nationale (Latin) 5132', *EHR* 103 (1988), 640–57.

26   The Latin text may be found in *RHC Oc.* IV.265–713, or, better, in S.B. Edgington, *The Historia Iherosolimitana of Albert of Aachen: a critical edition*, unpublished Ph.D. thesis, University of London 1991, to be published by Oxford Medieval Texts with English translation.

27   *Anonymi Gesta Francorum*, ed. Hagenmeyer, pp. 62–92; FC, p. 80.

28   B. Kugler, *Albert von Aachen* (Stuttgart, Kohlhammer, 1885).

29   *La Chanson d'Antioche*, ed. S. Duparc-Quioc, 2 vols (Paris, Librairie Orientaliste Paul Geuthner, 1977–8).

30   P. Meyer (ed.), 'Fragment d'une chanson d'Antioche en Provençal', *Archives de l'Orient Latin* 2 (1884), 467–509; S. Duparc-Quioc, *Chanson d'Antioche*, 171–205.

31   S. Duparc-Quioc, *Chanson d'Antioche*, 11/2, pp. 148–70.

32   R.F. Cook, *'Chanson d'Antioche', chanson de geste: le cycle de la croisade est-il épique?* (Amsterdam, Benjamins, 1980).

33   E.O. Blake and C. Morris, 'A hermit goes to war: Peter and the origins of the First Crusade', *Monks, Hermits and the Ascetic Tradition*, in W.J. Shiels, Studies in Church History 22 (Oxford, Blackwell, 1985), pp. 79–107.

34   Cf. the comment on *Gesta Francorum* above.

35   Knoch, *Studien*, pp. 116–19 and 125.

36   C. Morris, 'The aims and spirituality of the first crusade as seen through the eyes of Albert of Aix', *Reading Medieval Studies* 16 (1990), 99–117.

37   Runciman, I, *passim*.

38   R.-J. Lilie, *Byzantium and the Crusader States 1096–1204*, trans. J.C. Morris and J.E. Ridings (Oxford, Clarendon Press, 1993).

39   Sewter, *Alexiad*.

40   B. Ebels-Hoving, *Byzantium in Westerse Ogen 1096–1204*, Ph.D. thesis: University of Groningen (Assen 1971), especially pp. 84–8.

41   Sewter, *Alexiad*, pp. 308–9.

42   Sewter, *Alexiad*, pp. 318–19; 322–4.

43   Runciman, I, pp. 149–50.

44   But see Lilie, *Byzantium*, p. 52, who argues that the relationship was a later development.

45   GF, p. 17.

46   GF, pp. 63–5.

47   Sewter, *Alexiad*, p. 349.

48 GF, p. 65.

49 Runciman, I, pp. 239–40.

50 For an excellent attempt at untangling the question of Latakia, see Lilie, *Byzantium*, Appendix 1, pp. 259–76.

51 E.A.S. Dawes (trans.), *The Alexiad of the Princess Anna Comnena* (London, Kegan Paul, 1928), pp. 261–8; Sewter, *Alexiad*, pp. 322–31.

52 France, *Victory*, p. 382.

53 Matthew of Edessa, 'Chronicle', in, *Armenia and the Crusades: Tenth to Twelfth Centuries:* trans. A.E. Dostourian (Lanham, Maryland, University Press of America, 1993).

54 C. Cahen, *Orient et Occident au Temps des Croisades* (Paris, Aubier Montaigne, 1983), pp. 221–2.

55 Michael the Syrian, pp. 182–9.

56 A.S. Tritton, 'First and Second Crusades from an anonymous Syriac chronicle', *Journal of the Royal Asiatic Society* (London, 1933) 69–101; 273–305.

57 R. Chazan, *European Jewry and the First Crusade* (Berkeley, University of California Press, 1987). The chronicles are printed as an appendix, pp. 225–97.

58 S. Goitein, 'Contemporary Letters on the capture of Jerusalem', *Journal of Jewish Studies*, 3 (1952), 162–77.

59 For an account of sources not available except to readers of Arabic, see Dr Carole Hillenbrand's paper in this volume.

60 Ibn al-Qalānisī, *Damascus Chronicle*, extracts ed. and trans. H.A.R. Gibb as *The Damascus Chronicle of the Crusades* (London, Luzac and Co., 1932).

61 F. Gabrieli, *Arab Historians of the Crusades* (London, Routledge and Kegan Paul, 1969).

5

The Chronicle of Zimmern as a source for the First Crusade

The evidence of MS Stuttgart, Württembergische Landesbibliothek, Cod. Don. 580

Alan V. Murray

When Pope Urban II proclaimed his expedition to the East at Clermont on 27 November 1095 he probably did not intend Germans to be part of it; the kingdom of Germany was still riven by the great struggle between empire and papacy which had arisen between the Emperor Henry IV and Urban's predecessor Gregory VII. This conflict, which came to be known as the Investiture Contest, together with the many local and regional feuds which interacted with it, helps explain the ambivalent German response to the pope's appeal. For most German lords and prelates, this would have been an inopportune time to leave their responsibilities, whether temporal or spiritual. The German episcopate stayed away from Clermont, and in many parts of Germany the first substantial news of the crusade must have arrived from France along with the first of the so-called 'People's Crusades', those expeditions which left the West before the official starting date of 15 August 1096. Some Germans joined up with the armies led by Peter the Hermit and Walter Sans-Avoir, while others left with German leaders such as Emicho, Folkmar and Gottschalk. It is significant that we can say little about the status or origins of these three; they and most of their followers were killed or dispersed long before they could reach the Holy Land, and posterity was not too interested in such failure.[1] Most of the chroniclers who described the expedition to Jerusalem devoted their attention to the 'official' or 'Princes' Crusades'. It is thanks to one of these full-length accounts, that of Albert of Aachen, that we are extremely well informed about the army of Godfrey of Bouillon, duke of Lower Lotharingia, which represented the main contribution to the crusade from the kingdom of Germany, although it should be noted that while most of his followers may have been subjects of Henry IV, the majority of the lords and knights were probably French-speakers from the duchies of Lower and Upper Lotharingia.[2] It is therefore remarkable that there should survive a source from the sixteenth century which apparently provides unique evidence of the participation in the crusade of a large number of lords and knights from southern Germany. It is the reliability of this source, generally known as the *Zimmerische Chronik* or Chronicle of Zimmern, which I intend to examine here.

The *Zimmerische Chronik* is a chronicle written in Early New High German (ENHG), the work of Froben Christoph, count of Zimmern (now Herrenzimmern, Baden–Württemberg) and lord of Meßkirch and Wildenstein (1519–66), which treats the history of his family from the time of the Roman republic up to his own day. It survives in two manuscripts which were formerly kept in the library of the princes of Fürstenberg at Donaueschingen and which were recently acquired by the Württemberg State Library in Stuttgart.[3] The first printed edition of the chronicle was published by the Donaueschingen librarian, Karl August Barack, and was immediately noticed by Reinhold Röhricht who pointed out its importance for the German involvement in the First and Second Crusades.[4] However, it was only in 1884 that Heinrich Hagenmeyer published the section of the chronicle dealing with the First Crusade, along with a translation into French (by Furcy Raynaud) and a detailed discussion endorsing its value as a source. Hagenmeyer was able to include references to Barack's second edition which had appeared in the meantime.[5] In 1964 a new edition was begun, which is scheduled to be completed by the year 2000.[6]

Since Hagenmeyer's discussion, some key studies have appeared which have thrown considerable light on Froben Christoph of Zimmern and his methods. It is clear that he made extensive use of materials written or compiled by his uncle, the jurist and historian Wilhelm Werner of Zimmern (1485–1575), although these were not always acknowledged by him. Beat Jenny has demonstrated that Froben Christoph frequently 'improved' his sources, especially when they evidently failed to reflect the prominence that he thought his family deserved. One of the recurring themes of the chronicle is his conviction that the Zimmern family originally had comital or even ducal status rather than that of free lords, which was their rank until Zimmern was raised to a county by Charles V in 1538 (see I, pp. 43–4; III, pp. 126–9).[7]

As far as scholarship on the First Crusade is concerned, almost every citation of the Chronicle of Zimmern and its evidence derives from and relies on Hagenmeyer's translation and discussion of 1884. One of the greatest problems in evaluating the Zimmern account is that research on the crusades has not kept pace with that on German local and regional history; conversely, most of the German historians who have discussed the chronicle have not really been concerned with its treatment of the crusade, which is fairly peripheral to the general concerns of the work. Thus, the evidence of the Chronicle of Zimmern has been accepted as genuine by most historians of the First Crusade since Hagenmeyer, and almost all modern accounts of the People's Crusades make use of names or events supplied solely by Froben Christoph.[8] A critical evaluation of this source is long overdue. In so far as the limitations of length permit, I would like at least to initiate this evaluation in two respects: firstly, to re-examine the question of the sources used by the account of the crusade, and secondly, to provide an English translation of the relevant text which is more literal than the French version by Hagenmeyer and Furcy Raynaud, as a means of making the ENHG text more accessible. This new translation is given in the Appendix below.

The chronicle describes the crusade in four chapters (I, pp. 74–85), each with a summary heading. After establishing the chronology of the expedition in relation to the Investiture Contest in the bishopric of Konstanz, Froben Christoph begins his account with a programmatic discussion, claiming that the crusade has been described at great length by *Guido Remensis*, Robert the Monk and particularly William of Tyre. However, since these and other writers (he continues) originated in France and the Low Countries they have tended to give most attention to the nobles of their own countries, to the neglect of the nobility of southern Germany. After a discussion of two local sources (to which I will return) he tells how the crusade originated in a vow made by Godfrey of Bouillon after he contracted an illness during the siege of Rome by Henry IV in 1081. In the course of the next twelve years Godfrey laboured to raise funds for the expedition, and when his intention became known, he was chosen unanimously as leader by the crusaders. There follows a list of German bishops, princes and lords who took the cross. Among the other participants, we are told, were three brothers, Albrecht, Conrad and Frederick, lords of Zimmern. The second chapter (I, pp. 77–8) describes their departure, but is mostly concerned with a pestilence which killed several members of the Zimmern family in Germany.

The third chapter (I, pp. 78–9) tells how Godfrey of Bouillon led the entire army to Asia Minor. After an initial victory over the Turks, the crusaders advanced into hostile territory towards Nicaea. The German contingent, initially cautious, grew ever bolder, until a foraging expedition of 200 knights and 4,000 foot-soldiers was surrounded and massacred by the Turks. The German leaders, Hugh of Tübingen and Walter of Teck, were unable to calm the indignation of the rest of the army, which marched out to avenge the defeat. Although the Germans fought more bravely than those from other countries, the majority of the army was killed, and a list of casualties is given, which includes most of those previously named, including the two commanders. The surviving Germans took service with Godfrey of Bouillon. These included Frederick of Zimmern, on whom the remainder of the story now focuses. After some time in the service of King Baldwin I of Jerusalem (1100–18), Frederick returned to Germany. The final chapter (I, pp. 80–5) relates his growing discontentment and resolution to go again to Syria. To finance his journey, he demanded a share of the family estates from his brothers. He greatly oppressed the people of his lands, and eventually disposed of his entire inheritance, raising a large number of followers. On arriving in Syria, they fought in the siege of Acre (supposedly in 1106), where Frederick was grievously wounded and his entire retinue killed. He lamented his fate until told by a priest that it was a divine punishment for his exactions on his peasants in Germany. Frederick then did penance for these misdeeds and spent the rest of his life in the service of Baldwin II of Jerusalem (1118–31).

At a superficial level this account seems extremely valuable, since it contains considerable detail which is not known from any other source, particularly in three respects: the participation of a large number of nobles and their followers from southern Germany, the defeat of the German contingent by the Turks before Nicaea, and the deeds of Frederick of Zimmern in the service of three rulers of Jerusalem. Since this account of the crusade was written down over 450 years after the events it describes, we cannot judge it by the same criteria as the major primary accounts, which were mostly written within a few decades of the crusade. Hagenmeyer recognised that the Chronicle of Zimmern drew on a variety of earlier sources, some of them mentioned at the beginning of the account, that is Robert the Monk, William of Tyre and the unidentified *Guido Remensis*. Others are listed at the end of MS B. Of these, some are fairly late, such as the humanist Aventinus (1477–1534), who gives a very confused account of the crusade.[9] Others are simply described as *Monumenta* of a particular place, and evidently relate to archives of various noble families, although in the absence of further detail it is impossible to tell precisely which documents were used or how reliable they were. Above all, we must recognise the importance of Count Wilhelm Werner's work as a source, even when this is not explicitly cited by his nephew.[10]

It is thus clear that Froben Christoph's account of the crusade is a compilation drawing on various sources, some named, some unacknowledged. Probably because of this he did not always understand how events narrated by different authors related to one another. It has always been assumed that the Germans described by the Chronicle of Zimmern left the West in one or more of the various groups which belonged to the People's Crusades, rather than as part of the main expedition. However, there is no explicit information to suggest that the author himself was aware of this. He describes the crusade as one expedition, led by Godfrey of Bouillon, which passed through Hungary and Bulgaria to Constantinople and crossed to Asia Minor, where it quickly defeated its first Turkish opposition. The chronicle then goes on to describe in considerable detail two battles involving the Germans, fought near Nicaea. The first was an extended foraging expedition which was ambushed by the Turks. The second was a major attempt to avenge this first defeat, involving Germans and others, in which a large number of the Germans were killed. We are then told that the survivors entered the service of Godfrey of Bouillon.

These events have usually been identified as a description of the fate of a combined French and German army, led by Peter the Hermit and the French knight Walter Sans-Avoir, which was defeated in October 1096 and whose survivors joined the main expedition a year later. This army and its fate are described in greatest detail by Albert of Aachen and William of Tyre, although they are also mentioned in various other accounts. Froben Christoph describes these events as if they occurred during the main expedition rather than a full year before the princes arrived in Asia Minor. It is likely that he elaborated on the account of the expedition of

Peter the Hermit and Walter Sans-Avoir given in two of his named sources. The history of William of Tyre was readily available in an edition printed at Basel in 1549. This would certainly explain the figure of 200 knights and 3,000 foot for the foraging raid, which is the number given by William of Tyre.[11] The chronicle of Robert the Monk was available in German translation in four separate manuscript versions and a printed edition.[12] The reason why Froben Christoph chose to concentrate on this expedition was probably because both William and Robert repeatedly make allusions to Germans being in it; it thus fitted into his purpose in writing the account of the crusade, which, as we have seen, was to highlight the role of the High German nobility.

However, it is the sources unique to the Zimmern account which are central to our discussion, particularly in view of the weight accorded to them by Hagenmeyer. Froben Christoph mentions two particular sources which had come into the possession of the monastery of Alpirsbach from the lordship of Zimmern. The first is *ain alt geschriben buoch*, that is 'an old hand-written book', which he claims was written by one of the three Zimmern brothers who had been on crusade. The second was a tapestry embroidered with pictorial roundels and an accompanying Latin text; both pictures and text supposedly corresponded with the content of the book. We are told that the following account, in so far as it concerns the lords of Zimmern, was drawn from these two interdependent sources (I, p. 74).

In his analysis, Hagenmeyer recognised that several of the names included in the list of German crusaders could not be genuine since they relate to the crusade of 1101. These include Thiemo, bishop of Salzburg, Conrad, bishop of Chur, and Eckhart, count of Scheyern. He argued that they therefore could not have derived from the Alpirsbach codex (the 'old hand-written book'), but that other names did, certainly from Walter of Teck to the unnamed count of Zweibrücken, along with most of the rest of the Zimmern account. Thus the bulk of the German account published by Hagenmeyer is set in italics to indicate his belief that it was translated from the putative Latin text of the Alpirsbach codex.[13] Elsewhere I have tried to demonstrate that most of the names of crusaders given are anachronistic or doubtful, and that only one of them, Hartmann of Dillingen, can be confirmed from other sources.[14] For the present, however, I would like to address the question of the transmission and reliability of the two putative key sources, the tapestry and codex of Alpirsbach, in the light of the claims made for them by Froben Christoph himself.

The actual manufacture of the tapestry is described elsewhere in the chronicle (I, p. 90), which reveals that it was woven over a period of nine years by Elisabeth of Teck, the wife of Godfrey of Zimmern, and nine of her ladies, with the purpose of recording the deeds of Godfrey's three brothers, Conrad, Albrecht and Frederick. The tapestry supposedly illustrated *die ganz historia des zugs geen Jerusalem* ('the entire history of the expedition to Jerusalem') and, according to Froben Christoph, its content corresponded with that of the codex (I, p. 74).[15] However, the chronicle reveals that while the tapestry was still extant at Alpirsbach in 1520, it was torn up and burned during the Peasants' War (1524–25), and that only a few pieces survived which were kept at Herrenzimmern (I, p. 90). Froben Christoph was born in 1519 and therefore could have known the tapestry in its pristine state. However, at this early age he would have been dependent on older members of the Zimmern family or household to explain the significance of the illustrations and the accompanying text. His interpretation of the tapestry probably owed far more to family tradition rather than to his own independent historical research, which does not seem to have been the case with the codex. Certainly the detail that it took nine ladies nine years to complete the tapestry is suggestive of oral rather than written traditions.

The marriage between Godfrey and Elisabeth was evidently of great importance to Froben Christoph, and it is hardly surprising that the lords of Zimmern and dukes of Teck are the two families which figure most prominently in his account of the crusade. We have already seen how much of the account describes the deeds of the three Zimmern brothers, and towards the end it concentrates solely on the second pilgrimage of Frederick of Zimmern. The family of the dukes of Teck plays an important role both in the account of the crusade and the creation of one of the ancient sources, the tapestry. The joint leader of the German contingent, along with Count Palatine Hugh of Tübingen, is given as Walter, duke of Teck (*herzog Walther von Tegk*), who is named on five occasions (I, pp. 75, 76, 77, 78, 79). The tapestry was created by Elisabeth, daughter of Duke Frederick of Teck and wife of Godfrey of Zimmern, a marriage which supposedly dated from before the

departure of Godfrey's brothers on crusade (I, pp. 71, 90). Godfrey's brother Frederick of Zimmern mortgages the lordship of
Rosenfeld to Frederick of Teck, who here is described as the
former's brother-in-law (I, p. 81). There is no indication given that
these two Fredericks were father and son, which would explain the
apparent contradiction.

This is not the only such problem. The chronicle makes no
attempt to describe the family relationship between the leader of the
German crusaders, Duke Walter, and the other named members of
the Teck dynasty, Duke Frederick and Elisabeth, the wife of Godfrey
of Zimmern. This omission clearly troubled Hagenmeyer, who suggested that Walter may not have been a member of the Teck family
at all; rather, in this one case the name *Tegk* may have been a mis-
reading of *Rugk* in the codex, and therefore referred to Walter of
Ruck, lord of a castle situated near Blaubeuren in Swabia and
belonging to a family of *Edelfreie* (free lords).[16] There was a documented Walter, son of Sigiboto of Ruck (d. *c.* 1085), but this identification would mean that Walter's ducal title had been supplied by
a subsequent reader as a result of a mistaken identification with a
member of the Teck dynasty.[17] What is quite unconvincing about
Hagenmeyer's proposed solution is why, if the codex referred to a
Walter of Ruck, a large number of supposed crusaders of comital
rank should have been willing to accord leadership, even joint leadership, to someone of mere baronial rank.

A more likely explanation is that, once again, the information
came from Froben Christoph's uncle. During the 1540s, Wilhelm
Werner of Zimmern compiled a so-called *Heiratenbuch* (Book of
Marriages) recording the marital connections of the Teck dynasty.
The original has been lost, but Rolf Götz has shown that a surviving
copy of this was made sometime before 1575 by the archivist
Andreas Rüttel the Younger (d. 1587).[18] This records the information that a Walter of Teck was a leader of the Germans who left on
crusade in 1096.[19] It is impossible to say on what basis Wilhelm
Werner made his identification. However, what we can say with
complete confidence is that all references to dukes of Teck at the
time of the First Crusade are completely anachronistic, since at that
time there was no noble family, ducal or otherwise, named after the
castle of Teck.

The Teck dynasty was a cadet branch of the dukes of Zähringen.
On the death of Duke Berthold IV in 1186, the Zähringen inheri-

tance was divided between his son Berthold V and his two brothers Adalbert and Hugh. Adalbert received a collection of lordships centred on the castle of Teck and the neighbouring towns of Owen and Kirchheim, and from around 1188 began to use the title 'duke of Teck'. By the end of the thirteenth century the dynasty had split into two separate lines, respectively concentrated around the territorial clusters of Oberndorf and Owen.[20] The name Walter is unknown in either line.[21] However, it is not only the name of the crusader *Walther von Tegk* which is questionable. The Teck family and the repeated references to it are a vital part of the absolute chronology of the account of the crusade. Yet it is impossible for a member of the Zimmern family to have been married to a daughter of a Duke Frederick of Teck at the end of the eleventh century. If there was ever a marriage between the two families, it could not have been at the time of the First Crusade. Conversely, if three of the Zimmern males did take part in the crusade, their brother Godfrey cannot have been married to a Teck. There is a clear conflict between evidence for the Zimmerns on crusade, and the marriage to Elisabeth of Teck. The indications are that the latter was the more plausible event.

The marriage is mentioned repeatedly in the chronicle (I, pp. 71, 81, 82, 89, 90); it is also represented in an illustration in MS B (p. 54) which combines the arms of Zimmern (dexter) and Teck (sinister), which, according to the pattern regularly employed in MS B, symbolises a marriage between a Zimmern male and a Teck female. Independent testimony to such a marriage is also provided by Wilhelm Werner, who recorded (undated) information probably derived from a necrology of Alpirsbach: *Obiit Godefridus de Zimbarn liber dominus, sepultus in monasterio Alpirsbach una cum uxore Elisabete ducisse de Deck.*[22] The absolute *terminus a quo* for the marriage would be 1186 (the date when Adalbert I inherited part of the Zähringen territories). If we accept the chronicle's insistence that Elisabeth of Teck's father was named Frederick, this pushes the chronology even further forward. The name Frederick occurs several times in the Teck line of descent. The first known Frederick belonged to the Owen line, and was a younger son of Duke Conrad II (d. 1292). He was still a minor in 1296 and was dead by February 1303. In view of this short lifespan and the fact that no wife of his is recorded, it is unlikely that Elisabeth could have been his daughter.[23] The earliest realistic candidate is probably

Frederick II, of the Oberndorf line, who is first documented in 1319 in his capacity as advocate of Alpirsbach, and is named as having died in a charter of his brother Ludwig IV issued on 6 November 1343. He was married to Anna, the daughter of William, count of Montfort–Tettnang.[24] The Elisabeth mentioned by the Chronicle of Zimmern may have been an otherwise unrecorded daughter of this Frederick, or one of the later dukes of this name, Frederick III (*c.* 1325–1390) or Frederick IV (*c.* 1370–1410/1413).[26] However, this would mean that any marriage with a Godfrey of Zimmern must necessarily have occurred in the fourteenth rather than the eleventh century.

If the Alpirsbach tapestry was indeed woven by Elisabeth of Teck and her ladies, as the chronicle claims, then it, too, must have belonged to this period rather than the years following the First Crusade. It is possible that circumstantial evidence from elsewhere within the chronicle may also point to a much later dating than the one claimed by Froben Christoph. There is a strong possibility that any tapestry woven in the fourteenth century and illustrating a military expedition would have depicted heraldic devices, since these would have permitted the use of strong, bright colours. Coats of arms began to appear in Europe in the second quarter of the twelfth century. The earliest sigillographic evidence indicates that the use of armorial devices originated in the 1130s among the great nobles of northern France. There was some delay before the new fashion spread to Germany, where it was first taken up by the rank of imperial princes around the middle of the century and gradually spread to the comital and untitled nobility. Given this chronology, it is quite improbable that those crusaders named in the chronicle bore coats of arms in 1096 or indeed for a full half-century thereafter. How likely is it, then, that the crusade tapestry included coats of arms? There is no direct evidence but the chronicle itself gives another revealing case of a heraldic tapestry for which Froben Christoph claims a date in the pre-heraldic age, thus raising doubts about his reliability in dating such evidence. He earlier relates how in the year 1041 a Werner of Zimmern took part in an expedition of the Emperor Henry III against Duke Vratislav of Bohemia (I, pp. 58–9). The army was defeated by the Bohemians, and Werner and many of his compatriots were taken prisoner and kept in shackles by their captors. Thanks to the intervention of Saint Leonard the prisoners were miraculously released, and to commemorate their escape, the

Swabians commissioned a tapestry depicting them along with their shackles and also 'their coats of arms according to which they could be recognised'.[26] This tapestry was kept at the monastery of Ettenheimmünster, but was destroyed in 1525 during the Peasants' War like that kept at Alpirsbach.

Thus the Ettenheimmünster tapestry clearly did show coats of arms, and therefore could not have been commissioned soon after 1041 – in the pre-heraldic age – as the chronicle claims. If this tapestry existed in the form described, then Froben Christoph was claiming a date for it which was at least a hundred years too early. It is more than possible that he did something similar with the Alpirsbach tapestry. One of the striking features of the list of crusaders he gives is that many of them are recorded on the pattern, 'a lord of X', that is without any personal name – for example, *ain grave von Salm* or *ain herr von Bolanden*. If the tapestry showed heraldic devices, then Froben Christoph (or rather Wilhelm Werner) would have been able to recognise the titles or families of the figures depicted, but of course would not have been able to tell their names, which would explain why so many of the nobles listed in the chronicle are referred to by their title alone, without any forename. If this was the case, then a significant number of the listed crusaders derived from the tapestry rather than from the codex; this might also explain why, as I have suggested elsewhere, several of the names mentioned in the list, such as the *grave von Zwaibrucken*, date from several decades after the crusade.[27] All indications suggest that the tapestry was of late medieval manufacture. It may have incorporated family crusading traditions – real or imagined – but it certainly could not have had the direct relationship to the testimony of the crusading generation claimed for it by the chronicle.

We are left, then, with the ancient codex of Alpirsbach. Froben Christoph is considerably less specific about the provenance of the *alt geschriben buoch* than that of the tapestry: it is *gütlich zu glauben* (well believable) that it was written by one of the three lords on crusade, that is Frederick, Conrad, or Albrecht (I, p. 74). Hagenmeyer points out that it could not have been either of the latter two, since they were killed at Nicaea (I, p. 79), while the authorship of Frederick should be discounted, given that the account is so unfavourable to him and that it records his death. One might add that it was extremely doubtful whether any members of a family of free lords in Germany in the early twelfth century possessed the education to write an account of their deeds. Hagenmeyer's suggestion was that the codex was written by an unknown author, probably a member of Frederick's retinue, on the basis of testimony furnished by the latter personally; the codex further provided the subject-matter for the tapestry, which thus must have been roughly contemporaneous with the codex. Hagenmeyer argued that since the codex must have described the second pilgrimage and death of Frederick of Zimmern, it could not have been completed before the beginning of the reign of Baldwin II of Jerusalem at the earliest (that is, 1118).[20]

Even if we accept the existence of such a codex written in the first half of the twelfth century, it is difficult to decide how much of Froben Christoph's account derives from it rather than from other sources. When he first introduces the tapestry and the codex, the chronicler asserts that the following chapters, in so far as they concern the lords of Zimmern, are drawn from these two sources: *aus disen baiden dise nachvolgende capitl, so vil es die freiherrn von Zimbern belangen thut, gezogen worden* (I, p. 74). No distinction is made between the testimony of the tapestry and that of the codex. If any information at all derived from an ancient codex, then it must at least have included the most detailed stories concerning the Zimmern family, yet here too, the chronicle's evidence is problematic. One of the main themes of the story of Frederick of Zimmern is an explanation of how the family lost several of its lordships. That of Rosenfeld, for example, was supposedly mortgaged by him to Frederick of Teck to finance his second pilgrimage. The town of Rosenfeld developed on land which originally belonged to the dukes of Zähringen and which passed to the dukes of Teck in 1186/88. Rosenfeld is first mentioned in 1255, and it seems to have been a foundation of the dukes of Teck. In 1305 it was mortgaged, and in 1317 sold along with neighbouring estates, to the count of Württemberg, in whose possession it remained. It is thus very difficult to claim, as the Chronicle of Zimmern does, that Rosenfeld passed to the dukes of Teck from the Zimmern family at the time of the crusade.[29]

It is equally doubtful that Frederick sold tithes at Rosenfeld, Ehrlach and Eisingen to the house of the Hospitallers (*Johannserhaus*) at Rottweil (I, p. 81). This occurred supposedly during the reign of Baldwin II of Jerusalem (1118–31), a time when the Order of St John was still in its infancy. The Hospitallers did not begin to spread to Germany until the time of the Second Crusade, and the first documentary evidence of the commandery in Rottweil dates from 1274. The most recent study of the order at Rottweil argues convincingly that a leaden bull of Pope Innocent IV discovered in 1926 on a piece of land which once belonged to the Hospitallers may have originally been attached to the papal confirmation of foundation of the commandery, which would then have occurred in the period 1244 to 1253.[30] A final piece of evidence connected with Rosenfeld points to an even later chronology. Frederick of Zimmern supposedly granted the castle of Tiefenberg to a nobleman called Eisenhart Brandhoch as a fief. However, the Brandhoch family is only documented in the Rosenfeld area from 1433 onwards.[31]

These objections raise weighty doubts as to the nature – and indeed the existence – of the *alt geschriben buoch*. One might question whether the text contained in it was a detailed narrative, as Hagenmeyer assumed. His main argument for this was a number of participial phrases in the German text of the chronicle, which, he argued, were probably direct translations from Latin.[32] However, we should bear in mind how much the written German language was influenced by Latin in the sixteenth century, and with a university-educated, humanistic author like Froben Christoph we should quite naturally expect a strong Latin influence on both vocabulary and syntax. Certainly Froben Christoph's information about the Alpirsbach codex is vague in the extreme, and as we have just seen, his speculation about its authorship is contradicted by information provided about the three Zimmern brothers elsewhere in the chronicle. Could the lack of detail about the codex have been because the information contained in it was so terse or fragmentary that Froben Christoph was unable to say more about it? It is quite possible that the ancient codex could have been a necrology, a cartulary, a register of donations, or something similar, and that it yielded fairly exiguous information which Froben Christoph was obliged to combine with the fruits of his researches on other sources. Certainly the fragmentary details normally recorded in a manuscript of one of these types would have lent itself to the kind of elaboration and 'improvement' that Froben Christoph is known to have indulged in elsewhere.

Finally, we should not discount the possibility that the *alt geschriben buoch* may have never actually existed. In the Middle Ages an allusion to an ancient book, usually in very vague terms, was a common enough literary technique employed to claim a spurious authority for relatively new material.[33] It is possible that the ancient codex was an invention of Froben Christoph designed to provide authenticity and antiquity for an anachronistic account of the crusading history of his own family and their prestigious relatives, the dukes of Teck.

The overall chronological framework and most of the detail of the Zimmern account of the crusade is so anachronistic, contradictory or simply doubtful that it should not be regarded as a reliable witness to German participation in the First Crusade or settlement in Outremer. It is conceivable that some elements of the account have some degree of veracity. However, these cannot be identified without a thorough study of all the possible sources used by Froben Christoph and his uncle, insofar as they can be identified with any certainty. Unless we disregard its testimony completely, I suggest that this source will distort our perception of the crusade and the German response to it. Since it is impossible or near-impossible to establish the precise sources of any given section of the account we have to doubt it in its entirety. Its unreliability means that we have to revise our opinion of the People's Crusades. As far as their German element is concerned, these expeditions probably had far fewer nobles and retinues of knights than has been assumed for over a century; the participation of a duke, a count palatine, and numerous bishops, counts and lords from Germany is questionable in the extreme, and is most likely a product of the inventiveness of Froben Christoph and Wilhelm Werner of Zimmern. The dubiety of the Chronicle of Zimmern highlights the even greater importance we have to accord to Albert of Aachen, as the only reliable full-length account which deals with the crusade from a German perspective.

What the Chronicle of Zimmern *does* reveal is the perception of the First Crusade in Germany in the late medieval and early modern period. This was a time which saw a growing preoccupation with crusading in German literature. The steady advance of the Ottoman Turks across mainland Europe in the sixteenth century meant that the German-speaking countries were increasingly aware of a major Muslim threat, and this perception seems to have led to a reflection on the successes of the past and a desire to exalt the rather meagre German contribution to the one crusade which was an unqualified success, the First. The chronicle of Zimmern virtually negates the role of the papacy and the Council of Clermont, and transforms the genesis of the entire crusading movement into an enterprise initiated by a faithful servant of the German emperor, in which the bravest and best fighters were Germans. This was a patriotism at both national and family levels. Like those members of the Victorian aristocracy who claimed an ancestor who had fought with William the Conqueror at Hastings, the Zimmern family desired forebears on the expedition to Jerusalem. The Chronicle of Zimmern tells us far more about the conceits and inventiveness of the early modern nobility of Swabia than about the German response to the appeal of Pope Urban II.

Appendix
The account of the First Crusade in the Chronicle of Zimmern[34] (English translation)

In this chapter is recorded when the glorious expedition against the heathens first began under the Emperor Henry III, and also from what sources the following chapters are drawn [I, pp. 74–7 = Hagenmeyer, 'Étude', I–IV].

At the time when these events involving the two bishops of Konstanz were taking place, there began, in the year of the incarnation of Christ Our Lord 1095, the greatest expedition against the heathens of which one finds written. There were a great many princes, both spiritual and temporal, and also counts, lords, knights and squires, from High and Low Germany, from Gaul, Italy, and from the whole of Christendom generally, so that the army was estimated at approximately three hundred thousand fighting men on horse and foot. The unspeakable difficulties and trials, the worries and dangers that they endured until they conquered the city of Jerusalem and the land of Judaea have all been described at great length by Guy of Rheims and also Robert the Monk and in particular by William of Tyre, some of whom lived at that time and took part, so that it is not necessary to introduce such matter here. But since these historians named here and others were not High Germans, but Frenchmen or Netherlanders, they have mostly paid particular attention to the lords of their own lands who took part, recording their names and histories with great diligence; but as for the High German nobility, who did not risk life and limb any the less, and who performed nobler and more laudable deeds, these they have not mentioned at all except in the most general and cursory terms.

This is why it should be known that in the monastery at Alpirsbach in the Black Forest there was an old handwritten book as well
as a large woven tapestry, both of which came from the lordship of
Zimmern and were given to the monastery many years before. The
content of the entire book is a description of the expedition, and it
can well be believed that this was described and recorded by one of
the lords of Zimmern, of whom three, that is Sir Frederick, Sir
Conrad and Sir Albrecht, took part. Similarly, large figures were
woven in round panels into this aforesaid tapestry, with a Latin text
whose content corresponds to the book; the following chapters, in
so far as they concern the lords of Zimmern, are taken from these
two sources.

However, the cause and the origin of the glorious, laudable and
Christian expedition was principally the following: The laudable,
estimable prince, Duke Godfrey of Lotharingia, by descent and
origin a count of Bouillon, had always faithfully served the Emperor
Henry IV of blessed memory, and when Emperor Henry descended
in force into Italy and besieged Rome in the year 1081 that same
Duke Godfrey also accompanied him, and after some time when the
city of Rome had been assaulted, and a good part of the walls and
fortifications cast down, he had acted with such valour in the assault
that he was the first to mount the walls, a distinguished and honourable deed which led to the conquest of the city of Rome by the
imperial troops. Duke Godfrey had exerted himself to such an
extent during this assault, which occurred in the month of June, that
he succumbed to a deadly sickness, with the result that he vowed to
Almighty God that, if he should recover and remain in good health,
then he would journey to the Holy Sepulchre and attempt to take it
back again out of the hands of the heathens. Thereupon he quickly
made an amazing recovery, and as soon as he returned to Germany,
he took leave of the emperor, and tried every means of raising the
money to pay for a contingent of soldiers. And after he had been
engaged in this task for twelve years, he finally sold, with the consent of his two brothers, Sir Baldwin and Sir Eustace, all of their
estates with the intention of using this considerable sum of money
against the heathen for the good of all Christendom. A further
reason for this intention was the great bloodshed and the continual
warfare between the emperor and the German princes which had
been brought about by the intrigues of the papacy.

When the princes of Gaul and the other nations heard of the honourable, Christian undertaking, they (who had also been encouraged by Pope Urban at Clermont in Auvergne) unanimously chose Duke Godfrey as their leader over the entire army. As soon as this became known in Germany, several bishops took the cross, namely Bishop Conrad of Chur and Bishop Otto of Strasbourg, brothers of Duke Frederick of Swabia. These and other bishops were joined by Bishop Thiemo of Salzburg, and also Duke Eckhart of Bavaria, son of Count Otto of Scheyern, and Duke Walter of Teck. With them went likewise the following counts and lords: Count Henry of Schwarzenburg, Count Palatine Hugh of Tübingen, Count Rudolf and Count Ulrich of Saarwerden, Count Hartmann of Dillingen and Kyburg, Count Thiemo of Eschenloch, Count Henry of Helfenstein, Count Adalbrecht of Kirchberg, Count Henry of Heiligenberg, a count of Fanen, Sir Arnold lord of Bussnang, a lord of Fridau, Sir Rudolf lord of Brandis, a lord of Westerburg, Count Berthold of Neuffen, Sir Albrecht lord of Stöffeln; also a count of Salm, a count of Viernenberg, a lord of Bolanden; also Count Emicho of Leiningen, a count of Rötteln and a count of Zweibrücken, as well as a considerable number of knights who all desired to fight against the heathen for the salvation of the Christian faith.

At the time when these tidings were heard in Germany, the brothers Sir Frederick and Sir Conrad of Zimmern were at the court of the Emperor Henry, where they had served for several years alongside other counts and lords from Swabia; despite the great damage which the lordship of Zimmern had suffered at the hands of Duke Berthold of Zähringen, they had remained loyally with their lord through good times and bad. As soon as the expedition began, they took their leave with all due respect and went as quickly as possible to their father, Sir Godfrey, whom they found at Herrenzimmern along with their two brothers Sir Godfrey and Sir Albrecht. To them, but first of all to their lord father they revealed their intention to take part in this honourable Christian expedition and to prove their knightly spirit alongside the other counts, lords and nobles of the German nation against the dreadful arch-enemy of the faith and of all Christian people; thus they wanted to ask him as their lord and father to provide them with the necessities for the journey. With these and similar words they persuaded their brother, Sir Albrecht, who had lived for some time at Herrenzimmern, to accompany his two brothers, Sir Frederick and Sir Conrad. When their father had recognised the spirit of his sons he no longer wished to dissuade them, but agreed faithfully to provide whatever he was able, so that they would be prepared for the Christian journey. In his generosity he provided for them handsomely with harness, horses and other things useful for such a long journey.

But since Sir Frederick of Zimmern had always been an extravagant lord, both at the imperial court where he had resided since his youth, and also in wars, he was not content with what had been provided by his father for himself and his two brothers, Sir Conrad and Sir Albrecht; on the contrary, without the knowledge of his father or his brothers, he took money by force from several of the vassals who resided in the lordship, especially in the village of Rulinghofen, where at that time there were very wealthy and prosperous people who bore the name of Zoppen. Because of this a great complaint arose from the common people after his departure, and also, as shall be described, he suffered a great misadventure. After this they at last joined their leader Hugh, Count Palatine of Tübingen, with whom they found Duke Walter of Teck, the standard-bearer, and a great number of counts and lords and a considerable number of knights. With them they travelled through Hungary and Bulgaria to Constantinople.

How Sir George, lord of Zimmern, before the marriage between him and Lady Adelgund, lady of Hohenklingen, died in a pestilence along with his mother and his brother Cuno, and how they were buried at St. Georgen [I, pp. 77–8 = Hagenmeyer, 'Étude', V].

Just a few days before the brothers Sir Frederick, Sir Conrad and Sir Albrecht of Zimmern departed with Duke Walter of Teck and Count Palatine Hugh of Tübingen, the leaders of the German army, their brother, Sir George of Zimmern, who had been staying for some time at Klingen with Sir Hartmann of Klingen, as was fitting, now learned of their intentions. While the patriarch of Aquileia, as well as Count Henry of Heiligenberg and the others were acting as they wished, he took leave of Sir Hartmann and his wife, and also from their son, Sir Henry, and from his betrothed, Lady Adelgund, in order to ride to Herrenzimmern and visit and bid farewell to his brothers before they began their long and arduous journey; also, since he had become betrothed to Lady Adelgund of Klingen, he wished to enquire of the views of his father and brothers in this matter. When he arrived at Herrenzimmern he discovered that his brothers, whom he had hoped to find, had left a few days before, and was greatly grieved by such an unexpected and sudden departure. Nevertheless he reported to his father and his two brothers, Sir Godfrey and Sir Cuno, who were at Herrenzimmern at that time, all that had occurred between the bishops, and related that he had spent some time at Hohenklingen, where Sir Hartmann of Klingen had promised him in marriage his only daughter, Lady Adelgund. And therefore since it was an honourable marriage which was appropriate to his estate, he wished to know all of their views, especially that of his lord father, as to how he should act in the matter. When his lord father and his two brothers had heard his mind, they happily agreed to this marriage, and it can be assumed that his lord father made over to him his share of the lordship with the consent of his brothers, although there is no evidence for this.

But when the wedding and marriage had been delayed for three years thereafter, a cruel and terrible pestilence came through the whole German nation, of a kind that had never been heard of in human memory, and from which both the wild and domesticated animals died as well as the people. During this mortality Almighty God called from this valley of sorrow the Lady Agnes, countess of Hohenberg, wife of the old Sir Godfrey, as well as their two sons, Sir George and Sir Cuno, who had already been ill for a long time. They were taken to the monastery of St. Georgen and laid to rest in their family burial-place in the chapel of Our Lady. After the death of his wife and two sons, Sir Godfrey the Elder was seized by such a sorrow that he withdrew from all worldly affairs and made over the entire lordship to his son, Sir Godfrey, and his wife, Lady Elisabeth duchess of Teck, who resided at Harhausen. Thereafter he went to the monastery of St. Georgen where he lived for many years until his own end. It was also after this that Lady Adelgund of Klingen was given in marriage to Eberhard, lord of Roseneck, to whom she bore many children.

> How the High Germans suffered a great defeat at Nicaea, in which Sir Conrad and Sir Albrecht lords of Zimmern were killed and Sir Frederick escaped with a terrible wound, and thereafter returned to Germany but did not remain there for long [I, pp. 78–9 = Hagenmeyer, 'Étude', VI–XII].

But when Duke Godfrey of Bouillon and the entire army came through Hungary and Bulgaria into Thrace, they lost many good people through the treachery of Emperor Alexius of Constantinople, yet they were able to cross safely into Asia over the Hellespont, the arm of the sea known as the Bosphorus, some three hundred thousand strong not counting women and children; and although several Saracen princes and potentates advanced towards them with a large number of troops in order to block the pass or entrance into Syria, yet they defeated them and killed a large number. After these victories they advanced towards the city of Nicaea. Yet on the way, and not far from Nicaea, the German force had run out of food and provisions, and when they had learned of the strength of the Turks and of their camp which was not far away, they went foraging with great caution and apprehension, but thereafter they went further each day, until finally they went plundering and robbing some ten miles distant from the camp. At last, when they no longer had any fear of Suleiman the Turkish king, who had carefully held back until that time, and two hundred horse and three thousand foot left the camp in poor order, they were quickly surrounded by the Turk Suleiman and the greater part of them massacred.

When this news became known in the camp, a great indignation arose, so that the ordinary soldiers wanted to advance against the enemy without any kind of battle order; and although Count Palatine Hugh of Tübingen and Duke Walter of Teck in their capacity as commanders wanted to hold back the army in view of the rapid defeat and of the might of the enemy, they were so little able to assert themselves that they were finally forced to draw up the army in battle order; therefore they advanced against the enemy with four thousand horse and twenty-five thousand foot in the hope, since there was no alternative, of winning honour or else dying in the attempt; and although the Germans, especially the nobles, fought most keenly, in the desire to distinguish themselves from other nations by honourable and knightly deeds, yet the Turks in their countless numbers were so superior to them, and pressed in on them with their poisoned arrows – in addition to which the relief from the other Christians came so slowly – that in the end the majority of them were killed. Among them were the two commanders, Count Palatine Hugh of Tübingen and Duke Walter of Teck, and the majority of all the previously named counts and lords, that is to say Count Ulrich and Count Rudolf of Saarwerden, the brothers Sir Conrad and Sir Albrecht, lords of Zimmern, Sir Albrecht lord of Stöffeln, Count Berthold of Neuffen, with many others of the nobility of High Germany. However, those who escaped from this force included Count Henry of Schwarzenburg, Sir Frederick of Zimmern, a lord of Brandis named Rudolf, a nobleman of Ems and one of Fridingen, who escaped with severe wounds. As soon as their wounds had healed, they entered the service of Duke Godfrey, their commander-in-chief, in view of the fact that the majority of the Germans along with their captains and commanders had died in this battle.

Some time after the capture of the city of Antioch, the Christians arrived before the city of Jerusalem, which was besieged and captured by force after great effort and travail, in the year of the incarnation of Our Lord 1099. There Duke Godfrey was unanimously elected king. Yet the pious, estimable prince ruled for only a year. His brother Duke Baldwin was chosen in his place; he ruled for eighteen years. Sir Frederick of Zimmern remained with him for several years. However, after Bohemond of Apulia, duke of Antioch, resolved to take ship for France, Sir Frederick of Zimmern, who had never intended to remain in that country, took his leave, in order to go with that prince to France and thence home to Germany. This he did, but did not remain for long, as will be described here.

In the monastery of Alpirsbach one can find written in a very old book, that many years before a lord of Zimmern had given to the monastery a golden candelabrum, a magnificent piece of work such as is known in Latin as *candelabrum miri operis*, for his eternal memory. But what his name was, how long ago he lived, or where the candelabrum ended up, are not known. Yet it is conceivable that the frequently aforementioned Sir Frederick of Zimmern brought it with him from Syria and afterwards presented it to the monastery.

How Sir Frederick, lord of Zimmern, returned to King Baldwin in Syria, but had previously mortgaged the lordship of Rosenfeld with its appurtenances, to the disadvantage of his brothers [I, pp. 80–5 = Hagenmeyer, 'Étude', XIII–XVI].

When Sir Frederick of Zimmern returned home and sought out his father Lord Godfrey at St. Georgen, whom he found healthy and well, and had spent some time in idleness and without any activity, and since he had been used to courts and warfare since the time of his youth, he began to become melancholy and to regret deeply that had come back across the sea, leaving the other Germans, considering that he had spent his youth at the imperial court, and then served other princes, and finally two kings of Jerusalem, where he had been highly honoured and had enjoyed a reputation greater than others. Thus he often thought about how and with what means he might return across the sea, so that he would not need to spend the rest of his life so uselessly and in melancholy. He thought especially of the deaths of his two brothers, the late Sir Conrad and Sir Albrecht, and of all those who had shed their blood for the name of Christ at Nicaea and in Syria and in many other places, among whom he had himself been, and thought also how many of the German nobility (who were well known to him) had settled in Outremer, and had prospered and been honoured in the eyes of other nations. He was preoccupied with these thoughts by day and night, until he finally resolved to travel across the sea and to spend the rest of his days faithfully helping the Christians there.

Once he had finally resolved on this course in his heart, although he gave no outward sign of it, he wrote to his brother, Sir William, who the whole time had been at the court of the prince of Swabia, that he wished to come immediately to him and to Sir Godfrey the Younger at Herrenzimmern. As soon as this happened, he revealed to his two brothers the various reasons which moved him to seek from them the share of the inheritance which was due to him, since he proposed to retire and to spend some time on his own; this desire of his would bring no disadvantage to them since he wanted nothing from them which had not been divided. Yet his mind and intention were very different. He was allocated as his portion (at the behest of their lord father, with whom all three had been at St. Georgen) the lordship of Rosenfeld and the castles of Harhausen and Tiefenberg together with their villages, tithes and serfs as well as the rights which belonged to them. But as soon as the poor people had sworn allegiance to him he began to oppress them sorely, and showed no mercy in all the means he employed to wring money from them. His retinue of nobles as well as others, of whom he had not a few because of his journey, and who were aware of his purpose, helped him in this to the best of their ability.

Finally, without his brothers' knowledge, he mortgaged everything, that is the lordship of Rosenfeld with its villages and all its appurtenances, to Duke Frederick of Teck, his brother-in-law, as a result of which a great dispute and enmity occurred, lasting several years, between the dukes of Teck and the lordship of Zimmern concerning the repayment. This enmity was resolved by an abbot of St. Gallen, from whom the dukes of Teck held the office of butler in fee, to the effect that the lordship of Rosenfeld remained with the dukes of Teck; but the castle and village of Harhausen which he had allowed to decline, he gave with all their appurtenances to be sold to the nuns of Oberndorf on the Neckar, which had been built by his brother Sir Godfrey's brother-in-law, the old duke of Teck, for the sake of one of his daughters who had been born blind. The deeds of sale are still extant. He [Frederick of Zimmern] still possessed some tithes at Rosenfeld, Erlach and Eisingen which he mortgaged with all of his rights and *jus patronatus* to the house of the Hospitallers at Rottweil. He gave the castle of Tiefenberg to a nobleman named Brandhoch for him and his children, daughters as well as sons, to hold from the lordship of Zimmern. This Eisenhart Brandhoch had long been an official of his father at Rosenfeld and had a son with Sir Frederick, who later went with him across the sea; he [Brandhoch] had previously had a residence near the castle of Tiefenberg known as Untreues Ziel, which had been burned by his enemies and rivals. After a long time Tiefenberg passed from the Brandhochs into other hands and finally fell into ruin.

But since Sir Frederick had mortgaged his lordship completely and thus deprived himself of all possessions, he again decided to leave for Syria, in the hope that he could join King Baldwin (if he was still alive) and fight against the heathens to the praise of God and the good of all Christendom. Several nobles and others who had learned of his intention had come to him, and joined the expedition and desired to travel with him, some for the will of God, some to perform deeds of chivalry, and some for the money and wages which he paid them as free persons. With these and his own servants he made ready as best he might, and departed on the named day, making his way at first along the Rhine valley, where his force increased, for Sir Gerold lord of Vaz and others joined him, and then on to Milan. There he learned that the Genoese and Venetians were recruiting soldiers whom they wanted to send to the assistance of King Baldwin at his request. Therefore he did not delay, but journeyed on towards Genoa, from where the troops – now a considerable number – wanted to start. With them he sailed across the sea, and found King Baldwin with his forces before the city of Acre (known in Latin as Ptolomais). As soon as the Venetians and Genoese arrived, the city was invested so effectively by land and sea that it was taken by assault within two months, and a great number of the heathens slain, although with great losses to the Christians.

Again Sir Frederick of Zimmern survived with severe wounds; he had lost all of his retinue, particularly his faithful companion Sir Gerold of Vaz. This battle was fought in the seventh year after the conquest of the city of Jerusalem in the year of the Lord 1106. Soon afterwards Sir Frederick came to the city of Caesarea; there he lodged with a knight from Germany, a certain von Horn, who gave him assistance and counsel until his wounds healed.

Once he was walking beyond the gate in this city of Caesarea, thinking now and again of the great loss of his good friends and faithful servants whom he had brought from Germany, and all of his possessions which he had lost to the heathens. Absorbed in these thoughts he was sent by the providence of God a priest, whom, after a kindly greeting, he led into a nearby chapel. There he lamented his great misfortune: of how he had several times fought against the heathens with the loss of his men; how he had lost his two brothers against the heathens; how now he had lost his servants and soldiers whom he had brought from his own lands which he had mortgaged, as well as all his personal belongings; and how he had been near fatally wounded and barely survived. He then began to confess in great earnest all of the sins that he could think of. The priest asked him where this money had come from and how he had raised it. He then confessed that he had raised the greatest part through frequent exactions and oppressions on the poor people of his lord father and his brothers as well as his own; finally in his greed he had mortgaged away his paternal inheritance to the disadvantage of his brothers and all of his family. The priest set about punishing him severely for this, making clear that certainly the assessment and the hard exactions on the poor people were a cause of his great losses and misfortune; although he may have thought that he had not done any wrong, since he had used these funds solely to fight the heathens, unless he did sincere penance for them, these things would be so repellent to God that they would cause him to suffer more misfortunes during the rest of his mortal life and would need to be atoned with eternal punishment in the next life. Sir Frederick examined his soul, and promised the priest to change his life for the better, and thus comforted, left him and returned to King Baldwin, with whom he remained thereafter. He ended his life under King Baldwin, the second of that name, and was buried in Syria.

As has been heard in this chapter, Sir Frederick lord of Zimmern mortgaged the fief of Rosenfeld to his brother-in-law Duke Frederick of Teck, with whom it remained; but it should be known that Duke Frederick's descendants were not able to hold it, for the brothers Duke Conrad and Duke Ludwig of Teck sold it along with the castle at Beron which had been their hunting-lodge, as well as the castle of Aichsteig and all its appurtenances to Count Eberhard of Württemberg for 4,000 pounds of Schwäbisch Hall. This was done in the year of the Lord 1317.

Notes

1 For a recent overview of the People's Crusades, see France, *Victory*, pp. 88–95.

2 A.V. Murray, 'The army of Godfrey of Bouillon, 1096–1099: structure and dynamics of a contingent on the First Crusade', *Revue Belge de Philologie et d'Histoire*, 70 (1992), 301–29. For the importance of Albert of Aachen, see the chapter by Susan Edgington in this volume.

3 MS Stuttgart, Württembergische Landesbibliothek, Cod. Don. 580 (= B), now bound as two separate volumes, is the final revised version of the chronicle, dictated by Froben Christoph to his secretary, Hans Müller, in 1566. The account of the crusade is at pp. 59–70. The second manuscript, Cod. Don. 581 (= A), is an earlier fair copy which subsequently underwent considerable revision; it contains numerous corrections in Froben Christoph's hand, and evidently served as the examplar for B. References to the text of the chronicle in this paper are to the most recent edition: *Die Chronik der Grafen von Zimmern: Handschriften 580 und 581 der Fürstlich Fürstenbergischen Hofbibliothek Donaueschingen*, ed. H. Decker-Hauff, A. Holtorf, S. Lorenz and R. Seigel, 7 vols (Konstanz, Stuttgart, Sigmaringen, Thorbecke, 1964–).

4 *Zimmerische Chronik*, ed. K.A. Barack, 4 vols (Tübingen, Litterarischer Verein in Stuttgart, 1869); R. Röhricht, 'Die Deutschen auf den Kreuzzügen', *Zeitschrift für deutsche Philologie*, 7 (1876), 125–74, 296–329.

5 H. Hagenmeyer, 'Étude sur la Chronique de Zimmern: Renseignements qu'elle fournit sur la première croisade', *Archives de l'Orient Latin*, 2 (1884), 20–36; *Zimmerische Chronik*, ed. Barack, 2nd edn, 4 vols (Freiburg im Breisgau, Tübingen, Akademische Verlagsbuchhandlung Mohr, 1881–2).

6 *Chronik der Grafen von Zimmern*, ed. Decker-Hauff et al. The rarely cited *Zimmerische Chronik*, ed. P. Herrmann, 2 vols (Meersburg, Hendel, 1937) is essentially a reproduction of Barack's second edition.

7 H. Baumgart, 'Studien zur Zimmerischen Chronik des Grafen

Christoph und zur Mainzer Bistumschronik des Grafen Wilhelm Werner von Zimmern' (unpublished Ph.D. thesis, University of Freiburg, 1923); B.R. Jenny, *Graf Froben Christoph von Zimmern, 1519–1566: Geschichtsschreiber-Erzähler-Dynast* (Konstanz, Thorbecke, 1959), esp. pp. 123–74.

8   R. Röhricht, *Geschichte des Ersten Kreuzzuges* (Innsbruck, Wagner'sche Universitäts-Buchhandlung, 1901), pp. 55–8; F. Duncalf, 'The Peasants' Crusade', *American Historical Review*, 26 for 1920–1 (1921), 440–53; F. Chalandon, *Histoire de la première croisade jusqu'à l'élection de Godefroi de Bouillon* (Paris, Picard, 1925), pp. 75–116; R. Grousset, *Histoire des croisades et du royaume franc de Jérusalem*, 3 vols (Paris, Librarie Plon, 1934–6), I, 5–9; Runciman, I, 121–2, 131–2; S. Runciman, 'The First Crusade: Constantinople to Antioch', *A History of the Crusades*, ed. K.M. Setton and M.W. Baldwin (Madison, University of Wisconsin Press, 1969), I, pp. 280–304; A. Waas, *Geschichte der Kreuzzüge*, 2 vols (Freiburg, Herder, 1956), I, 119–21; J.S.C. Riley-Smith, 'The motives of the earliest crusaders and the settlement of Latin Palestine, 1095–1100', *EHR*, 98 (1983), 725; Riley-Smith, *The First Crusade and the Idea of Crusading* (London, Athlone Press, 1986), pp. 50–1.

9   *Johannes Turmair's genannt Aventinus Annales Ducum Boiariae*, ed. S. Riezler, 2 vols (Munich, Chr. Kaiser 1882–84), I, 149–50.

10 Thus the erroneous name of Bishop Conrad of Chur in the list of crusaders derives from Wilhelm Werner's chronicle of the archbishopric of Mainz (Jenny, *Graf Froben Christoph von Zimmern*, p. 146). In the discussion below I hope to show that was by no means an isolated instance.

11 Hagenmeyer, 'Étude', p. 38; WT, pp. 149–52.

12 RM, pp. 733–6; *Historia Hierosolymitana von Robertus Monachus in deutscher Übersetzung*, ed. B. Haupt (Wiesbaden, Steiner, 1972), pp. 217–30; F. Kraft, *Heinrich Steinhöwels Verdeutschung der Historia Hierosolymitana des Robertus Monachus: Eine literarhistorische Untersuchung* (Strassburg, Trübner, 1905), pp. 22–45; S. Fuchs, 'Die St. Galler Übersetzung der Historia Hierosolymitana des Robertus Monachus' (unpublished M.A. dissertation, University of Frankfurt, 1990).

13 Hagenmeyer, 'Étude', p. 56: 'Ce fait nous donne à supposer que le chroniqueur a bien trouvé dans le *Codex d'Alpirsbach* les noms des nobles allemands, c'est-à-dire tous les noms cités au chap. III, depuis le duc Walther de Tegk jusqu'au comte de Deux-Ponts'; p. 62: 'Il y a, du reste, des raisons positives d'admettre l'authenticité de cette liste, depuis le nom du duc de Tegk jusqu'à celui du comte de Deux-Ponts'.

14 Murray, 'Army of Godfrey of Bouillon', pp. 315–22.

15 The one detail Froben Christoph actually gives about the tapestry is that it included the inscription 'Gottifredus dux de Zimbris', which is advanced as proof that Godfrey of Zimmern had a status higher than that of a free lord (I, 90).

16 Hagenmeyer, 'Étude', pp. 77–8. It is noticeable that while Hagenmeyer expressed doubts about this identification, those accounts of the First Crusade which rely on his work have invariably spoken of Walter as duke of Teck (see above, note 8).

17 I. Eberl. 'Die Edelfreien von Ruck und die Grafen von Tübingen: Untersuchungen zu Besitz und Herrschaft im Blaubeurer Raum bis zum Ausgang des 13. Jahrhunderts', Zeitschrift für Württembergische Landesgeschichte, 38 (1979), 5–63.

18 R. Götz, 'Die Stammtafel der Herzöge von Teck im städtischen Museum Kirchheim u. T. – eine Arbeit des Stuttgarter Archivars Andreas Rüttel (†1587)', Schriftenreihe des Stadtarchivs Kirchheim unter Teck, 6 (1987), 45–59, here p. 52.

19 MS Stuttgart, Hauptstaatsarchiv, J.7.27: 'Von den alten unnd ersten herzogen von Deckh findt man das ainer mit namen Walther gewesen ist ain hauptman unnd hertzog och heerfuerer teutschen volcks under denen etlich gaistlich unnd weltlich fürsten unnd sunnst vil namhaffter graven auch hern on die von der Ritterschaft in großer anzal gewesen bej zeiten unnd Regierung Kayser Heynrichs des vierdten dises Namens unnd umb das jar als man zalt nach Christi geburt MXCVI mit denen diser fürst uber mer gezogen helffen die ungleubigen bekrüegen und die haylgen statt Jerusalem gewinnen'. I am grateful to Dr Rolf Götz (of Weilheim an der Teck) for drawing my attention to this archival source.

20 E. Heyck, Geschichte der Herzöge von Zähringen (Freiburg im Breisgau, Mohr, 1891), p. 418; I. Gründer, Studien zur Geschichte der Herrschaft Teck (Stuttgart, Müller und Gräff, 1963), p. 3; H. Heinemann, 'Das Erbe der Zähringer', in Die Zähringer: Schweizer Vorträge und neue Forschungen, ed. K. Schmid (Sigmaringen, Thorbecke, 1990), pp. 215–65, here 217–18.

21 For the most recent study of the family see the genealogical tables given in A. Wolf, König für einen Tag: Konrad von Teck. Gewählt, ermordet (?) und vergessen (Kirchheim unter Teck, Stadtarchiv, 1993), which should be consulted in conjunction with the calendared documents listed in Gründer, Studien zur Geschichte der Herrschaft Teck (Regesten).

22 F.J. Mone, Quellensammlung der badischen Geschichte, II (Karlsruhe, Germany, 1854), 134.

23 Wolf, König für Einen Tag, p. 121 n. 113.

24 Gründer, Studien zur Geschichte der Herrschaft Teck. Regesten, nos.

91, 145, 160, 165, 166, 171, 173, 178, 179, 181, 182, 184, 185, 189, 190–3, 195, 201.

25 For the later Fredericks see Wolf, *König für einen Tag*, genealogical table.

26 I, 59: 'Und damit dise wunderzaichen in ewigkait nit vergessen, sonder zu ainer zeugnus der ehr und macht Gottes denen nachkomen kundt thon wurd, *liesen sie sich alle mit iren wappen, bei denen sie erkannt werden mechten*, in ain aufschlag wurken, denen etliche die ketten an füeßen, etlichen an armen oder an leiben hiengen, nachdem dann ain iegclicher gefangen und eingeschmidt gelegen war' (*my emphasis, A.V.M.*). For the chronology of the appearance of heraldry, see L. Fenske, 'Adel und Rittertum im Spiegel früher heraldischer Formen und deren Entwicklung', in *Das ritterliche Turnier im Mittelalter: Beiträge zu einer vergleichenden Formen- und Verhaltengeschichte des Rittertums*, ed. J. Fleckenstein (Göttingen: Vandenhoeck und Ruprecht, 1985), pp. 75–160.

27 Murray, 'Army of Godfrey of Bouillon', pp. 318–20.

28 Hagenmeyer, 'Étude', pp. 50–1.

29 K.-O. Bull, 'Die württembergischen Amtsstädte am oberen Neckar und ihre Vermögensverhältnisse vom 15. bis zum 17. Jahrhundert', in *Zwischen Schwarzwald und Schwäbischer Alb: Das Land am Oberen Neckar*, ed. F. Quarthal (Sigmaringen, Thorbecke, 1984), pp. 469–82.

30 W. Hecht, *Die Johanniterkommende Rottweil* (Rottweil, Germany, Stadtarchiv, 1971), pp. 21–6.

31 *Der Landkreis Balingen: Amtliche Kreisbeschreibung*, 3 vols (Stuttgart, Statistisches Landesamt Baden-Württemberg, 1960–1), II, 676–7.

32 Hagenmeyer, 'Étude', p. 51.

33 D.R. Howlett, 'The literary context of Geoffrey of Monmouth: an essay on the fabrication of sources', *Arthuriana*, 5 (1995), 25–69.

34 The English translation given here corresponds to the ENHG text as found in the following manuscript and editions: (1) MS Stuttgart, Württembergische Landesbibliothek [formerly Donaueschingen, Fürstlich Fürstenbergische Hofbibliothek], Cod. Don. 580 (= B), pp. 59–70; (2) *Zimmerische Chronik*. ed. Barack, 1st edn, I, 78–90 and 2nd edn, I, 85–96; (3) Hagenmeyer, 'Étude', pp. 20–36; (4) *Chronik der Grafen von Zimmern*, ed. Decker-Hauff et al., I, 74–83. MS B is divided into unnumbered chapters, a practice which is followed by the Decker-Hauff edition; Hagenmeyer subdivided his translation of the four chapters dealing with the crusade into eighteen numbered sections. Although these subdivisions are quite arbitrary, I have given references to them in the chapter headings to allow easier comparison. In the translation I have purposely tried as far as possible to retain the syntax and phraseology of the original (sometimes at the expense of

elegance), again to facilitate comparison with the ENHG text. I am grateful to Dr Richard Byrn (University of Leeds) for checking my translation and making many valuable suggestions. Any errors are, of course, my own.

6

Cross-purposes: Alexius Comnenus and the First Crusade

Jonathan Shepard

Our narrative sources for the First Crusade focus on the person, policy and conduct of Alexius Comnenus. He was assumed by Latin writers to be behind most of the actions of his agents, for good or ill, and by the time of the expeditions of 1101 participants such as Ekkehard of Aura supposed that the Turks' attacks on them and mishaps at sea were alike at Alexius's behest.[1] Conversely, the early Latin narratives have little to say about 'the Greeks' in general or the city of Constantinople.[2] The chroniclers who wrote up the story without first-hand experience essentially made Alexius, rather than the Greeks in general, the villain of the piece. Even Guibert of Nogent, who does make defamatory remarks about Greeks, attributes their need for Western military aid to 'a celebrated edict' of Alexius: 'one of every so many daughters of all throughout his empire' was made a prostitute, with the profits going to Alexius's treasury, while one of the sons was castrated and thus ruled out for military service. The consequent shortage of soldiers was Alexius's fault, rather than an inherent deficiency of the Greeks: 'he who has damaged his own [resources] is now justly compelled to seek those of others', that is, to turn to the West for help.[3]

We shall examine why Alexius features so prominently in an adversarial role in the main sources and consider certain aspects of his actual role: in what sense did he instigate the First Crusade and what was his strategic situation on the eve of the expedition? What were his dealings with individual westerners at that time and may these have influenced his appeals for aid? Finally, if Alexius and the crusading leaders did have divergent goals, need this necessarily have given rise to the confrontation which our sources depict?

One must first belabour the obvious. Our knowledge of Alexius's relations with the crusaders rests on a very narrow range of sources. The handful of early narratives is ill-balanced, partisan and often polemical, each having its own 'agendas' or heroes. Our one detailed Byzantine account was written by Alexius's daughter, Anna Comnena. Her work, comprising fifteen 'books', gained its present form in the mid-twelfth century. The hero confronts wave upon wave of attackers and misfortunes, steering the ship of state through them all more or less single-handedly, in the mould of Odysseus. The spiritual motivation of 'the simpler folk' who set off to 'venerate the Tomb of the Lord and to visit the Holy Places' is recognised, but the crusade is treated as tantamount to a barbarian invasion: leaders such as 'Bohemond and like-minded men' were aiming to use the mass-movement to seize Constantinople and thus take over the empire, though pretending 'to set off against the Turks and in defence of the Holy Sepulchre'.[4]

Fortunately, they met their match in Alexius: well-aware of the greedy and volatile temperament of the 'Celts', he was alert to the schemes of leaders such as Bohemond and although he humoured them, he did not trust them. He shuttled them across the Bosphoros as fast as possible, once he had extracted from each an oath to hand over 'whatever cities, districts or forts formerly belonging to the Roman empire they might happen to take'.[5] The westerners flouted their oaths at Antioch, failing to hand it over, and Bohemond spurned Alexius's demand that he should give up the city.[6] However, Alexius triumphed in the end, foiling Bohemond's invasion in 1107–8. A sizeable portion of Book XIII of the *Alexiad* is given up to the text of an agreement drafted in Bohemond's name. Bohemond repents of his actions at the time of the crusade, 'now that I have regained my senses and, virtually from the point of your spear, recovered my sanity'.[7] Bohemond pledges loyalty to Alexius, receiving the conditional grant of Antioch and other places in exchange. Thus Anna's depiction of the crusade belongs to a kind of triptych of episodes from Alexius's struggle against Robert Guiscard and Bohemond. First, he fends off their attacks in the early 1080s;[8] then he thwarts Bohemond's designs on Constantinople at the time of the crusade, albeit losing Antioch to him; finally, he defeats him humiliatingly at Dyrrachium and gains recognition of his own lordship over Antioch.

Thus the First Crusade in the *Alexiad* forms one of the hero's setpiece confrontations with barbarians in general and Bohemond in particular.[9] The latter is, in effect, the 'anti-hero' of the work. At the same time, Anna is conducting a polemic on one, probably two levels. As John France pointed out, she is rebutting the charge lodged against Alexius that he had let the westerners down:[10] the guidance and advice given to the crusaders is highlighted, and so are the huge amounts of money spent on them. It was they who were the oath-breaker, and not Alexius; the oath-breaking was symbolised by the crusaders' retention of Antioch, still a live issue at the time when she was writing.[11] Anna is probably also conducting a 'domestic' polemic: by the time when she did much of the drafting of the *Alexiad*, the 1140s, westerners were prominent at the imperial court. Her depiction of the cultural inferiority of the 'Latins' and her insistence on her father's wariness of them may well represent a thrust at latter-day regimes which she detested and which, especially under Manuel Comnenus (1143–80), were developing cultural as well as diplomatic ties with Western and Levantine Frankish courts. Alexius, her message seems to be, knew how to keep the Latins in their place whereas his successors did not.[12]

No other Greek source is detailed or independent enough to serve as a 'control' on Anna Comnena. John Zonaras's 'Epitome of the Histories', written in the mid-twelfth century, offers important qualifications to Anna's eulogy of Alexius; but while he conducts a kind of silent polemic against her, his account of the reign is succinct and does not rest on a major alternative source. Zonaras seems to imply that the 'Franks' were, like the locust-hordes which heralded them, intent on journeying from east to west without hostile designs on Constantinople. In contradiction to Anna, he maintains that the crusaders were wholly responsible for the capture of Nicaea, storming it and handing it over 'to the emperor in return for much money'.[13] But he apparently found no evidence to suggest that the First Crusade was other than a bizarre natural phenomenon, on a par with the locusts: he gives no hint that Alexius might have had a hand in unleashing it. Alexius Comnenus seems successfully to have projected an image of himself as essentially 'reactive'. The crusade is treated as just another barbarian incursion in a poem which was, in my view, commissioned by Alexius, even if he did not fashion every verse in it. The poem, addressed to his son John II, urged him to store up valuables 'so that with these you may stop the greed of the nations, when they are on the move around us just as long ago, … attempting to consume in their vast numbers the envied city [Constantinople]'.[14] Alexius urges John to reflect upon his own experiences, 'the great concourse hither from the west, lest the time of necessity should arise, put to shame and abase the proud heights of New Rome and the majesty of the throne'. Thus Alexius recalls the episode as one of epic confrontation, in which he defended his 'envied city' against 'the open jaws ... of the barbarians.'[15]

If the *Alexiad* should be viewed primarily as the 'literary' construction of an heroic image for Alexius, aimed at quite a broad audience, the thwarting of the crusading leaders' alleged intentions is an important component in that image.[16] Recent scholarship has also highlighted literary qualities in what amounts to the key early Latin source, the *Gesta Francorum*. This work is said to contain many features of the *chansons de geste*, including a penchant for 'the dramatic encounter of speakers in confrontation'. It now appears that the *Gesta* was written in a fairly sophisticated style, with an eye to both edification and entertainment.[17] Colin Morris suggested that the author was, through constant use of the words *nos* and *nostri*, expressing 'a powerful *wir-Gefühl*'.[18] One may suspect that the author was deliberately promoting a sense of 'us-ness' and manifest destiny, preferring terms such as *milites Christi* to names denoting the ethnic or regional origins of groupings. The desire to present the crusading hosts as united in Christ may well also account for the *Gesta*'s omission of virtually all mention of internal disputes, notably that concerning the authenticity of the Holy Lance at Antioch.

The only dispute between the leaders to receive repeated coverage is that between Bohemond and Raymond of St Gilles, count of Toulouse, over Bohemond's possession of Antioch: it is represented as turning on the oath which Raymond had sworn to Alexius at Constantinople and which he invoked, producing the written words of an agreement with Alexius and of his oath.[19] Our concern here is not whether Raymond really was primarily motivated by scruples over the oath. What matters is the role which the *Gesta* assigns to the oath, as being the source of discord in an otherwise united host on its 'sacred journey': the emperor is the begetter of Raymond's and the other leaders' oaths, and the *Gesta* attends closely to the circumstances in which they were sworn at Constantinople. It is probable that by the time the *Gesta* was written up, Raymond was staying at – or soon to depart for – Constantinople, aligning himself with Alexius against Bohemond and Tancred. The seeds of so bitter a division between leading crusaders in the Levant would then have been of keenest concern.[20]

The *Gesta* is congruent with Anna's *Alexiad* in so far as each pays serious attention to the oath-taking and the figures of Alexius, Bohemond and Raymond, devising more or less the same narrative framework. Each is interested in set-piece confrontations involving these characters, playing up their feats or misdeeds The fact that the *Alexiad* sounds a similar – more precisely, contrapuntal – note to the *Gesta* and its derivatives has encouraged some historians to view the First Crusade essentially in terms of confrontation. Of course, we also have eye-witness accounts from Raymond of Aguilers and Fulcher of Chartres, while Ralph of Caen could draw on the recollections of Tancred; and the value of Albert of Aachen's early sources is being 'rehabilitated' by Susan Edgington. But one must underline two points. First, three of these authors had access to the *Gesta*:[21] It seems to me that they were, with the significant exception of Fulcher, influenced by its narrative structure: they recount the oath-swearing under pressure but have nothing to say about the grand *levée* which Alexius staged for nearly all the leaders after the capture of Nicaea (June 1097) and which seems to have been a convivial affair.[22] Their silence is broken only by Ralph of Caen. It is true that even without, apparently, drawing on the *Gesta*, Ralph rails against Alexius's insistence on oaths of *fidelitas* and homage and celebrates Tancred's attempt to evade the emperor by slipping across the Bosphoros in disguise.[23] But this leads to a second point. Ralph's work is a eulogy of Tancred, who resisted swearing an oath even at the *levée* and later took over Antioch.

Thus two of our main narrative sources were closely associated with what were, in a sense, the 'loose cannons' of the expedition, Bohemond and his nephew.[24] Moreover, two other prime narratives of the doings at Constantinople originated in the *entourages* of leading *dramatis personae* in them: firstly, Raymond of Aguilers, a chaplain of the chief 'conscientious objector' to the oaths and preeminent opponent of Alexius's conduct in 1097–8; and secondly, by way of Albert of Aachen, 'arms-bearers' associated with the commander whose men most spectacularly came to blows with Alexius's forces at Constantinople, Godfrey of Bouillon. Moreover, Count Raymond and Godfrey had sold, mortgaged or handed over their properties at home and, assuming that they intended to settle in the

Levant, they might be expected to have had strong reservations about making sweeping sworn commitments, unless Alexius would fully commit himself to leading or aiding them.[25]

I suggest that there is, so to speak, a 'missing middle ground' among our narrative sources, whether Greek or Latin. We have little detailed narrative from those who journeyed to Jerusalem, said their prayers at the Holy Sepulchre, and then returned via Constantinople. We do not have a 'chronicle' from the immediate entourages of Count Robert II of Flanders, Duke Robert of Normandy or Count Eustace of Boulogne, all of whom were important enough to be parties – together with Bohemond, Godfrey and Count Raymond – to the letter sent to Pope Urban II in September 1098. A chronicle composed by someone in Count Stephen of Blois' company might perhaps have waxed as eloquent on the emperor's hospitality and largesse as Stephen does.[26] But it is no less possible that it would have passed over the stay at Constantinople without making a drama of it. This is, in effect, what is done by the sole Latin eye-witness chronicler who did not have an axe of one sort or another to grind against Alexius, Fulcher of Chartres.

Of course one should not take Fulcher as the mouthpiece of the rank-and-file in 1096 – or as wholly objective: he was writing his second redaction some thirty years later in the light of hindsight and of the political realities of the land in which he had settled. But whereas the other four more or less 'settler-linked' narratives discussed earlier make much of the oaths and Alexius's obstruction and perfidy, Fulcher offers an explanation why nearly 'all' the leaders made a sworn 'treaty' (*foedus*): this was to be the means of establishing 'friendship' (*amicitia*) with the emperor, without whose 'counsel and aid' the journey could not have been accomplished, either by them 'or by those who were to follow after us by the same route', presumably right up to the time of writing.[27] He thereby highlights a specific reason for Alexius's indispensability to the crusaders: his virtual stranglehold on communications between the Levant and western Europe, which the fragile, expensive vessels of the Genoese, Pisan and other mariners could not, in 1096–7, be expected to circumvent.[28] And if, as is likely, the pivotal role of Alexius and his swarms of Pechenegs and Turopoles in controlling communications and the flow of reinforcements was recognised by most crusading leaders at the time, we have part of the answer to the question of why he looms so large in the principal sources.

Fulcher is deliberately presenting what might be called the 'realistic' line taken by many leaders of varying shades of opinion: that the establishment of a *pax* of some sort with the Greeks' ruler was necessitated by his ability to help or to hinder the crusaders, however far they advanced towards Jerusalem and however long they remained in the Holy Land. An alternative response to the underlying problem of communications was, in effect, to exaggerate Alexius's command of events and to blame him for the setbacks in Asia Minor in 1097–8 and the disasters which subsequent companies of crusaders (in 1101) also suffered at the hands of the Turks. As Jonathan Riley-Smith has pointed out, only a small minority of the crusaders stayed in the Levant.[29] It is Alexius's misfortune that the early Latin narratives were so heavily influenced, if not shaped, by this minority: sympathisers with or encomiasts of Norman fortune-seekers, respectively the author of the *Gesta* and Ralph of Caen; or former associates or followers of two magnates outstandingly committed to the conquest of the Holy Land and thereby drawn into spectacular confrontations with Alexius. Raymond of Toulouse's large force had fallen prey to the Pechenegs while he was confronting the emperor at Constantinople and he thereupon formally charged Alexius with 'treason'; Godfrey of Bouillon's exchanges with Alexius were coloured by outbreaks of fighting which were in large part due to his forces' massive provisioning needs.[30]

The preoccupations of, and 'scapegoating' by, the early Latin narratives generally serve to obscure the part played by Alexius in the origins of the crusade. Only Raymond of Aguilers gives a hint that there might have been significant preliminary contacts.[31] This in turn obfuscates the nature of Alexius's overtures towards and initial expectations of the westerners, as well as his strategic position on the eve of the First Crusade. From their different vantage-points, Anna Comnena and the Latin writers had a common interest in side-stepping the question of any imperial, earthly, causation of 'the great stirring of heart'.[32] That Alexius was sending messages to the West in quest of military aid is stated by near-contemporary sources and there is no reason wholly to reject their testimony. But if the Byzantine emperor is the likeliest source of the 'frequent messages concerning the oppression of the Lord's Sepulchre' mentioned by Frutolf, it remains unclear to whom such 'messages' were addressed.[33] The objective which Ekkehard of Aura ascribes to Alexius, appealing to Pope Urban in 'not a few letters', 'if possible to call on the whole West ... to help him' in defending 'the eastern churches' is similar to that reported by Bernold of St Blaise: the Byzantine embassy at Piazenza 'humbly implored' for assistance against the pagans 'for the defence of Holy Church'. But Bernold also ascribes to the envoys the report that 'the pagans ... had almost annihilated [Holy Church] ... [and] had occupied those parts up to the walls of Constantinople.[34] By the time of the Council of Piacenza (March 1095) no 'pagans', Pechenegs or Turks had been at large beneath the walls for some four years. Thus the envoys' report, taken literally, appears to have been exaggerating the parlousness of the Eastern Christians' plight.

Study of Alexius's position on the eve of the crusade might be expected to shed light on his purpose in sending to the West and determining whether he had a particular project in hand in 1095. Unfortunately, the evidence as to his position then and, more pertinently, as to Alexius's own assessment of his problems and prospects, is almost entirely indirect. A number of immediate threats had abated: the Pechenegs were crushingly defeated in 1091 and the Turkish emir of Smyrna, Tzachas (Çaka) perished not long afterwards, apparently as a result of Alexius's intrigues. Alexius's brother-in-law, John Ducas, achieved the reconquest of Mytilene, Samos and other islands off the west coast of Asia Minor. By the end of 1092 Crete and maybe Cyprus, too, were restored to imperial rule, having broken away two or more years earlier.[35] And events in the Muslim world could be viewed as working to Alexius's advantage: Malikshāh, the Great Seljuq sultan, died in November 1092, and in 1094 the ruling elite of Fātimid Egypt was preoccupied with a succession-struggle. Moreover, the disputes among the Seljuq leaders which Malikshāh's death unleashed allowed some local dynasts to look to Alexius as their formal overlord. Judging by a Greek inscription in Edessa apparently datable to 1094, leading elements in the town were still looking to the authority of 'Alexius Comnenus, the Christ-loving *autokrator* of the Romans'. Around that time, Toros, of Armenian stock but a 'Roman official' in Matthew of Edessa's account, was trying to seize the town's citadel.[36] A few years later the crusaders travelling south-east from Caesarea would come upon a town 'which the Turks had been besieging for three weeks a little before our arrival'.[37]

If Alexius was aware of this state of affairs, he might be expected to have taken advantage of it. There were, however, serious constraints on his freedom of action, while the outlook in Asia Minor may well have appeared to him uncertain, and not altogether favourable. Firstly, his strategic position in the Balkans was still exposed to external challenges. In 1094, he was torn between leading an expedition against a truculent Serb prince and remaining on the alert for a Cumans' incursion which was expected. In, most probably, the first half of 1095 – while his embassy to Piacenza was underway – the Cuman invasion took place and they presumed to beleaguer Adrianople, a key fortress some 200 km (120 ml) northwest of Constantinople, for almost seven weeks.[38] Alexius hesitated to go to its relief in person, partly for lack of commensurate forces, but probably also for political reasons. He had reason to be wary of engaging in heavy fighting, when the loyalty of his own troops was questionable. The previous year, much of his officer corps and a substantial number of the rank-and-file had been implicated in a plot by a senior commander to murder Alexius and seize the throne.

Even after Alexius discovered the conspiracy and extracted a confession from the commander, Nicephorus Diogenes, son of Emperor Romanus IV (1068–71), he forebore from widespread reprisals. Reportedly, Alexius's supporters 'were now reduced to a handful of men and his life was in danger'; he realised that he had 'insufficient forces to guard so many prisoners and he was most unwilling to mutilate a great mass of people'.[39] The charisma attaching to the name of Diogenes remained potent: the Cumans' invasion was ostensibly in support of a bid for the throne by a pretender claiming to be another son of Romanus IV.[40] Thus a tangled mass of external and internal challenges confronted Alexius: he had been leading his army to deal with the Serb prince Bolkan when Nicephorus Diogenes conspired to kill him. This was scarcely a propitious time for Alexius either to lead an expedition far into Asia Minor himself or to entrust troops of uncertain disposition to another experienced commander, however loyal he personally might be towards Alexius. Furthermore, a major offensive against the Turks was likely to be costly; and while Alexius's finances were eventually strengthened by such measures as his currency reform of c. 1092, he was probably all the more open to the accusations of 'unjust tax-collection' voiced so bitterly by John the Oxite early in 1091: the welcome given by townsfolk in Thrace to the Cumans and the false Diogenes in 1095 may well have owed something to Alexius's tax regime.[41] Fiscal and political considerations accordingly pointed in the direction of prudence and modesty of scale in military enterprises to the east.

However, a gradualist approach to the *reconquista* was not without its problems. As Claude Cahen noted, the death of Malikshāh had a limited impact in western Asia Minor.[42] The Turks' incursions were piecemeal and they often took the form of the devastation of towns and dispersal of their populations, rather than occupation. Nonetheless, from the mid-1080s the Turks were in a position to dominate the military road between Nicaea and Cilicia, the Danishmendids became established in the region of Sebastaea, while individual emirs were trying to seize ports on the west coast and to build fleets. As we have seen, Tzachas was dealt with by 'diplomatic' means and Alexius reacted swiftly to the seizure of Cyzicus and Apollonias by another Turk, 'Elchanes': his commanders succeeded – after an initial disaster – in regaining them.[43] But the pressure from opportunistic emirs did not let up and effective responses were less easy to mount beyond the Sea of Marmara. Islands in the Aegean were exposed to pirates' raids in 1094 and the Turkish emir Tengribermesh seems still to have been extending his sway from Ephesus and raiding the islands in the later 1090s.[44] This implies that Turkish dominion was not yet complete in the central sector of Asia Minor's west coast, but it also highlights the urgent need for action, of which Alexius was probably aware. The longer he delayed, the harder it would be for Byzantine fortified centres to hold out; even if he managed to relieve them, the task of reconstructing towns subject to protracted raiding would be arduous and costly.

Alexius's overall position thus appears to have been ambivalent in the mid-1090s, despite the removal of direct threats such as Tzachas's. He may well have baulked at the political risks which a large-scale expedition led by himself might incur: ostensibly well-disposed centres of resistance against the Seljuqs such as Edessa lay far away, beyond a plateau overrun by Turks. Further light on Alexius's objectives and methods is cast by a text briefly noted by Alfons Becker in 1988 but generally ignored. Our text corroborates what the *Alexiad* already gives grounds for supposing: that Alexius made heavy use of westerners in the recovery of north-west Asia Minor. It allows one to suggest that he might have envisaged the employment or manipulation of still more substantial numbers of westerners to take speedy advantage of the opportunities opening up in the mid-1090s. The text relates how various relics were brought to the monastery of Cormery (near Tours) in 1103. The account was composed soon afterwards, most probably on the strength of information from the donor, Guillermus, a former monk of Cormery. As Becker pointed out, the narrative makes no mention of the crusade itself.[45] Only the salient features of the 'Cormery text' will be noted here.

First, Emperor Alexius, in response to Turkish inroads 'sent envoys everywhere with letters full of immense complaints and tears, and weepingly sought the aid of the entire Christian people (*totius populi christiani*), promising very great rewards to those who would help'.[46] This statement is (barring the mention of 'rewards') reminiscent of statements of Bernold, Ekkehard and Frutolf, but there is no reason to suppose that it derives from them; nor the description of Turkish atrocities, the destruction of churches and slaughter or violation of monks and clergy, which likewise appear in the Cormery text. Second, we are told that Alexius gathered 'a multitude of armies' and with their help and 'merciful God's' drove the Turks back from the lands which they had overrun 'right up to the Arm of St George' (the Gulf of Nicomedia).[47] Part of Alexius's host is assigned to Nicomedia; work begins on refortifying it; and after six months some of its former inhabitants begin to return. The implication is that the 'multitude of armies' were drawn from 'the Christian people' who had received Alexius's messages, and this would suggest a number of companies from the West, rather than just one or two. According to Anna Comnena, the 500 or so horsemen sent by Robert of Flanders were dispatched by Alexius to protect the district of Nicomedia from Turkish raids: Nicomedia is regarded as already back in Byzantine hands. Anna is capable of chronological confusion and she could have omitted the Flemings' role in first recapturing the city, before they took on guard-duties. But her information about them is fairly precise and to some extent verifiable; so the Flemings probably were sent as reinforcements to an already-captured position.[48] The Cormery text states that only 'part' of the 'multitude of armies' was assigned to guarding Nicomedia, and this suggests that the number of westerners in Alexius's service was quite large by 1090; in or before that year Nicomedia was retaken.[49]

A third item of information takes us back to the likely source of the text, Guillermus. He was already on friendly terms with the emperor and his court at the time of arrival of the 'multitude of armies'. Alexius detailed him, too, to Nicomedia 'so that he might look after the army as chaplain and priest, and so that he might restore that ruined city in accordance with the emperor's orders'.[50] One of the buildings which he set about restoring at considerable cost was a once-rich monastery, whose few surviving monks gave him advice on how to carry out the task. Thus a Frankish cleric was delegated by Alexius to provide spiritually for the westerners garrisoning Nicomedia and to see to the rebuilding of the town. Finally, our text indicates that Guillermus went to Jerusalem and obtained a considerable number of relics, for example from the Holy Sepulchre, Mount Calvary, the 'sepulchre of the mother of Christ' and the tomb of Lazarus. These were all presented to Cormery.[51] No indication is given as to whether Guillermus made his journey to Jerusalem before or after its liberation from the Saracens. One consideration weighing in favour of a pre-1099 dating is that Guillermus visited Cormery in July 1103 as the 'bishop of the *Salpinae civitatis*'. He was most probably already bishop of Salpi (in the ecclesiastical province of Bari) a year or two earlier and one should allow for the lapse of some time between Guillermus' arrival and installation there and his journey to his old monastery near Tours.[52]

If the Cormery text is taken at face value, it offers a counterbalance to the posturings of the *Alexiad* and the *Gesta*, but it also suggests that Alexius really was a central figure in Byzantium's dealings with the West, before as well as during the Crusade: by the late 1080s, he had adopted a kind of 'scatter-gun' approach, sending off messengers with 'letters ... full of tears' 'everywhere'. Alexius seems to have been aiming at men of substance – lay or cleric – capable of marshalling persons within their lordship, diocese or monastic affiliation to form an *exercitus* and lead or send it east. Comparing the Cormery text with Frutolf, Bernold and Ekkehard, one may infer that Alexius's messages constantly emphasised the damage inflicted on the clergy and churches, and that several years before 1095 he was seeking aid 'for the defence of Holy Church'. He did not lack advisers on the ecclesiastical hierarchy and religious sentiments in western Europe. Other literate westerners besides Guillermus were on familiar terms with the emperor: he was introduced to Alexius by another former monk of Cormery, a certain Goibert, 'who was dear enough to the emperor and his courtiers on account of his probity and his nobility of character'.[53]

This was not the only meeting of friends of Western origin in Alexius's entourage: around 1090 a monk of Canterbury, Joseph, returning from a pilgrimage to Jerusalem visited Constantinople and came upon a number of 'friends' who were now 'in the emperor's household' and on friendly terms with the officer in charge of guarding 'the emperor's chapel'. It is possible that some of these 'friends' were, like Joseph, churchmen rather than guardsmen.[54] Guillermus had travelled to Constantinople 'intent on more prolonged scholarly study'.[55] At least one other literate westerner resided there in the late eleventh century. Besides recounting in detail the relics and processions of the city, he indicates that he spent time at the church of St Sophia 'in order that I might learn Greek letters and the Greek language', skills which he used to hear about the history of the church 'from very many' as well as reading about it.[56] It was presumably from these informants rather than exclusively the written word that he gleaned the significance of the equestrian statue of Justinian outside St Sophia. Justinian held 'his hand most proudly raised against Jerusalem on a lofty column as he seems to swear, or to threaten [it]'.[57] The text's editor infers that the description was written before Jerusalem was liberated and this, together with other details, points towards a later eleventh-century dating.[58] It also suggests that Jerusalem was a topic of discussion in Constantinople at that time. The author of the text himself paid a visit to Jerusalem, presumably on pilgrimage.[59]

It would not be surprising if such talk about Jerusalem reached the ears of Alexius Comnenus. He may even have fostered it, seeing that he made as if to believe a prophecy that he would go and venerate the Holy Sepulchre before laying down his crown.[60] At any event there were literate Western-born churchmen accessible to Alexius, as well as a number of warriors, and our Cormery text suggests that they were aware of, perhaps actively involved with, the appeals for *auxilium* being put out.[61] Our text is referring to events of the later 1080s but Alexius's position, political as well as strategic, remained very uncertain and the more ground he regained in Asia Minor the more capable, trustworthy warriors would be required to garrison its forts and towns. We lack firm figures for the number of warriors serving in the East at any one time between the late 1080s and the mid-1090s, but our Cormery text gives reason to believe that the 500 horsemen who arrived from Flanders in, most probably, 1090 represent the tip, if not of an 'iceberg', then at least of a cluster of other Western companies in the emperor's service before 1095. It further indicates that the warriors were promised 'most lavish gifts' and it depicts Alexius as leading them in person. It was in terms of such direct leadership that Alexius continued to pitch his appeals. At, or just after, Piacenza Urban II induced 'many' to swear on oath 'that they would render most faithful aid (*fidelissimum adiutorium*) to the same emperor [Alexius] against the pagans to the best of their ability'.[62]

At the same time, Alexius had good reason to stress that he was well-disposed towards pilgrims making for Jerusalem. He might thereby avoid the sort of complaints over excessive exactions and requisitions which Pope Victor III (1086–7) had relayed to his government during Victor's pontificate and substantiate his theme that Eastern and Western Christians shared a common faith.[63] Alexius could also hope that some of the pilgrimages would generate military aid, as Robert of Flanders's had done. It is quite possible that Kibotos, the fortress built on the coast of the Gulf of Nicomedia in the second half of the 1080s, was from the first equipped with a Latin monastery and one may surmise that a hospice for pilgrims was also built there. Guillermus was then or soon afterwards supervising building-work at Nicomedia, including the restoration of its pre-eminent monastery, and in 1097 Alexius pledged to build 'a Latin monastery and a hospice for the poor among the Franks' at Nicaea.[64] The existence of a hospice in addition to a monastery at Kibotos before the crusade could explain how the followers of Peter the Hermit were accommodated there without apparent hardship or grievances against the Byzantines for several months in 1096.[65]

At any rate, our Cormery text suggests that Alexius employed – and often led – diverse companies of Western warriors, amounting to perhaps several thousand men at any one time, and that he received the counsel and enjoyed the respect of churchmen such as Guillermus. Some of them sooner or later went back – including Goibert as well as Guillermus[66] – and they presumably supplemented the reports of returning pilgrims, whose notables sometimes received gifts of relics from the emperor.[67] It would thus have been against the background of a not unsympathetic image of Alexius among the arms-bearing elites of Francia that Urban II pitched his call-to-arms at Clermont. Urban's appeal, of course, carried overtones which Alexius could scarcely have foreseen in the round or fully accepted, and the forces which it unleashed gained a momentum of their own. Even so, members of the elite could well have believed not only that Alexius was as committed to their well-being as he had been to earlier bands of Western warriors and pilgrims, but also that he shared their preoccupation with Jerusalem. Raymond of Toulouse's apparent expectation that Alexius would join in the *iter* may well convey traces of such assumptions.[68] It is not unlikely that Alexius's messages to the West had fostered them,[69] and they were in any case nurtured by his general stance before 1095.

The grounds which Alexius gave Raymond for remaining at Constantinople – the threat from 'Hungarians, Cumans and other ferocious peoples' – were, as we have seen, not wholly spurious,[70] and they seem to have been taken for granted by many leaders at the time, as they later were by Fulcher of Chartres, writing from a rather different perspective:[71] communications with the West depended partly on Alexius's survival as well as on his benevolence. Nonetheless, a sense of disenchantment or worse was already in the air in June 1097, as Anselm of Ribemont's letter to Archbishop Manasses of Rheims indicates.[72] This probably amounted to more than disgruntlement over the shares of spoils and gifts distributed after the capture of Nicaea or the conduct of the emperor's officials and Pechenegs. I suggest that, paradoxically, the disenchantment owed much to widespread regard for Alexius's words and deeds in the West on the eve of the crusade. In failing to offer leadership, or a substantial number of troops for the *iter*, after insisting on fealty and homage from all the leading crusaders except Raymond, Alexius may well have inspired distrust in those formerly disposed to regard him as an ally. And through his lavish distribution of gifts and array of attempts at personal bonding, Alexius may well have heightened that distrust among some. His dazzling show of wealth and effective supply of necessities to the besiegers of Nicaea could have been taken to imply that he had the means to honour his oath to keep the crusaders well-supplied throughout their journey. His adoption of the leading crusaders as his 'sons' and social intercourse with them probably raised expectations of an overriding personal commitment to their well-being.[73] He could scarcely satisfy them, when his essential objective was the continuance of the *reconquista* so far as opportunities would allow.

Anna seems to convey Alexius's thinking accurately enough in citing his reasons for aiding the expedition: firstly, to save them as fellow-Christians from the Turks' swords, and secondly, 'so that under our organisation they might destroy the cities of the Ish-maelites and hand over those which were subject to the emperors of the Romans and thereby extend the boundaries of the Romans'.[74] The interests of the Byzantine state were discrete from the prolon-gation of the crusaders' venture, as was shown by, for example, Alexius's decision not to press on from Philomeliun to try and relieve them at Antioch: according to Anna, such a venture might have cost him Constantinople itself.[75]

The discrepancy between Alexius's ritualised profession of per-sonal solicitousness for his 'sons' and his *raison d'état* seems to have eluded, or at least been tolerated by, many crusaders. But it played into the hands of those interested in blackening Alexius's reputation in the West, notably Bohemond. In what seems to have been a post-script to the letter addressed by leading crusaders to Urban II, Bohe-mond inveighed against 'the unjust emperor, who promised us many good things, but did very little. For all sorts of ills and obsta-cles, whatever he could manage, these he inflicted upon us'.[76] At the time of writing, September 1098, the author of the *Gesta Franco-rum* probably still had links with Bohemond's entourage, and the theme of breach of promise was developed and broadcast through works which drew on the *Gesta*. The accusations against Alexius transmit a strain of opinion which was all the more virulent for not being predominant among the crusaders in 1096–8. Its rapid spread in the West owed much to the striking literary qualities of the *Gesta* and to Bohemond's talent for black propaganda. But it probably also fed off a certain sense of bewilderment among some who had returned from the Levant without ever voicing hostility towards the Greeks during the crusade. Alexius had done much in response to the complaints of molestation of pilgrims levelled against him in 1086/7. But his very reputation as a brave commander of warriors and protector of pilgrims, together with his subsequent insistence on personal bonds with the crusading leaders, made him the more vulnerable to charges of betrayal if he appeared less than wholly committed to their cause. And while the westerners' fervour for their journey to Jerusalem opened up new opportunities for a speedy *reconquista*, the safeguarding of the 'pilgrims' and the welfare of those staying on in the Levant could scarcely over-ride the emperor's concern for 'New Rome and the majesty of the throne'.

Notes

1 EA, p. 30; cf. p. 31.
2 An exception is Fulcher of Chartres' apostrophe to Constantinople: FC, pp. 176–7. See also the derisive apostrophe in EA, p. 13.
3 GN, p. 133.
4 Anna Comnena (hereafter AC), II, pp. 209, 212, 221; Sewter, *Alexiad*, pp. 311, 313, 319.
5 AC, II, p. 226; Sewter, *Alexiad*, p. 323.
6 AC, III, pp. 39–40; Sewter, *Alexiad*, pp. 357–8.
7 AC, III, p. 125; Sewter, *Alexiad*, p. 424.
8 AC, I, pp. 143–68; AC, II, pp. 13–32, 50–60; Sewter, *Alexiad*, pp. 135–53, 160–73, 188–96.
9 See J. Shepard, 'When Greek meets Greek: Alexius Comnenus and Bohemond in 1097–98', *Byzantine and Modern Greek Studies*, 12 (1988), 189–98; *idem*, '"Father" or "Scorpion"? Style and substance in Alexios's diplomacy' in M.E. Mullett and D. Smythe (eds), *Alexios I Komnenos*, Belfast Byzantine Texts and Translations, 4.1 (Belfast, 1996), pp. 69, 74; R.-J. Lilie, 'Der erste Kreuzzug in der Darstellung Anna Komnenes', *Poikila Byzantina* 6 (= Varia II) (Bonn, 1987), pp. 55–63, 90–1, 95–100, 146–8; *idem*, 'Anna Komnene und die Lateiner', *Byzantinoslavica*, 54 (1993), 176–9.
10 AC, III, pp. 39–40; Sewter, *Alexiad*, p. 358; J. France, 'Anna Comnena, the *Alexiad* and the First Crusade', *Reading Medieval Studies*, 10 (1984), 20–1, 30–2; R.-J. Lilie, *Byzantium and the Crusader States 1096–1204*, trans. J.C. Morris and J.E. Ridings (Oxford, Clarendon Press, 1993), pp. 36–7, 46, 52–3.
11 AC, II, pp. 230, 234; AC, III, pp. 17–18, 27, 49, 146–7; Sewter, *Alexiad*, pp. 326, 329, 341, 348–9, 365, 439; France, 'Anna Comnena', 21; Lilie, *Byzantium and Crusader States*, pp. 138–45, 163–9.
12 R.D. Thomas, 'Anna Comnena's account of the First Crusade', *Byzantine and Modern Greek Studies*, 15 (1991), 273, 293–4, 300–5, 309–11; P. Magdalino, *The Empire of Manuel I Komnenos (1143–1180)* (Cambridge, Cambridge University Press, 1993), pp. 52–3, 55–6, 90–1, 209, 221–3, 385–6; M. and E. Jeffreys, 'Who was Eirene the Sevastokratorissa?' *Byzantion*, 64 (1994), 51–65.
13 John Zonaras, *Epitome Historiarum*, ed. T. Büttner-Wobst, III (Bonn, 1897), pp. 742–3. See H. Hunger, *Die hochsprachliche profane Literatur der Byzantiner*, I (Munich, C.H. Beck'sche Verlagsbuchhandlung 1978), pp. 416–17. See also below, n. 69.
14 P. Maas, 'Die Musen des Kaisers Alexios I.', *Byzantinische Zeitschrift*, 22 (1913), 357, lines 324–7.
15 Maas, 'Musen', 358, lines 330–3, 335–6.
16 Lilie, 'Erste Kreuzzug', pp. 146–8. Anna is thought to have written up

the work after the death of her husband, Nicephorus Bryennius in 1136/7: Hunger, *Profane Literatur*, I, p. 403; Thomas, 'Anna Comnena's account', 293–4. The earlier part drew heavily on the unfinished work of Bryennius: J.D. Howard-Johnston, 'Anna Komnene and the *Alexiad*', in Mullett and Smythe (eds), *Alexios I Komnenos*, pp. 276–88, 300–1.

17 C. Morris, 'The *Gesta Francorum* as narrative history', *Reading Medieval Studies*, 19 (1993), 62. See also GF, p. xv (introduction); K.B. Wolf, 'Crusade and narrative: Bohemond and the *Gesta Francorum*', *JMH*, 17 (1991), 207–9, 214–16.

18 Morris, '*Gesta Francorum*', 68.

19 GF, p. 75; cf. pp. 80–1.

20 GF, pp. 6, 11–13. See also pp. 75–6, 80–1. The *Gesta* may well have been finished before the end of 1099 (Morris, '*Gesta Francorum*', 66), while Raymond is thought to have stayed in Byzantium from spring 1100 until spring 1102: Lilie, *Byzantium and Crusader States*, pp. 265, 268–9, 275.

21 See GF, pp. x–xi (introduction); J.S.C. Riley-Smith, *The First Crusade and the Idea of Crusading* (London, Athlone Press 1986), pp. 60–1; V. Epp, *Fulcher von Chartres: Studien zur Geschichtsschreibung des Ersten Kreuzzuges* (Düsseldorf, Droste 1990), p. 145.

22 The reception is, in contrast, mentioned in two contemporary letters: Hagenmeyer, *Epistulae*, p. 140 (Stephen of Blois); pp. 144–5 (Anselm of Ribemont). See also AC, III, pp. 16–17; Sewter, *Alexiad*, p. 340.

23 RC, pp. 612–13. On Ralph's likely independence of the GF, see Shepard, 'Greek meets Greek', 231–2.

24 The GF's author most probably set off in the company led by Bohemond and Tancred, who 'surpassed the others in fighting prowess' (GF, p. 56). He is more deferential towards, and informative about, Bohemond than any other leader: Wolf, 'Crusade', 208, 211–15.

25 This may have been one – though not the sole – reason why Raymond made Alexius's participation in the *iter* to Jerusalem a precondition of his performance of homage: RA, p. 41. See below, p. 121. On Raymond's and Godfrey's disposal of their properties, see Riley-Smith, *First Crusade*, p. 37; Lilie, *Byzantium and Crusader States*, pp. 13–14 and n. 65.

26 Hagenmeyer, *Epistulae*, pp. 138–9.

27 FC, pp. 178–9. On Fulcher's omission of the oaths from his revised version, see Epp, *Fulcher*, pp. 294–5.

28 On the limitations of twelfth-century galleys, see J.H. Pryor, *Geography, Technology and War: Studies in the Maritime History of the Mediterranean, 649–1571* (Cambridge, Cambridge University Press, 1988), pp. 37–8, 116–20. Byzantine co-operation along the sea-routes

was of correspondingly great importance: *ibid.*, pp. 112–13.

29 Riley-Smith, *First Crusade*, p. 42.
30 RA, pp. 40–1; AA, II.10–13, II.18.
31 Raymond expected Alexius and his agents to be 'brothers to us, and allies', upon his company's arrival at Dyrrachium: RA, p. 38.
32 GF, p. 1. According to Anna, Peter the Hermit made every 'Celt' believe that they had heard a 'divine voice in their hearts', so that they set off for Jerusalem: AC, II, p. 207; Sewter, *Alexiad*, p. 309.
33 Frutolf in *Frutolfi et Ekkehardi Chronica*, ed. F.-J. Schmale and I. Schmale-Ott, Ausgewählte Quellen zur deutschen Geschichte des Mittelalters 15 (Darmstadt, Germany, Wissenschaftliche Buchgesellschaft 1972), p. 106.
34 EA, p. 15; Bernold, *Chronicon, MGHSS*, V, p. 462.
35 AC, II, pp. 162–4; Sewter, *Alexiad*, pp. 272–4; P. Gautier, 'Défection et soumission de la Crète sous Alexis Comnène', *REB*, 35 (1977), 219, 220–1, 225, 227.
36 Matthew of Edessa 'Chronicle', in *Armenia and the Crusades, Tenth to Twelfth Centuries*, trans. A.E. Dostourian (Lanham, Maryland, University Press of America, 1993), pp. 161–2. On the inscription, see W. Saunders, 'The Greek inscription on the Harran Gate at Edessa: some further evidence', *Byzantinische Forschungen*, 21 (1995), 301–4. Cf. Runciman, I, pp. 195–6, 202–4. J.H. Forse, 'Armenians and the First Crusade', *JMH*, 17 (1991), 15.
37 GF, p. 25. On the town Plasta (modern Elbistan) see F. Hild and M. Restle, *Kappadokien*, Tabula Imperii Byzantini 2. Österreichische Akademie der Wissenschaften philosophisch-historische Klasse. Denkschriften 149 (Vienna, 1981), pp. 109, 260.
38 AC, II, p. 197; Sewter, *Alexiad*, p. 301. P. Gautier adduced strong reasons for dating the Cuman invasion to the first half of 1095: 'Le synode des Blachernes (fin 1094). Étude prosopographique', *REB*, 29 (1971), 281–3.
39 AC, II, pp. 179, 180; Sewter, *Alexiad*, p. 286; J.-C. Cheynet, *Pouvoir et contestations à Byzance (963–1210)*, Byzantina Sorbonensia 9 (Paris, Publications de la Sorbonne, 1990), pp. 98–9, 276, 365, 367.
40 AC, II, pp. 190–1, 196; Sewter, *Alexiad*, pp. 296–7, 300; Cheynet, *Pouvoir*, pp. 99–100, 365–6. See now P. Magdalino, '*Digenes Akrites* and Byzantine literature', in *Digenes Akrites. New Approaches to Byzantine Heroic Poetry*, R. Beaton and D. Ricks (eds), (Aldershot, Varorium, 1993), pp. 10–11.
41 P. Gautier, 'Diatribes de Jean l'Oxite contre Alexis I Comnène', *REB*, 28 (1970), 43, line 12; AC, II, pp. 194–5; Sewter, *Alexiad*, p. 299. John the Oxite noted that 'not a few' persons had been driven by State exactions to desert to the barbarians: Gautier, 'Diatribes', 33, lines

26–7. On efforts to increase revenues from the 1080s to the early 1100s, see also R. Morris, *Monks and Laymen in Byzantium 843–1118* (Cambridge, Cambridge University Press, 1995), pp. 283–6; A. Harvey, 'Financial crisis and the rural economy', in Mullet and Smythe (eds), *Alexios I Komnenos*, pp. 177–82.

42 C. Cahen, *La Turquie pré-ottomane*, Varia Turcica 7 (Istanbul and Paris, Institut français d'études anatoliennes d'Istanbul 1988), p. 15.

43 AC, II, pp. 79–81; Sewter, *Alexiad*, pp. 210–11; J.-C. Cheynet, 'La résistance aux Turcs en Asie Mineure entre Mantzikert et la Première Croisade', in *Mélanges H. Ahrweiler* (Paris, 1996, forthcoming). I am most grateful to Dr Cheynet for letting me use the typescript of this.

44 F. Miklosich and I. Müller (eds), *Acta et Diplomata Graeca Medii Aevi*, VI (Vienna, Carolus Gerold, 1890), p. 91; AC, III, pp. 23, 26; Sewter, *Alexiad*, pp. 345, 347; Gautier, 'Diatribes', 14, n. 56; Cheynet, 'Résistance aux Turcs'.

45 A. Becker, *Papst Urban II (1088–1099), Teil II* (MGH Schriften 19.II) (Stuttgart, Anton Hiersmann, 1988), p. 183 and n. 345 (a).

46 *Acta translationis SS. Reliquiarum in Monasterium Cormaricenum*, *Gallia Christiana*, XIV (Paris, 1856, reprinted Farnborough, Hants., Gregg International 1970), *Instrumenta Ecclesiae Turonensis*, no. 58, col. 76.

47 *Acta translationis*, col. 76.

48 AC, II, pp. 109–10; Sewter, *Alexiad*, pp. 232–3; F. Ganshof, 'Robert le Frison et Alexis Comnène', *Byzantion*, 31 (1961), 72–4; J. Shepard, 'Aspects of Byzantine attitudes and policy towards the West in the 10th and 11th centuries', in J.D. Howard-Johnston (ed.), *Byzantium and the West, c. 850–1200* (Amsterdam, Adolf M. Hakkert, 1988), p. 103. The text gives grounds for revising my view that the number of Franks in Alexius's service before 1095 'seem[s] to have been quite modest': 'The uses of the Franks in 11th century Byzantium', *Anglo-Norman Studies* 15 (1993), 303.

49 The Flemings sent by Robert spent some time at Nicomedia before being summoned to participate in the campaign against the Pechenegs in the spring of 1091: AC, II, p. 135; Sewter, *Alexiad*, p. 252: see above n. 48. So Nicomedia is most likely to have been in Byzantine hands by 1090, and maybe several years earlier: Cheynet, 'Résistance aux Turcs'. J. Lefort noted Nicomedia's importance as a communications-hub: 'Les communications entre Constantinople et la Bithynie', in C. Mango and G. Dagron (eds), *Constantinople and its Hinterland* (Aldershot, Hants., Variorum, 1995), pp. 215–16; J.-C. Cheynet, 'Résistance aux Turcs'. Anna herself gives hints that other companies besides the Flemings were expected: AC, II, p. 139; Sewter, *Alexiad*,

p. 256; Shepard, 'Attitudes and policy', pp. 103–4.

50 *Acta translationis*, col. 76.

51 *Acta translationis*, col. 78.

52 *Acta translationis*, cols 76, 78. Guillermus can reasonably be identified with the *Guilielmus Salpitanus episcopus* named among those invited to attend the consecration of Canosa's church in a text bearing the date September 1101 or 1102: G.B. Nitto de Rossi and F. Nitti di Vito (eds), *Codice diplomatico barese*, II (Bari, Commissione provinciale di archeologia e storia patria, 1899), *appendice II, Le carte di Canosa (1102–1264)*, no. 1**, p. 212. Doubts as to the text's authenticity were justifiably raised by J.-M. Martin, *La Pouille du VI au XII siècle*, Collection de l'école française de Rome 179 (Rome, École française de Rome, 1993), p. 573 and no. 65. But it could well have drawn on an authentic list of signatories or witnesses of the beginning of the twelfth century, for at least two of the named bishops beside Guilielmus were *en poste* about that time, Robert of Cannae and Bisantius of Trani: Martin, *La Pouille*, p. 596 and n. 219, p. 620 and n. 394.

53 *Acta translationis*, col. 76.

54 C. Haskins, 'A Canterbury monk at Constantinople, c. 1090', *EHR*, 25 (1910), 295.

55 *Acta translationis*, col. 76.

56 K. Ciggaar, 'Une description de Constantinople dans le *Tarragonensis* 55', *REB*, 53 (1995), 125.

57 Ciggaar, 'Description', 127. That Justinian's gesture towards 'the Persians' was regarded as *defensive*, warning them not to invade, was stated in a tenth-century collection of tales about Constantinople's monuments: T. Preger (ed.), *Scriptores Originum Constantinopolitanarum*, II (Leipzig, Teubner, 1907), p. 159; cf. C. Mango, 'The columns of Justinian and his successors', in Mango's *Studies on Constantinople* (Aldershot, Hants., Variorum, 1993), no. 10, pp. 4–5.

58 The equation of *Garengi*, 'Varangians' with *Angli* suggests a date some time after the arrival of Anglo-Saxon exiles at Byzantium in the 1070s, whereas the mention of 'residences' of the Amalfitans and silence about the Venetians suggests a date not long after Alexius's grant of landing stages and properties to the Venetians in 1082: Ciggaar, 'Description', 119; D.M. Nicol, *Byzantium and Venice: A Study in Diplomatic and Cultural Relations* (Cambridge, Cambridge University Press, 1988), pp. 60–3.

59 Ciggaar, 'Description', 119; cf. *ibid.*, 122, 134 (commentary).

60 Zonaras, *Epitome*, III, p. 760; Magdalino, *Empire*, p. 34.

61 Ciggaar pointed out that several relics mentioned in the anonymous description feature in the letter purporting to be from Alexius to Robert of Flanders: 'Description', 129–31; cf. 120–1 (text); Hagen-

meyer, *Epistulae*, p. 134; M. de Waha, 'La lettre d'Alexis Comnène à Robert le Frison', *Byzantion*, 47 (1977), 121–2.

62 Bernold, p. 462.

63 H.E.J. Cowdrey, 'Pope Victor and the Empress A.', *Byzantinische Zeitschrift*, 84–5 (1991–2), 43–8; Becker, *Urban II*, pp. 131–2, 144–54, 184–8.

64 RA, p. 44.

65 On the building of Kibotos and installation of Anglo-Saxons there, see OV, II.202; cf. Lefort, 'Communications', p. 213; Cheynet, 'Résistance aux Turcs'. For the Latin monastery 'next to that imperial *civitas*', see G. Constable (ed.), *The Letters of Peter the Venerable* (Cambridge, Mass., Harvard University Press, 1967), I, p. 209; II, p. 292 (commentary). On Peter the Hermit at Kibotos, see GF, pp. 4–5.

66 *Acta translationis*, col. 76.

67 *Gesta Episcoporum Tullensium*, *MGHSS*, VIII.647; Shepard, 'Attitudes and policy', p. 103.

68 RA, p. 41; above, n. 25.

69 According to Ekkehard of Aura, Alexius was trying to defend 'the eastern churches' (*orientalium ecclesiarum*), EA, p. 15. Presumably the plural was intended to denote Antioch and Jerusalem as well as Constantinople. Jerusalem and the Holy Sepulchre are mentioned in the aforesaid letter from Alexius to Robert of Flanders: Hagenmeyer, *Epistulae*, pp. 132, 136; de Waha, 'Lettre d'Alexis', 120, 122–3; Becker, *Urban II*, p. 182 and n. 345 (scepticism about the letter). This evidence might suggest that Jerusalem had a place, albeit still peripheral, in Alexius's propaganda in the earlier 1090s: Shepard, 'Attitudes and policy', pp. 105, 110–12. The question whether Alexius's appeals to the West in 1095 now made Jerusalem the prime objective deserves further study: see Theodore Scutariotes, *Synopsis Chronike*, ed. K.N. Sathas, *Mesaionike Bibliotheke*, VII (Venice, Phoinix, 1894), pp. 184–5; P. Charanis, 'Byzantium, the West and the origins of the First Crusade', *Byzantion*, 19 (1949), 30–6. Scutariotes seems to have used unidentified sources besides an early twelfth-century work apparently also available to Zonaras: Hunger, *Profane Literatur*, I, pp. 477–8. See also below, n. 71.

70 RA, p. 41; above, p. 115.

71 FC, p. 179. The letter of Alexius to Robert of Flanders seems to warn that the loss of Byzantium would jeopardise westerners' access to the Holy Sepulchre: Hagenmeyer, *Epistulae*, pp. 136, 209 (commentary). This could well have been a device whereby Alexius associated his regime's survival with the westerners' evident veneration for the Holy Sepulchre.

72 Hagenmeyer, *Epistulae*, pp. 144–5.

73 Hagenmeyer, *Epistulae*, pp. 138–9; RA, p. 38; AA, II.16; Shepard, '"Father" or "Scorpion"', 96–8, 111–13, 120–9.
74 AC, III, p. 146; Sewter, *Alexiad*, p. 439. Anna reaffirms Alexius's whole-hearted anxiety 'to extend the frontiers of the Roman empire': AC, III, p. 147; Sewter, p. 439.
75 AC, III, p. 29; Sewter, *Alexiad*, pp. 349–50.
76 Hagenmeyer, *Epistulae*, p. 165.

7

The First Crusade: the Muslim perspective

Carole Hillenbrand

It is an impossible task to deal in a short chapter with the impact of the First Crusade on the Islamic world. This chapter will therefore be limited to the following three aims: a brief discussion of the Arabic sources, an analysis of the state of the Islamic world around the year 1095 and some insights into the impact of the First Crusade on its direct victims, the Muslims of Syria and Palestine.

Runciman writes: 'Arabic sources, though numerous and highly important for the later crusades, give us very little assistance over the first .... The great encyclopaedias and geographies, so popular with the Arabs, are barely concerned with these years.'[1] According to Runciman, only three works are of real value: the chronicles of Ibn al-Qalānisī, Ibn al-Athīr and Kamalāl-Dīn,[2] known more commonly amongst Orientalists as Ibn al-ʾAdīm. With the greatest respect to Runciman, whose *magnum opus* has inspired many to embark on serious study of the crusades, these statements of his require modification or downright contradiction. He is right, of course, in one sense: one looks in vain in the Islamic sources for a detailed account of the battles of the First Crusade.

This dearth of information does not, however, stem from any desire on the Muslims' part to pass over a series of ignominious defeats at the hand of the crusaders.[3] It is, rather, a general characteristic of medieval Islamic historiography which stresses propagandistic themes, skating hazily over military details. One is forcefully reminded that most Islamic historians were by training religious scholars or administrators, not military strategists. But the worst of it is that modern Western scholarship on the crusades must still rely, inevitably, on the limited canon of Arabic works which *happen* to have been translated into European languages. Moreover, despite the undeniable usefulness of the *Recueil des historiens des croisades*, one should recall that the passages translated in it are only excerpts of much fuller texts personally selected by the editors and sometimes badly edited and mistranslated.

Some sources remain unexploited. An important, if fragmentary source, the chronicle of al-'Aẓīmī (d. 1160), published by Claude Cahen in 1938 in Arabic handwritten form and recently published in printed form,[4] is barely cited in recent scholarship. New texts have been published. The great biographical dictionary of Ibn al-'Adīm, the *Bughya*, has recently been published in full.[5] Some of his entries *were* included in the *Recueil* but his biography of Riḍwān of Aleppo, for example, remains unexploited. *Pace* Runciman, much of interest is to be found in the Arabic encyclopaedias and geographies, as for instance in the section of Ibn Shaddād's geography which deals with northern Syria.[6] There is, moreover, some useful information to be gleaned from a range of untranslated and unexploited Mamlūk histories, such as those of the prolific al-Maqrīzī[7] and the administrator, Ibn al-Dawādārī.[8] It is also most worthwhile to read the *whole* of Ibn Taghribirdī.[9] It could be argued that these are later works, reflecting the preoccupations of the fourteenth rather than the twelfth century, but such writers draw heavily on earlier named and unnamed lost historiographical texts, and the works of the fourteenth- and fifteenth-century chroniclers certainly repay a laborious trawl, if their information is then evaluated judiciously. The extant Arabic poetry of the period of the First Crusade also remains largely unexploited.[10] Some of it, usually the same lines in each case, has been translated or summarised by Emmanuel Sivan, Francesco Gabrieli and Hadia Dajani-Shakeel, but there is more work to be done on this small yet important corpus of writing. Taken altogether, this mass of extra historical material cannot fail to give a fuller and more nuanced view than we have had so far of the composite Islamic historiographical contribution to our knowledge of the First Crusade.

It is a truism of crusader history that the warriors of the First Crusade succeeded because of Muslim disunity and weakness. Had the First Crusade arrived even ten years earlier, it would have met strong, unified resistance from the East under Malikshāh, the last of the three so-called Great Seljuq sultans. To what extent was the Islamic world bereft of unity and weakened by a complete lack of powerful overall leadership and by religious schism? First, the issue of leadership. It has often been said that the centrifugal forces at the heart of the Seljuq government machine all worked towards the fragmentation of the once unified Seljuq empire after 1092. Thus the crusaders found in Syria and Palestine small territorial units under the nominal suzerainty of the Seljuqs but ruled by mutually hostile Seljuq princelings and military commanders.

Seljuq weakness should be further contextualised and emphasised. In the space of less than two years, beginning in 1092, there was a total sweep of *all* the major political pieces on the Islamic chessboard from Egypt eastwards. In 1092 the greatest figure of Seljuq history, the vizier, Niẓām al-Mulk, the *de facto* ruler of the Seljuq empire for over thirty years, was murdered. A month later, Malikshāh, the third Seljuq sultan, died in suspicious circumstances, after a successful twenty-year reign, followed closely by his wife, grandson and other powerful political figures. In the ensuing turbulence, Seljuq pretenders fought fratricidal and familial struggles to gain supreme power, struggles which monopolised their energies and military resources.[11] The Muslim sources view the year 1094 as even more doom-laden, for in this year yet another era was brought to an end with the death of the Fāṭimid caliph of Egypt, al-Mustanṣir, the arch-enemy of the Seljuqs, who had ruled for fifty-eight years. His death was closely followed by that of *his* vizier, Badr al-Jamālī. Also in 1094 the ʿAbbāsid Sunni caliph, al-Muqtadī, died. As Ibn Taghribirdī put it: 'This year is called the year of the death of caliphs and commanders'.[12] This succession of deaths in both the key power centres of the Islamic world, the Seljuq and Fāṭimid empires, occurring at exactly the same time, must have had the same impact as the disintegration of the Iron Curtain in recent years: known political entities and certainties gave way to disorientation and anarchy. The timing of the First Crusade could not have been more propitious. Could one suggest that the Europeans had somehow been briefed that *this* was the perfect moment to pounce?

Religious schism was not removed by the deaths of the major political figures of the time. It permeated Islamic life at every level of society and was indeed exacerbated by the political vacuum which developed in the years 1092–4. As 'good Sunni Islamic rulers' the Seljuqs had pursued a vigorous foreign policy in the period 1063–92, the main thrust of which had been to wage war but not against Byzantium or the Christian kingdoms of the Caucasus, although such initiatives did occur. The prime Seljuq obsession on the military front had been the 'heretical' Fāṭimid Shi'ite caliphate of Cairo and a protracted struggle was fought out in Syria and Palestine. The ideological and political enmity between Fāṭimid Ismaili Shi'ites and the Seljuq Sunnis died hard. Indeed, the crusaders, once they were established in the Levant, would prove, for a while at least, preferable as allies for both Sunnis and Shi'ites; it was almost unthinkable to form a united Islamic front against the outside invaders, as might have been expected, for example, at the siege of Antioch. As for Jerusalem itself, in 1095 it was not the cynosure of Muslim eyes that it was to become in the build-up to its reconquest by Saladin in 1187. The concept of *jihād*, sharpened in the tenth and eleventh centuries on the frontiers with the nomadic Turks of Central Asia in the east and with Byzantium in the west, was flagging now, a rhetorical term rather than a politico-religious rallying-cry.[13]

The same disunity characterised other areas of the Islamic world. The Turks of Asia Minor were the first Muslim foe to be encountered by the crusaders. The information in Muslim sources on their activities is scattered in the chronicles of the Seljuqs of Iraq and Iran and in Ayyūbid and Mamlūk histories written from the vantage point of Syria and Egypt. The battle of Manzikert in 1071 is usually taken as a convenient date to symbolise the beginning of a gradual but steady process by which diverse groups of nomadic Turks infiltrated the Byzantine empire, pursuing their time-honoured lifestyle of pastoralism and raiding.[14] We do not know how numerous these groups were: some were authorised to raid by the Seljuq sultans, others progressed unchecked by any allegiance, even nominal, to a supra-tribal authority. The Seljuq ruler of western Asia Minor, Qilij Arslan (ruled 1092–1107), called 'sultan' retrospectively in the sources, came from a renegade branch of the great Seljuq family, and even though he was far from Iran he was still attached emotionally to his tribal heritage in the east. In the political instability of the post-1092 period he interfered whenever possible in the affairs of the Seljuq sultanate in the east, to exploit its weakness and to gain territory for himself. This was of far greater moment to him than to contemplate campaigns across the mountains into Syria and Palestine to fight the crusaders. Even within Asia Minor there was no semblance of overall political unity between the disparate nomadic Turkish groups vying for territory there in the aftermath of the battle of Manzikert in 1071. The Danishmendids, who held sway in central Anatolia, between Sivas and Malatya, did, it is true, form a temporary alliance with the Seljuqs of western Anatolia for the battle of Dorylaeum (July 1097), but such alliances were always ephemeral. Any concerted Turcoman initiative into Palestine or Syria was inconceivable.[15]

As for the Fāṭimids of Egypt, they are portrayed most unfavourably by the great Sunni historians of the Islamic Middle Ages, for the Fāṭimids had begun life as a secretive, esoteric, extremist Ismaili Shi'ite sect and they had become the major enemies of the Seljuqs who presented themselves as the 'defenders of Sunni Islam'. At the time of the First Crusade, the Fāṭimids were experiencing difficulties. Their religious persuasion usually cut them off from alliances with neighbouring Sunni Muslim powers. Their *de facto* ruler, the vizier al-Afḍal, chose to rule through young puppet caliphs. As already mentioned, al-Maqrīzī, the great Mamlūk historian, wrote a complete history of the Fāṭimids, *Itti'āẓ al-ḥunafā'*. For the period of the First Crusade it is noteworthy that he mentions that Egypt was laid low by famine and plague, in 490/1096–7 and especially in 493/1099–1100. He also stresses further religious schism with the formation of the breakaway Fāṭimid group, the Assassins, after al-Mustansir's death in 1094. In these difficult circumstances it is hardly surprising that the Fāṭimid war effort against the crusaders was to prove less than creditable.[16]

Unfortunately, the Muslim chroniclers indicate no motivation for the Fāṭimids' sending out an army in 1098 to seize Jerusalem from the two Turcoman chiefs who were holding the city on behalf of the Seljuq sultan. But the most likely reason is that al-Afḍal was making a pre-emptive strike. In view of Seljuq weakness and the imminent arrival of the crusaders, al-Afḍal wanted to secure again the Fāṭimid hold on Jerusalem. It had, after all, been in Fāṭimid hands for a good part of the eleventh century and they had beautified its major buildings. Between 1099 and 1107, as is well known, the Fāṭimids did send a number of expeditions to Palestine by way of Ascalon to fight the crusaders. However, with one notable exception, these campaigns achieved nothing.[17]

What of the eastern perspective after 1092? The Seljuqs, and especially two sons of Malikshāh, Barkyaruq and Muḥammad, were locked in a protracted military conflict which lasted until Barkyaruq's death in 1105. This conflict gobbled up almost all the available military resources. It was fought out in western Iran, but its repercussions were felt in Iraq, the traditional seat of the Sunni caliph, in eastern Iran and Central Asia, and, by default, in distant Syria and Palestine, earlier a centre of Seljuq activity. Most Sunni Islamic sources try to whitewash Seljuq indifference to the loss of Jerusalem and the Syrian ports and they stress the fact that some campaigns were sent out under the auspices of the Seljuq sultan to wage *jihād* against the crusaders.

An exception to this approach is the historian, Ibn al-Jawzī. Writing from the vantage-point of Baghdad, he notes as early as the year 491/1097-8, that is, *before* the fall of Jerusalem: 'There were many calls to go out and fight against the Franks and complaints multiplied in every place'.[18] He records that on the orders of the Seljuq sultan, Barkyaruq, commanders assembled: 'But then his resoluteness fizzled out'.[19] Ibn al-Jawzī also notes succinctly that after the fall of Jerusalem, when a Syrian delegation came to ask for military assistance, the sultan's army held themselves aloof, or to render the Arabic text more closely, they remained sitting on their backsides.[20]

The implications of Seljuq political weakness and lack of concern for the plight of the Muslims of Syria and Palestine were far-reaching. It has often been pointed out that it was the Turkish warriors, not the Fāṭimid armies, who posed a military threat to the crusaders. Only the Seljuq armies could seriously have arrested Latin Christian expansion in the Levant. Whilst the Seljuq sultans, first Barkyaruq and then his brother Muhammad, paid lip service to the cause and sent some armies to fight the Frankish settlers in the period 1100-18, neither sultan took the field himself at the head of an army, as Alp Arslan had done at the battle of Manzikert in 1071. Neither dared to leave his power base in the east undefended. And that was the territory that counted for them, not Palestine. The fate of Jerusalem was sealed, therefore, in Iṣfahān. The disparate nature of the Seljuq army – composed as it was of the standing troops, provincial contingents under local commanders, and groups of nomadic Turcomans organised on tribal lines – necessitated strong military leadership, epitomised in the figure of the sultan. Otherwise, and this often proved the case, there was dissension and defection and the Turcomans would disappear as soon as they had been paid.

Philip Hitti speaks of the Crusaders as 'a strange and unexpected enemy'.[21] This is an apt description of the initial reaction of the Muslims most in the firing line of the First Crusade. Just as, a little more than a century later, the essentially alien Mongols would strike the Islamic world like a thunderbolt, this time from the east, so too, as the First Crusade unfolded, waves of fear, shock and incomprehension spread from the areas most affected across the whole Islamic world. But the impact of the catastrophe diminished the further afield the news of it spread. The waves became ripples. There was confusion in Baghdad about the identity of the enemy: al-Abīwardī, the Seljuq poet, writing a lament after the fall of Jerusalem, calls the malefactors al-Rūm, the usual Arabic term for the Byzantines,[22] and Ibn Shaddād also confuses Byzantines and Franks in his geography of northern Syria.[23] This is not surprising, since the Muslims' centuries-old struggle with their close neighbours, Byzantium, had been waged in the very same frontier areas now penetrated by the crusaders.

Nor is this the only evidence that the Muslim world as a whole failed to grasp what was happening. It is especially noticeable that the Islamic sources, with a few exceptions, notably Ibn al-Athīr,[24] do not evince any curiosity as to the motivation for the Latin Christian presence in Muslim territory. The correlation of the concepts of crusade/*jihād* never crosses the mind of the medieval Muslim chronicler. Crusader activities are narrated as an inevitable fact of life in the Muslim context from the First Crusade onwards, but occasion little or no special comment or digression. There is no sense that the crusaders are an unusual kind of enemy, with a fundamentally new agenda.

Thus, under the year 489/1095–6, al-'Azīmī writes laconically: 'The Franks came out from their country and Saturn was in Virgo .... Alexius, the Byzantine emperor, wrote to the Muslims, informing them of the appearance of the Franks'.[25] However, even in this brief entry the author manages to intimate foreboding and alarm to those of his readership acquainted with astrology. As the Muslim encyclopaedist, al-Qazwīnī, was to write: 'The astrologers call Saturn the largest star of misfortune ... and they ascribe to it devastation, ruin, grief and cares'.[26] One is left, moreover, to speculate on the motive of the Byzantine emperor (was the letter sent out of solicitude or was it a threat?) and on the identity of the group of the Muslims to whom it was addressed. The Fāṭimids seem to be the most likely target, but this is not overtly expressed.

Two contemporary sources exist. Sivan made extensive use of a work entitled the *Kitāb al-jihād* written in the early years of the twelfth century by a Damascene legal scholar and preacher, al-Sulamī. The two extant manuscripts of this text, both housed in a Damascus library, contain only small sections of a much longer original work. Given the crucial dating of this work, it is certainly time for an edition and translation of the complete text of the manuscripts; Sivan published and translated only selected excerpts of those sections which did survive. According to his summary of the contents, this work records the views of one contemporary religious scholar on the impact of the coming of the Franks, warning the Muslims of the dangers of military inactivity and pointing out that the Franks are aiming at seizing the Syrian ports and that the Muslims must rise in defensive *jihād* against them.[27] The other extant contemporary Islamic source which reveals the Muslim reaction to the First Crusade is a group of poems, by al-Abīwardī (died 1113), Ibn al-Khayyāṭ (who died in the 1120s) and an unnamed third poet. Gabrieli has already translated part of al-Abīwardī's lament on the loss of Jerusalem; so this chapter will concentrate on some so far untranslated texts of the other two poets.

The anonymous poet's lines are powerful even within the conventions of Arabic poetry, which is a highly conservative genre. The panegyric ode, normally addressed by the poet to his patron, is here, after the catastrophes of the First Crusade, transformed into an eloquent diatribe against the Muslims who have allowed these disasters to occur. These lines were, of course, intended to be declaimed publicly:

> The unbelief of the infidels has declared it lawful to inflict harm on Islam, causing prolonged lamentation for the faith.
> What is right is null and void and what is forbidden is [now] made licit.
> The sword is cutting and blood is spilt.
> How many Muslim men have become booty [*salīb*]?
> And how many Muslim women's inviolability has been plundered [*salīb*]?
> How many a mosque have they made into a church!
> The cross [*ṣalīb*] has been set up in the *miḥrab*.
> The blood of the pig is suitable for it.
> Qurans have been burned under the guise of incense.

[137]

Do you not owe an obligation to God and Islam,
Defending thereby young men and old?
Respond to God: woe on you! Respond![28]

The stereotypical images of the crusaders, who are portrayed as infidels, pork-lovers, rapists and despoilers of all that Islam holds sacred, are noteworthy; and there is much emphasis on the wordplay between ṣalīb ('cross') and salīb ('plunder').

The poet Ibn al-Khayyāṭ, who had served the rulers of Tripoli before the First Crusade, is equally forceful in an ode addressed to his patron, 'Aḍb al-Dawla, one of the commanders in Damascus, in his attempt to revive the flagging spirit of jihād in the early years of the twelfth century.[29] As Sivan merely summarised some of this fifty-five line ode,[30] the following gives a fuller flavour of it:

The polytheists [mushrikūn] have swelled in a torrent of terrifying extent.
How long will this continue?
Armies like mountains, coming again and again, have raged forth from the land of the Franks.

Ibn al-Khayyāṭ then alludes to the mutual rancour of the Muslim princes and to the Franks' ability to buy them off, before reaching the climax of his ode:

The tribe of polytheism do not reject [any kind] of corruption.
Nor do they recognise any moderation in tyranny ...
How many young girls have begun to beat their throats and necks out of fear of them [the Franks]?
How many nubile girls have not known the heat [of the day] nor felt the cold at night [until now]?
They are almost wasting away with fear and dying of grief and agitation.

The choice of imagery is apposite: the Arabic root nahara means 'to cut the throat of an animal for slaughter' but is here applied to that most sacred pillar of Islamic society, the sanctity of the womenfolk. So the poet continues:

Defend your religion and your ḥarīm, not counting death as a loss!
Block the frontiers by the piercing of throats!
The heads of the polytheists have already ripened,
So do not neglect them as a vintage and a harvest!

Finally the poet turns to the great hero of Manzikert as a role model for the Muslim warriors fighting the Franks:

> For in like circumstances Alp Arslan sallied forth,
> sharper-edged than the sword.

Sadly for the Muslims this eloquence went unheeded for several decades.

This chapter has first tried to suggest that the scholarship of Western crusader historians on the Muslim dimensions of their subject suffers from an over-reliance on a small and over-exploited body of translated source material which is itself excerpted from much longer works. There exists in fact a much larger body of relevant material than was suspected forty years ago. It is for Islamic historians to make these sources more readily available. They may add little enough to current knowledge about the crusaders themselves, but they will certainly reveal a lot more about their Muslim enemy. Second, the preceding discussion has emphasised that the years 1092–4 were utterly catastrophic for the Muslim world from Egypt to Afghanistan, for death removed literally all the major political figures from the scene. And many of them were seasoned, formidable leaders. They left behind them a total political vacuum. Third, it has been shown that Syria and Palestine were sacrificed on the altar of *Realpolitik* by the Seljuqs, who alone had the right kind of military capacity to save these territories, but who were to obsessed with their own power squabbles in Iran to take a global view of this unheralded invasion over a thousand miles away.

Notes

1 Runciman, I, p. 333.
2 *Ibid.*, pp. 333–4.
3 The medieval Muslim accounts of glorious victories, such as Manzikert or Hattin, are also vague on details of the course of the actual battles.
4 C. Cahen, 'La chronique abrégée d'al-'Aẓīmī', *Journal Asiatique*, 230 (1938), 353–448; ed. I. Za'rur, *Tārīkh Ḥalab* (Damascus, 1984).
5 Ibn al-'Adīm, *Bughyat al-ṭalab fītārīkh Ḥalab*, ed. S. Zakkar, 11 vols (Beirut, Dar al-Fikr, 1988).
6 Ibn Shaddād, *Description de la Syrie du Nord*, trans. A.M. Eddé-Terrasse (Damascus, Institut Français de Damas, 1984).
7 Most notable in this context is the work of al-Maqrīzī which is

devoted to the history of the Fāṭimids, the *Itti'āẓ al-ḥunafā'*, ed. J. Al-Shayyal (Cairo, Dār al-fikr al-'arabī, 1948). Also worthy of mention is his massive biographical dictionary, the *Kitāb al-muqaffā' al-kabīr*, ed. M. al-Ya'lawi, 8 vols (Beirut, 1990).

8   Ibn al-Dawādārī, *Die Chronik des Ibn al-Dawādārī*, vol. 6, ed. S. Munaǧǧid (Cairo, Deutsches Archäologisches Institut, 1961).

9   Although the *Recueil* provides translated excerpts from the history of Ibn Taghribirdī, this historian's contribution is much more extensive. CF. Ibn Taghribirdī, *Nujūm al-ẓāhira*, vol. 5 (Cairo, Maṭba'at dār al-kutub, 1939).

10 Cf. the lines of an anonymous poet quoted by Ibn Taghribirdī (*op. cit.*, 151–2) and discussed by H. Dajani-Shakeel, 'Jihad in twelfth-century Arabic poetry', *The Muslim World*, 66 (1976), 96–113; the ode of al-Abīwardī quoted by Ibn al-Jawzī, *Al-Muntaẓam*, vol. 9 (Hyderabad, 1940), 108, and by Ibn al-Athīr, *Al-Kāmil*, ed. C.J. Tornberg (Leiden and Uppsala), 1851–76, X, pp. 284–5, and partly translated by F. Gabrieli, *Arab Historians of the Crusades* (London, Routledge and Kegan Paul, 1969), p. 12; and the poems of Ibn al-Khayyāṭ, *Dīwān* (Damascus, Al-majma' al-'arabī, 1958), pp. 184–6. The importance of this poetry is discussed by E. Sivan, *L'Islam et la Croisade* (Paris, Librairie d'Amérique et d'Orient, 1968).

11 For a recent treatment of this topic, cf. C. Hillenbrand, '1092: a murderous year', in the *Proceedings of the 14th Congress of the Union Européenne des Arabisants et Islamisants*, vol. II (Budapest, 1995), 281–97.

12 Ibn Taghribirdī, *op. cit.*, p. 139.

13 In the tenth and eleventh centuries, a major area for *jihād* was the eastern border with Central Asia, where regular campaigns were conducted against the pagan Turks. This is widely attested in the works of medieval Islamic geographers and historians who speak about the popularity of frontier forts (*ribāṭs*) for housing *jihād* warriors; cf. R. Frye, *The History of Bukhara* (Cambridge, Mass., The Medieval Academy of America, 1954), p. 18 and n. 92. Archaeological evidence in the form of unprecedentedly large numbers of frontier forts in Central Asia testifies to the veracity of the written accounts; cf. R. Hillenbrand, *Islamic architecture* (Edinburgh, Edinburgh University Press, 1994), pp. 340–1 and S. Tolstov, *Auf den Spuren der altchoresmischen Kultur* (Berlin, Verlag Kultur und Fortschritt, 1953).

As for the Muslim–Byzantine border, it became famous in the tenth century because of the *jihād* activities of the Ḥamdānid dynasty (ruled 905–1004) in the Jazīra and Syria. This milieu produced the famous, though little studied, *jihād* sermons of Ibn Nubāta (d. 984) of Mayyā-fāriqīn (cf. *Sayf al Daula: Recueil de textes relatifs à l'emir Sayf al*

Daula le Hamdanide, ed. M. Canard (Algiers, Editions Jules Carbonel, 1934).

14 *Encyclopaedia of Islam*, 2nd edn, article: *Malāzgird*.
15 *Ibid.*, article: *Kilidj Arslān*.
16 Al-Maqrīzī, *op. cit.*, pp. 283–4.
17 S. Lane-Poole, *A History of Egypt in the Middle Ages* (London, Methuen, 1914), pp. 164–5.
18 Ibn al-Jawzī, *op. cit.*, p. 105.
19 *Ibid.*
20 *Ibid.*, p. 108.
21 P.K. Hitti, *History of Syria* (London, Macmillan, 1951), p. 589.
22 *Apud* Ibn al-Athīr, *op. cit.*, pp. 284–5.
23 Ibn Shaddād, *op. cit.*, p. 270. When referring to a place called Artāḥ in the 1060s, Ibn Shaddād mentions twice that it was in the hands of the Franks (instead of the Byzantines).
24 Ibn al-Athīr, *op. cit.*, p. 195.
25 Al-ʿAẓīmī (Cahen), *op. cit.*, p. 371.
26 *Encyclopaedia of Islam*, 1st edn, article: *Zuḥal*.
27 *Op. cit.*, pp. 30–2. In his original pioneering article on al-Sulamī ('La genèse de la contre-Croisade: un traité damasquin du début du XIIe siècle', *Journal Asiatique*, 254 (1966), 197–224), Sivan says that he has produced an edition of the 'texte original des passages essentiels de l'introduction, accompagné d'une traduction' (*ibid.*, 198).
28 Ibn Taghribirdī, *op. cit.*, pp. 151–2.
29 Ibn al-Khayyāṭ, *op. cit.*, pp. 184–6.
30 Sivan, *op. cit.*, p. 32.

8

The principality of Antioch and the Jabal as-Summāq

Thomas Asbridge

On 3 June 1098 the Latin participants in the First Crusade finally managed to gain entry into the city of Antioch after a tortuous and costly siege which had lasted almost eight months.[1] Soon after this the crusaders were themselves besieged within Antioch by Kerbogha's army until their victory in the battle of Antioch on 28 June 1098.[2] This chapter will examine the relationship between the Latin principality which was subsequently formed at Antioch and the Jabal as-Summāq, the plateau region to the south-east of the city, which extended from the Ruj valley and contained the towns of Albara, Kafarṭab and Maʿarrat-an-Nuʿmān. This area was of considerable political and strategic importance because, first, it controlled one of the two southern approaches to Antioch via the Ruj, and second, the town of Maʿarrat-an-Nuʿmān lay on a Roman road which acted as a major communications link between the Muslim city of Aleppo and its southern neighbours Shaizar and Homs. This paper will focus on the contest for control of Antioch and northern Syria which took place from 1098 to 1099 between Bohemond of Taranto and Raymond of St Gilles, count of Toulouse. This was a period in which both men were seeking to establish power-bases in the Levant. Its purpose is to expand our understanding of how and why Bohemond eventually prevailed, by re-evaluating the aims and importance of the Latin conquest of the Jabal as-Summāq region.

First, however, a number of introductory points need to be made in order to place the events which occurred in the Jabal as-Summāq into context. Bohemond initially established his claim to the city of Antioch through the agreement he negotiated with the majority of the other leaders of the crusade in the early summer of 1098. This apparently stated that he should be allowed to hold the city if he were able to orchestrate its fall.[3] There has been some scholarly debate about whether this agreement was ever really made, but I think the sources clearly demonstrate that it was.[4] Even Raymond of Aguilers, whose account was generally antagonistic to Bohemond, recorded that 'all the princes except the count [Raymond] offered Antioch to Bohemond in the event it was captured' – although he wrote that this promise was made in order to prevent Bohemond from leaving the siege of the city early in 1098.[5] After the fall of the city and the defeat of Kerbogha, the leaders of the crusade, with the exception of Raymond of Toulouse, seem eventually to have abided by this agreement. After envoys had been sent to the Byzantine Emperor Alexius I Comnenus they finally agreed to hand over the portions of the city which they controlled to Bohemond and did not dispute his occupation of the citadel. The willingness of Duke Godfrey of Bouillon, Count Robert II of Flanders and Count Robert of Normandy to allow him to take control of the points of strategic importance in Antioch, and their subsequent reluctance to dispute his retention of the city contrary to the oaths made to Alexius, clearly placed Bohemond in a strong position to exert his full authority over Antioch.

It should be realised, however, that, even in light of the promises Bohemond had received, he might not have succeeded in seizing control of Antioch if his campaign to occupy the commanding areas of the city had not been so tenacious. Crucially, Bohemond had moved almost immediately to raise his banner on the highest point possible above the city when it fell on 3 June and it was plainly visible in the dawn light when the rest of the Latins began entering Antioch.[6] Then, when the crusaders defeated Kerbogha, the citadel of Antioch surrendered to the Christians. Although Ralph of Caen wrote that this fortress surrendered to Raymond of Toulouse, it is clear that it surrendered to Bohemond. Raymond of Aguilers recorded that Bohemond seized control of the citadel, while the anonymous author of the *Gesta Francorum* reported that Raymond of Toulouse attempted to receive the surrender of the fortress, but was beaten to it by Bohemond who had his own banner raised above the citadel and 'put his followers into the citadel at once'. It should be noted that Raymond should have been in a good position to receive the surrender of the citadel as he remained in the city during the battle against Kerbogha.[7] Albert of Aachen noted that, after Bohemond made this acquisition, he was named 'lord and advocate of the city' and 'assumed power and lordship over the city'.[8] The vague title of lord probably indicates that Bohemond did not possess independent powers of rulership over Antioch at this point. 'Advocate' is an interesting term which may suggest that Bohemond was claiming to be the protector of the patriarch. Ralph of Caen stated that 'Bohemond gained the region [*principatum*] of Antioch'.[9]

In spite of this, Bohemond's position was still not secure. The threat to Bohemond's claim to the city came from Raymond of Toulouse, because he had also managed to gain his own foothold in Antioch when the city fell on 3 June. During the siege Raymond's troops had held the fortification built by the crusaders which was known as La Mahomerie.[10] This siege fort was particularly important because it controlled the bridge over the Orontes and thus access from the city to the roads to Alexandretta and St Simeon. Raymond's control of this site also helped him to take control of a quarter in the city. When Antioch fell, the count's men were camped in and around La Mahomerie and entered the city through the Bridge Gate.[11] Ralph of Caen recorded that during the sack the Provençals captured the finest buildings in the city.[12] Raymond subsequently concentrated his acquisitions in the section of the city closest to La Mahomerie, perhaps initially because this was the first area his troops reached, but probably also because he wished to build on his existing strength. Therefore it appears that the location of Raymond's quarter in the city was determined by the location of the fort he had held during the siege.

When the crusaders were themselves besieged within Antioch, La Mahomerie was temporarily abandoned, but Raymond does seem to have maintained control of a quarter in the city during this period. He certainly defended the Bridge Gate during the defence of the city. There is no doubt that, after the defeat of Kerbogha's army, the city of Antioch was divided between Bohemond and Raymond. Raymond continued to occupy the palace, the Bridge Gate and its tower, the fortified bridge across the Orontes and he moved to re-occupy La Mahomerie.[13] This placed him in a position to challenge Bohemond's right to the city, a challenge which he was clearly keen to press. Raymond made a failed attempt to gain over-riding control of the city when he tried to occupy the citadel of Antioch immediately after the defeat of Kerbogha.[14] He also tried to provoke a revolt against Bohemond in the city at some point after 1 August 1098.[15]

In this situation Bohemond could not hope to exert full authority over the city. The narrative sources reflect this fact. Ralph of Caen noted that at this point Bohemond was regarded by the people as only 'a half-prince' – *semiprincipem* – and 'not a real prince' as 'he called Raymond his colleague in the principality'.[16] The use of the phrase 'half-prince' is unusual but was probably meant to indicate that, to start with, Latin authority over the city was equally divided between Bohemond and Raymond of Toulouse. Albert of Aachen recorded that it was only after Bohemond actually expelled Raymond's troops that he truly gained 'sole lordship over Antioch', while Fulcher of Chartres noted that 'Bohemond afterwards possessed Antioch together with the whole area'.[17]

We have, therefore, a situation in which, by September 1098, both Raymond and Bohemond controlled sectors of Antioch and both appear to have been prepared to contend possession of the city. Traditionally, however, it has been suggested that something of a hiatus in this dispute occurred until Bohemond finally took full possession of the city in early 1099. While it is clear that conflict did largely come to a standstill in Antioch itself, it is my contention that the campaigns which took place in the Jabal as-Summāq between September 1098 and January 1099 were actually an important aspect of this dispute. The Latin conquest of the Jabal as-Summāq has been generally misrepresented in both the primary sources and the secondary literature. The evidence provided by Albert of Aachen and Ralph of Caen is misleading here because it gives the impression that Raymond's activities in this region took place as part of the journey to Jerusalem. This was, however, patently not the case, as he made two separate campaigns in the area, in between which he returned to the vicinity of Antioch, before leaving to continue his pilgrimage to Jerusalem. Recent historians have also suggested that these campaigns were opportunist ventures, without trying to analyse what deeper motives may have existed. John and Laurita Hill believed that Raymond's interest in the region was stimulated by the need to gather supplies for his troops, writing that 'hungry mouths had to be fed and the count took to the field'.[18]

I want to suggest that Raymond also had a political interest in the Jabal as-Summāq. I hope to show that he was trying to establish a new power-base there in order to counter Bohemond's dominance in Antioch and to prevent him gaining control over northern Syria. In essence, therefore, the conflict for the Jabal as-Summāq was, in fact, another expression of the struggle for overlordship of what was to become the principality of Antioch. In order to demonstrate this I will re-examine the campaigns between September 1098 and January 1099, showing that Raymond took detailed measures to ensure the creation of a Provençal enclave in this plateau area, that Bohemond attempted to challenge his hold over this region, and that Raymond hoped to use this power-base to threaten Bohemond's position in Antioch.

It is important to note that Raymond had already gained a foothold in the Ruj valley, to the south-east of Antioch, in the autumn of 1097, even before the crusade arrived at Antioch. The author of the *Gesta Francorum* recorded that while the crusade army was at Coxon in Armenia, Raymond sent an advance expedition to the region of Antioch, during which Peter of Roaix led a force into the Ruj valley and killed its Muslim inhabitants. The Armenians in the region then apparently surrendered to Peter and he took possession of 'the city of Rusa and a number of castles'.[19] It is likely that 'Rusa' was in fact the fortification known as Rugia.[20] The expedition established a base in the Ruj for Raymond and he seems to have used the area as a foraging centre and a staging post during the siege of Antioch. Clearly then, any gains which he subsequently made in the Jabal as-Summāq must be seen as extending from this initial position.

So, to the campaigns themselves. Raymond of Toulouse led foraging raids into the Jabal as-Summāq at the beginning of September 1098,[21] but his first direct attempt to expand into the region came at the end of September 1098 with an expedition against Albara. The town was still in Muslim hands when Raymond and a number of the other crusade leaders, probably including Bohemond, arrived there at the end of September 1098 and began a siege which led to the capture of Albara after a short time.[22] Raymond then proceeded to Latinise the town. The *Gesta Francorum* recorded that he converted the mosque in Albara into 'a temple of the true and living God': a Christian church.[23] It would also seem that he was determined to oversee the occupation of Albara and its new church, as he remained there until the beginning of November.

After discussion with his clergy and lay commanders, he nominated a priest from his army, Peter of Narbonne, to be elevated to the position of bishop of Albara.[24] Raymond of Aguilers related that Peter was informed in public that his duties as the bishop of Albara would require him 'to hold Albara even unto death' and went on to state that Raymond of Toulouse granted Peter 'one-half of Albara and its environs'.[25] Clearly, Peter was expected to wield both ecclesiastical and lay authority over the town. In the event he actually travelled with Raymond of Toulouse for the rest of the crusade, leaving Albara behind, because the count felt his presence would 'increase the number of knights who marched from Ma'arrat-an-Nu'mān to Jerusalem'.[26] Raymond of Aguilers noted that Peter left a garrison of seven knights and thirty footmen commanded by William of Cunhlat at Albara on his departure, and mentioned that William carried out his duties so well that he caused 'the bishop's interest to grow tenfold' so that the town was soon garrisoned by seventy infantry and sixty or more knights.[27]

The second expansion into the Jabal as-Summāq came after the council of the crusade's leaders at Antioch in early November 1098. Raymond of Toulouse and Robert of Flanders left Antioch on 23 November 1098 and travelled via Rugia and Albara to arrive at Ma'arrat-an-Nu'mān on 28 November.[28] The siege of the town was recorded in detail by a number of sources, most notably by Raymond of Aguilers and the *Gesta Francorum*.[29] There is some disagreement in the sources about who was present on this occasion, but apart from Raymond of Toulouse and Robert of Flanders, Bohemond was probably the only other leader involved and he may have arrived only one day after them.[30]

Siege engines played an important part in the capture of Ma'arrat-an-Nu'mān. A number of early Latin assaults failed primarily because of a lack of siege materials.[31] Raymond of Aguilers indicated that in one attack the crusaders would have 'seized Ma'arrat-an-Nu'mān if we had possessed four ladders'.[32] Perhaps the clearest demonstration of how crippled the crusaders were by this lack of siege equipment is provided by the marked change in their fortunes once these materials became available. It is important to note that Raymond of Toulouse was credited, even in the *Gesta Francorum* – a source usually hostile to the count – with the development of these siege resources. The fact that he could claim responsibility for building the engines which played so vital a part in the fall of Ma'arrat-an-Nu'mān must have strengthened his claim to the town, and may substantiate Raymond of Aguilers's accusation that Bohemond and the Normans 'were more of a hindrance than a help' and were 'only half-hearted in pressing the siege' of Ma'arrat.[33]

It is also worth pointing out that during the renewed attack upon Ma'arrat-an-Nu'mān this siege tower was noted to contain 'many knights', including Everard the Huntsman and William of Montpellier who were members of Count Raymond's retinue.[34] Both the anonymous author of the *Gesta Francorum* and Raymond of Aguilers also recorded that it was Gulpher of Lastours who first gained a foothold on the walls of Ma'arrat. This may have strengthened Raymond's claim to the town because, although Gulpher was a vassal of the duke of Aquitaine, his lord did not participate in the First Crusade and he may also, therefore, have gravitated towards the count of Toulouse's retinue.[35] The accounts of the subsequent seizure of Ma'arrat are quite confused. All the major sources agree that either on 11 December 1098, or more probably on the following day, the crusaders slaughtered a major proportion, if not all, of the Muslims at Ma'arrat. The anonymous author of the *Gesta Francorum* recorded that the Latins 'killed everyone, man or woman, whom they met in any place whatsoever'.[36] The sources also make it clear that the Latins pillaged Ma'arrat-an-Nu'mān with particular ruthlessness.[37] When dusk fell on 11 December, with Ma'arrat only partially captured and 'some towers and parts of the town in Saracen hands', the majority of the Latin army stopped their attacks for the night, with only the poorer people carrying on fighting in the dark and thereby gaining a considerable amount of booty.[38]

None of the accounts stated that any particular banner was raised above Ma'arrat to claim the town on either 11 or 12 December, but it seems that both Raymond of Toulouse and Bohemond seized control of considerable parts of the town. Some of the evidence presented in the sources suggests, perhaps misleadingly, that Bohemond took control of the greater section. Raymond of Aguilers recorded that he 'acquired the greater number of towers, horses and captives'.[39] Bohemond's deceitful implementation of the agreement with the town's Muslim leaders, in which he promised them safety during the night if they gathered with their possessions in the town's palace, and then proceeded on the following day to loot them all, killing some and selling others into slavery at Antioch, must also have brought him significant financial reward.[40] The accuracy of this story can surely not be doubted, given the author's bias in favour of Bohemond.

In spite of this Bohemond may not have taken a commanding share of Ma'arrat at this point. Raymond of Aguilers recorded only that Bohemond had possession of more towers than Raymond, not a greater proportion of the town as a whole. If he had taken possession of such an overwhelming share of Ma'arrat, his subsequent departure and relinquishment of any claim to the town would not make sense. Instead, it is likely that Bohemond managed to capture enough of Ma'arrat to prevent Raymond of Toulouse from exercising complete control over it. This is suggested by Raymond of Aguilers's report that the count wished to 'give the city [Ma'arrat-an-Nu'mān] to the bishop of Albara', Peter of Narbonne, but was unable to do so immediately as Bohemond 'held to some of his captured towers'.[41] It was at this point that Bohemond apparently informed the count of Toulouse that he would not hand over his possessions at Ma'arrat unless Raymond agreed to give up his remaining holdings in Antioch.[42]

The dispute over the possession of Ma'arrat-an-Nu'mān was, however, not quickly solved. The forces which Raymond of Toulouse had led there remained for one month and four days, and it was during this prolonged stay that supplies became so scarce and the ensuing famine so desperate that some of the Latins were reported to have resorted to cannibalism.[43] When it became clear that no agreement could be reached Bohemond left the town, although the date of his departure cannot be ascertained exactly.[44] At some point before the council held at Rugia, which itself cannot be dated other than the fact that it took place before 13 January 1099, Raymond of Toulouse decided to secure his control of Ma'arrat-an-Nu'mān. As we have seen, the count had expressed his desire to install Peter of Albara in command of the town, and Raymond and Peter now 'turned to providing a garrison' for the settlement 'determining both the number and choice of personnel'.[45] Then, after returning from Rugia, Raymond 'ordered his knights to fortify the palace and the castle' of Ma'arrat.[46] Raymond was clearly keen to ensure that his acquisitions in the Jabal as-Summāq were maintained in his absence.

Raymond of Toulouse may also have succeeded in gaining control of Kafarṭāb in January 1099. When he returned to Ma'arrat-an-Nu'mān after the council at Rugia he led a foraging expedition into what Raymond of Aguilers called 'Hispania'. After the success of this trip, and when Raymond of Toulouse was preparing to leave Ma'arrat, Raymond of Aguilers recalled that 'the foragers left their booty at Kafarṭāb'.[47]

It is clear that, during the First Crusade's extended sojourn in the region of Antioch, Raymond of Toulouse made a concerted effort to establish a power-base in the Jabal as-Summāq. What did he hope to gain by this? The fact that Bohemond connected the two disputes over possession of Antioch and Ma'arrat-an-Nu'mān might suggest that the region was to be used as a bargaining piece, but it seems that in this instance the impetus for such an exchange came from Bohemond himself.[48] It is more likely that Raymond hoped to use his control of the Jabal as-Summāq to threaten and destabilise Bohemond's position in Antioch. Raymond's motives for wishing to challenge Bohemond's authority in northern Syria are of course open to debate, and it is possible that he was acting for his own gain or even perhaps as a representative of Byzantine interests.

The key to understanding Raymond's interest in the region lies in an appreciation of its significance. The early history of the principality of Antioch clearly demonstrates that control of this plateau region was of enormous political and strategic importance, and it could be argued that, if Raymond had managed to maintain authority over this area, then Bohemond's ability to establish the principality would have been undermined. As it was, Raymond's plan failed for a number of reasons. In the short term, the count was compelled to continue the journey to Jerusalem both by popular opinion and his own desire to complete his pilgrimage. It was probably at this point, in early 1099, that Bohemond finally expelled Raymond's men from the tower over the Bridge Gate, the palace and La Mahomerie, and took full possession of the city of Antioch.[49]

In the long term, Raymond's attempts to secure the safety of his foothold in the Jabal as-Summāq also collapsed. His departure, along with the other leaders of the crusade, left a power vacuum in the region which Bohemond was able to fill, and crucially, the man whom Raymond had established as bishop of Albara, Peter of Narbonne, failed to maintain his allegiance. He seems to have fallen out with the count at Jerusalem when in 1099 he surrendered the Tower of David to Godfrey of Bouillon rather than to him.[50] On his return to Albara, Peter must have found it politically and militarily expedient to align himself with Antioch. Perhaps quite soon after the elevation of Bernard of Valence as the first Latin patriarch of Antioch in 1100, 'Peter transferred the allegiance of his own metropolis to that church'.[51] Peter's career was subsequently furthered by his elevation to the archiepiscopal see of Apamea, after its capture by Tancred in 1106.[52] In a charter of 1110 he appeared both as 'archbishop of Apamea', and 'archbishop of Albara'.[53] This elevation also provided another opportunity to ensure Peter's loyalty to Antioch, for on this occasion we hear that he 'received the *pallium* from Bernard'.[54]

Raymond's decision to focus his attention on the Jabal as-Summāq in 1098–9, and his failure to secure long-term control of the region, ultimately played into his rival's hands. Subsequently, the count devoted his attention to securing territory further south in the region that was to become the county of Tripoli. In contrast, Bohemond was able to gain lordship of the city of Antioch and to expand his holdings to form a principality.

Notes

1 GF, pp. 46–7; RA, pp. 64–6; FC, pp. 231–5; AA, IV.15–21; RC, pp. 654–5; France, *Victory*, pp. 257ff.
2 France, *Victory*, pp. 269ff.
3 GF, p. 45; RC, p. 654; AA, IV.15.
4 J.H. and L.L. Hill, *Raymond IV Count of Toulouse* (New York, Syracuse University Press, 1962), pp. 78–9; J. France, 'The crisis of the First Crusade: from the defeat of Kerbogha to the departure from Arqa', *Byzantion*, 40 (1970), 283.
5 RA, p. 55.
6 GF, p. 47; AA, IV.23; FC, p. 234.
7 RA, p. 83; GF, p. 71: FC, p. 263; RC, pp. 675, 678.
8 AA, V.2.
9 RC, p. 674.
10 GF, p. 42; RA, p. 62.
11 RC, p. 655.
12 RC, p. 660.
13 GF, p. 76; RC, p. 768.
14 GF, p. 68.
15 RC, p. 679. This date is inferred by the reference to the mediation of Arnulf of Chocques, which would seem to indicate that the event took place after the death of Adhémar of Le Puy.
16 RC, p. 675.
17 AA, V.26; FC, p. 268.
18 J.H. and L.L. Hill, *Raymond IV*, p. 101.
19 GF, pp. 26–7.
20 RA, p. 99. The fortification of Rugia has not been conclusively identified.

21 RA, p. 89.
22 GF, pp. 74–5; RA, p. 91; AA, V.26; FC, p. 266.
23 GF, p. 75.
24 RA, pp. 91–2.
25 RA, p. 92.
26 RA, pp. 104–5.
27 RA, p. 104–5.
28 GF, p. 77; RA, p. 94.
29 RA, pp. 94–102; GF, pp. 77–80; AA, V.26, 29–30; RC, pp. 674–5; FC, pp. 266–7.
30 GF, pp. 77–8; H. Hagenmeyer, *Chronologie de la Première Croisade (1094–1100)* (Paris, Ernest Leroux, 1902), pp. 195–6, no. 326.
31 GF, p. 78; RA, p. 94–5.
32 RA, p. 94.
33 RA, p. 98.
34 GF, pp. 78–9.
35 RA, p. 97; GF, p. 79. For more information about Gulpher, see M.G. Bull, *Knightly Piety and the Lay Response to the First Crusade: the Limousin and Gascony c. 970–c. 1130*, (Oxford, Clarendon Press, 1993), pp. 261ff.
36 GF, p. 80.
37 RA, p. 98; GF, pp. 79–80; RC, p. 679.
38 RA, p. 98.
39 RA, p. 98.
40 GF, pp. 79–80.
41 RA, p. 98–9.
42 RA, p. 99.
43 RA, p. 101; GF, p. 80.
44 RA, p. 99; Hagenmeyer, *Chronologie*, p. 202, no. 334.
45 RA, p. 99.
46 GF, p. 81.
47 RA, pp. 101–2.
48 RA, p. 99.
49 PT, p. 102; RC, p. 675; FC, pp. 267–8; RA, p. 125; AA, V.26. Albert believed that Bohemond did not attend the council at Rugia.
50 RA, p. 151.
51 WT, p. 353.
52 AA, X. 22–4; Kemal ed-Din, 'La chronique d'Alep', *RHC Or.* III, p. 595.
53 *La Cartulaire de Sainte-Sépulchre de Jérusalem*, ed. G. Bresc-Bautier (Paris, Librairie Orientalisté Paul Geuthner, 1984), pp. 197–9, n. 86.
54 WT, p. 353.

9

Captured property on the First Crusade

William G. Zajac

At almost every stage of the expedition to Jerusalem, the first crusaders depended upon plunder as a source of essential provisions and supplies. Even during their passage through Christian lands, many contingents resorted to looting when goods offered for sale proved inadequate or too costly, or markets were withheld entirely by the alarmed populace. Once they entered Muslim territory, however, the gains of war became critically important to the Christian forces. The pilgrims repeatedly found themselves with little or no access to markets or other friendly avenues of supply; in such situations, the Franks had to rely upon captured property for virtually all of their needs. On more than one occasion, foodstuffs taken as booty tipped the balance between starvation and survival for countless crusaders. Horses, arms, money and manifold other items were also avidly seized and used to make good losses or to replenish Frankish coffers.[1] Even when victuals and other merchandise were available for purchase, high prices often ensured that the poor in the crusader host remained dependent on supplies gathered through foraging. Plundering, in short, became 'a normal and absolutely necessary occupation' for the forces of the First Crusade.[2]

Historians have long appreciated the importance of captured property in the success of the expedition, and have often noted the powerful influence that the quest for loot had upon the conduct of the crusaders, particularly the poor. In recent years, the place of booty in the internal economy of the crusading army has also received attention, with scholars identifying mechanisms that operated within the host for the wider distribution of the money, provisions and other supplies that the Christians acquired as spoils of war. At one time or another during the expedition, sale, lordly largesse, almsgiving and tithing all played a part in channelling booty from the hands of its captors into the army at large.[3] These mechanisms, however, constituted a secondary stage in the dispersal of captured property amongst the crusaders; although the money and goods involved may have been obtained as spoils, they had become the personal possessions of crusaders before being thus redistributed for secular or spiritual ends.

Little consideration has yet been given to the important primary stage of that dispersal – the capture and initial disposition of the booty seized by the Franks, whether during foraging raids, on the field of battle, or in captured strongholds. The free seizure of plunder in captured cities like Ma'arrat-an-Nu'mān and Jerusalem has, it is true, often been remarked, but generally only to illustrate the chaos that ensued when a stronghold fell to the Franks, or to emphasise the desperate eagerness of the poor to lay their hands on provisions and riches.[4] Some authors, perhaps with Western practices in mind, have suggested that division of booty occurred within contingents of the crusade; but, with their principal concerns lying elsewhere, they have shown little interest in identifying or investigating instances of such division.[5]

A detailed treatment of the first crusaders' handling of newly-won spoils therefore remains wanting – this study is offered as an attempt to remedy that situation. In the pages that follow, a brief survey of contemporary Western usages will precede the examination of the practices employed within the pilgrim host for the disposition of captured moveables. This will not only emphasise the continuing influence of those Western usages on the conduct of the crusaders, but also point up the extent to which the extreme conditions and fragmented nature of command on the expedition led the Franks to adopt unusual, if not entirely novel, methods for the disposition of spoils. In addition to clarifying who was able to benefit directly from taking plunder, a more detailed understanding of the crusaders' treatment of booty will afford insights into the necessity for, and operation of, the secondary mechanisms for the distribution of captured property mentioned above.

While the money and goods seized from their foes may have assumed an exceptional importance for the first crusaders during the long and arduous march through the hostile lands that lay between Constantinople and Jerusalem, there can be no doubt that the spoils of war always preoccupied medieval warriors. Like the crusaders, European soldiers usually lived off the land while on campaign. In large part this reflected the central role of ravaging in the prosecution of warfare, but the logistical capabilities of even the most highly-organised medieval armies were unequal to supplying a force during extended operations in enemy territory.[6] Yet, captured property was more than just a source of sustenance for Western soldiers; it could also be a source of profit. Throughout the Middle Ages, fighting men of every rank and station marched off to war hoping to return as victors enriched with booty. Indeed, even though the indulgence formulated at the Council of Clermont seemed to withhold the spiritual reward from those who went to the East 'to acquire honour or money', those taking part in the First Crusade clearly continued to entertain such hopes.[7] There is no better expression of the fundamental equation between success in warfare and profit that existed in the minds of medieval men than the message of encouragement that Bohemond of Taranto passed to the hard-pressed crusaders at the battle of Dorylaeum in 1097: 'Stand fast together united in the faith of Christ and the victory of the Holy Cross, because today, God willing, you will all be made wealthy.'[8]

The fortunes of war often rendered illusory such dreams of riches to be won by the force of arms, but the lure of booty never lost its potency. As Bohemond's message shows, military leaders were well aware that the gains of war always offered a 'not inconsiderable inducement to martial ardour'.[9] Vassals, household warriors and others who owed military service to their lords no doubt fought all the more eagerly if rich prizes were in prospect, and soldiers of fortune – like the 'bellicose men' who, according to Orderic Vitalis, flocked to the banner of Duke William II of Normandy in 1066 'panting for the spoils of England'[10] – were plainly susceptible to the enticement of abundant plunder.[11] Yet, while mindful that the desire to win spoils could spur combatants to deeds of valour, medieval commanders were also conscious that it could pose a significant threat to the maintenance of military discipline. On the one hand, the cohesion of a force could be disrupted by disputes between its members over rights to captured property. On the other, men more intent on looting than fighting could easily expose themselves and their fellows to danger from the enemy. Distracted by plunder, soldiers might fail to maintain a proper watch while pillaging, or might abandon the pursuit of their adversaries before certain victory was achieved.[12] Such situations were most likely to arise if warriors could acquire spoils only by seizing them personally; under such conditions, men would have been constantly tempted to regard their comrades as competitors and to place private gain before military advantage.

In the light of the corrosive effect that plunder could have on military discipline, it is hardly surprising to find evidence for martial conventions governing its disposition in Western armies from an early date.[13] Much of the history of those conventions, however, has yet to be written. Scholars have concentrated most of their attention on the period of the Hundred Years War, when usages pertaining to booty and ransoms were widely regarded as 'laws of war' and abundant information about their character and operation was incorporated in narrative and documentary sources, legal codes, and juristic and chivalric treatises.[14] Research on earlier centuries has been limited, and, apart from some detailed studies on Spanish practices, historians have shown scant interest in the disposition of spoils at the time of the First Crusade.[15] Limitations of space dictate that a comprehensive examination of the handling of booty in eleventh-century Europe cannot be essayed here.[16] Nevertheless, even a brief discussion will help to inform the analysis of the Franks' conduct during the expedition to Jerusalem.

Any attempt to elucidate the conventions relating to the seizure and apportionment of spoils that would have been familiar to the men who joined the armies of the First Crusade is hampered by the fragmentary state of the available evidence. Some rules had appeared in legal texts in Spain – and perhaps in Wales – by the early twelfth century; but the principles governing the disposition of captured property in the rest of Europe seem to have persisted as unwritten customs until well after 1095.[17] Pertinent documentary sources are scarce, so one must rely almost entirely upon information garnered from historical narratives. Yet, while eleventh- and early twelfth-century chroniclers and annalists often reported the taking of plunder by victorious armies, they only occasionally recorded how the captors treated their prizes. Interpretation of many of the scattered accounts is further complicated by the possibility that their authors resorted to *topoi* or to half-remembered biblical passages describing the Israelites' seizure and division of booty in their composition. Nevertheless, in spite of the limitations of the evidence, the basic elements of the usages that would have shaped the crusaders' notions about captured property emerge with clarity.

Decisions about the disposition of spoils rested with a military force's leader, whether he was a monarch at the head of a royal host or a simple knight leading a raiding party. There are suggestions that commanders could act arbitrarily in such matters, but any general who disregarded his soldiers' expectations of booty ran the risk of creating serious disaffection in the ranks.[18] In the majority of cases, leaders must have conformed with time-honoured custom by overseeing the collection and apportionment of the moveables that had been seized by their men.[19] William of Apulia, for example, describes Robert Guiscard allotting booty to his Norman knights in Calabria around 1050: 'When anything was captured, he divided it equally with his men; all of his men were dear to him and he was dear to them.'[20] Guiscard was then little more than a captain of a brigand band, and such evenhandedness was no doubt advisable in a group where all would have been of roughly equal status.[21] In forces where distinctions of rank were more marked, the division of booty must usually have proceeded along different lines. Eleventh- and early twelfth-century sources are largely unforthcoming on the conventions that determined the proportions of shares of plunder awarded to army members, but social station was probably a significant factor.[22] By the beginning of the thirteenth century, it was certainly accepted as a matter of course that knights would receive larger shares than foot-soldiers.[23]

A commander supervising the apportionment of property taken from the enemy would not have been a disinterested party; like his men, he would have expected to reap some reward from their martial enterprise. If a figure of royal or princely rank, he might have had the right to a fixed fraction, or 'prince's portion', of the loot.[24] The fifth (*quinta*) that Spanish monarchs regularly collected from spoils taken by their subjects is the best-known example of a prince's portion at the time of the First Crusade, but a parallel can be cited in the third accorded to the king in the ancient Welsh laws.[25] Evidence for the claims that great lords could advance elsewhere in Europe is equivocal. William of Poitiers, for instance, recounts that Duke William II of Normandy (1035–1087) preferred to turn rich prizes over to his knights rather than retain them for himself.[26] Implicit in this celebration of lordly munificence is William II's unquestioned right to appropriate the booty, but there is no suggestion here or elsewhere that the duke could lay claim to a specific fraction of any property captured by his men.

Rather than expecting a precise proportion of the gains of war, many princes of William of Normandy's stature may have exercised a prescriptive claim to the 'best booty', or to particularly valuable types of plunder.[27] Whatever the exact nature of their prerogatives, one may confidently assume that, unless they chose to relinquish their rights in acts of largesse, monarchs and great nobles invariably received a significant portion of the spoils seized by their soldiers. Commanders of lower rank must have benefited from similar, though perhaps more modest, privileges, but the chroniclers offer negligible information on the handling of plunder by such men. One can only speculate that local martial custom and his personal standing dictated how large a share of the profits of war a lesser noble or knight could demand from his followers.[28]

The men who joined the armies of the First Crusade carried these usages with them to the East and established them in the newly-founded Latin principalities in Syria and Palestine. Fulcher of Chartres witnessed the veteran of the crusade, Baldwin of Boulogne, distributing spoils to his troops in October 1100, after the latter had defeated a Muslim force at Nahr al-Kalb in Syria while *en route* to claim the crown of Jerusalem. Fulcher tersely observes that 'our prince divided the ... plunder'; but Caffaro, the Genoese chronicler who visited the kingdom of Jerusalem less than a year after the battle, states that Baldwin 'took the arms and horses and all the belongings that they [the Turks] had carried with them, and he gave and distributed a portion to his knights and foot-soldiers according to the custom of warriors'.[29] Other chroniclers' reports of Frankish military successes during the first decades of the Latin presence in the East show that the division of booty was commonplace, and that the rulers of the nascent states, like their Western counterparts, took substantial shares of the gains made by their forces.[30]

The transplantation of these conventions to Syria and Palestine leaves little doubt that organised division was the martial norm for the disposition of captured moveables in the West at the time of the First Crusade. Indeed, the practice had much to recommend it to military leaders and fighting men alike. It contributed to the maintenance of discipline, and gave ordinary fighting men a degree of protection from the vagaries of war; all who contributed to an army's success could look forward to some part of the gains even if events had denied some the opportunity to take plunder personally. Nevertheless, in spite of these practical advantages, it is clear that not all booty taken by men of war around the year 1100 was subjected to formal apportionment. Avaricious soldiers would always have found opportunities to purloin some loot, but such theft is not in question here. Rather, one occasionally finds evidence for free seizure of booty in which every soldier simply retained whatever enemy possessions came into his hands. Some examples of such unregulated despoliation can easily be explained away as the result of a breakdown in military discipline in the wake of a victory,[31] but a few reports indicate that commanders sometimes deliberately chose to allow their warriors to pillage freely.

Thus, the Saxon chronicler, Bruno, relates that Otto of Northeim restrained the *pedites* under his command from despoiling their adversaries' camp before victory was assured in the battle at the River Elster in 1080. Once the last of King Henry IV's supporters had been put to flight, however, he turned his men loose on the spoils with the words: 'Now ... go search the camp in security: now, free from danger, take whatever you shall find, and call your own ... whatever was earlier today the enemy's.'[32] Bruno, one may assume, fabricated that address for rhetorical purposes, but there is no reason to doubt that Otto delivered the possessions of the Henricians to his followers in the manner described. Geoffrey Malaterra provides similar, if less vivid, evidence for the free seizure of booty in the Norman forces of Roger of Sicily and Robert Guiscard. He recounts, for instance, that Guiscard recalled his troops from the pursuit of the defeated forces of Alexius Comnenus at Dyrrachium in 1081, and returned with them to the Byzantine camp. 'The duke occupied the imperial tents, and the others who arrived first took possession of the richer lodgings with their spoils.'[33] With Guiscard in control, it is inconceivable that military discipline had dissolved in a scramble for plunder; he must have countenanced this method for the disposition of the spoils, just as Otto of Northeim had done in the preceding year.

Leaders who permitted the free seizure of captured property would have been aware that it posed a threat to order in the ranks. A general who declared before battle that all booty would remain in the possession of its captors in the hope of spurring his men to fight with more determination, could well have found that he had simply encouraged them to turn aside from the struggle in order to enrich themselves. Perhaps, like Otto of Northeim in Bruno's account, commanders generally gave licence for such pillaging only after their foes had been decisively vanquished. Even if that were the case, the practice of free seizure would not have been without drawbacks; if allowed, a leader would effectively have had to abandon any claim to a special share of the plunder, and disputes between soldiers over prizes would have been a natural result. It is surely no coincidence that in those cases where such unhindered looting is attested in Europe before the First Crusade, the spoils seem to have been sufficiently abundant to satisfy all the victors. These considerations must have ensured that free seizure was only infrequently preferred to orderly division for the disposition of captured property in Western armies.

Such are the broad outlines of the practices that would have shaped the fundamental ideas about the handling of captured moveable property harboured by the soldiers who answered Pope Urban II's crusade appeal. They would have grown familiar with these customs through their regular use in the armies with which they fought – armies that usually operated under the orders of a single commander (or at least a unified council of allied commanders) and rarely numbered more than a few thousand men.[34] One must now consider how they applied those familiar conventions to the booty taken under the exceptional conditions of the march to Jerusalem.

Indeed, once the entire army had assembled at Nicaea in Asia Minor in June 1097, the crusaders found themselves in circumstances that were radically different from anything that they would have known before their departure. The crusader host, at least during the first year or so of the pilgrimage, was vastly bigger than any army in which its members could have served in Europe.[35] Command was vested not in a single leader, to whom the soldiers owed obedience either as lord or paymaster, but in the council of the princes who led the disparate contingents loosely united behind the banner of Christ. Finally, a crowd of poor pilgrims and non-combatants that would have dwarfed any band of Western camp-followers accompanied the fighting men throughout the two-year march through hostile territory from Nicaea to Jerusalem. Therefore, booty – a vital source of essential supplies throughout the crusade – could not simply be a matter of concern for the men who bore arms against the Muslims. These factors were to have a profound effect on the crusaders' treatment of captured moveable property.

The Franks took plunder in a variety of situations during the journey to the Holy City. Much of the booty upon which they depended for their survival was seized in the foraging raids so often mentioned in the sources. Non-combatants as well as soldiers joined the forays, and one finds frequent references to foragers being slain by the Muslims.[36] On several occasions, the crusader princes provided groups with powerful escorts in order to minimise losses.[37] Encounters with the Muslims, of course, also afforded opportunities to secure booty. Even victories in minor skirmishes could leave some spoils in the hands of the Christians. Thus, after an inconclusive clash between the men of Baldwin of Boulogne and the troops of Balduk, emir of Samosata, in February 1098, one of the Frankish knights retained the horse of the Turk whom he had slain with a lance.[38] Major successes in the field, on the other hand, almost invariably brought abundant loot into the host.[39] The crusaders, however, found the richest prizes in the cities and strongholds that they conquered by the force of arms, and they could sack such places with horrifying thoroughness.[40]

The crusaders definitely subjected some of the moveables they took from the Muslims to apportionment in line with contemporary Western practices. Raymond of Aguilers is the sole eye-witness to mention division expressly. He recounts that in June 1099, during the siege of Jerusalem, a flotilla of Genoese ships arrived at Jaffa. Three of Count Raymond of Toulouse's captains – Raymond Pilet, Galdemar Carpinel and William Sabran – were dispatched to escort the mariners to the Holy City. Raymond Pilet and Galdemar Carpinel were figures of very considerable importance in the Provençal force, and one can safely assume that they were leading their own contingents.[41] On their way to the port, Carpinel's men were surprised by a Muslim force, and only rescued by the timely arrival of Raymond Pilet. The survivors 'collected and divided the spoils', and then continued together to Jaffa.[42]

Formal distribution of captured property is unequivocally attested in only one other instance during the crusade. Albert of Aachen and Ralph of Caen, both of whom had access to reliable information about events on the crusade, offer instructive accounts of Tancred's handling of the rich booty that he seized in the *Templum Domini* (the Dome of the Rock) during the sack of Jerusalem. While the rest of the crusading army ranged through the Holy City, Tancred and his followers acted alone in despoiling the *Templum Domini*, and Ralph of Caen relates in his florid Latin verse that the Norman leader allotted much of the booty to his men. Albert of Aachen adds the revealing detail that Tancred faithfully divided the spoils with Godfrey of Bouillon, 'whose knight he was'.[43]

In both of these cases the forces involved were relatively small, were acting under the command of respected leaders, and were effectively operating independently of the larger host. Under such circumstances, it must have been easy and natural for the crusaders to apportion the booty that they had won. Similar situations cannot have been unusual during the crusade, and there can be little doubt that the division of plunder occurred more frequently than the evidence would suggest. Indeed, it was very probably the norm within the military households of the princes, and of lesser leaders like Tancred, Raymond Pilet and Galdemar Carpinel, where there were tight bonds of loyalty and obligation between lords and followers. Just as they had done in Europe, those lords would have supervised the allotment of the booty seized by their men, and would have reserved some portion of it for themselves. It is difficult, in fact, to explain how many leaders maintained their positions during the expedition if one does not presume that they received fractions of the plunder taken by their followers. Albert of Aachen's assertion that Tancred rendered part of the spoil from the *Templum Domini* to Godfrey is, however, the only evidence for anything resembling a prince's portion from the First Crusade. Yet, even if one allows that division of booty was ordinarily practised amongst fighting men operating in small independent groups and in the households of the leaders of the crusade, the scanty evidence cannot be stretched any further. One must conclude that the regular apportionment of plunder as the Franks had known it in the West only occurred in limited circumstances during the march to Jerusalem.

The free seizure of captured property – a practice little employed in the West – was, however, commonplace during the crusade. The evidence for this is clearest in the context of the Christians' handling of booty taken in captured cities. At some point, the crusader princes, perhaps with the consent of the army or its representatives, decided that the possession of moveables in captured cities should be ceded to whoever could first secure them. The most explicit statement of this rule of free seizure is to be found in Fulcher of Chartres' relation of the sack of Jerusalem in 1099:

> They entered the houses of the citizens, seizing whatever they discovered in them. Indeed, this happened in such a fashion that whoever had first entered a house, whether he was rich or poor, in no way suffered injury from any other man. Rather, he was to hold and to possess that house or palace and whatever he had found in it as if the property were entirely his own. They had mutually approved this right [*ius*] of possession. Many needy men were thus made wealthy.[44]

Fulcher was not present at the capture of Jerusalem in July 1099, but he first visited the city at the end of that year and took up residence there as the chaplain of King Baldwin I in 1100.[45] He was, therefore, well-placed to learn of the crusaders' conduct in Jerusalem and of any resolutions that might have affected the treatment of property in the city. Moreover, Ralph of Caen, Albert of Aachen and other chroniclers furnish similar statements of the 'mutually approved right of possession'.[46] According to Ralph of Caen, Tancred invoked that right in his defence when Arnulf of Chocques accused him before the assembled leaders of the crusade of despoiling the holy place of the *Templum Domini*.[47]

Fulcher of Chartres gives no indication as to when the crusade leaders decided to license the uncontrolled taking of spoils in captured localities. The decision may have been taken as early as 1097, because the anonymous author of the *Gesta Francorum* recounts that Baldwin of Boulougne tried to persuade Tancred to join him in plundering Tarsus with the proposal: 'Let us enter together and pillage the city, and whoever can occupy most, let him occupy it, and whoever can seize most, let him seize it.' Tancred was appalled at the prospect of despoiling fellow Christians and declined Baldwin's offer.[48]

When Antioch was surprised, the poor, according to Fulcher of Chartres, were more concerned with gathering plunder in the streets and houses than pursuing the enemy, and Ralph of Caen depicts the Franks taking what they wished in the city.[49] It is at the capture of Ma'arrat-an-Nu'mān in December 1098, however, that the application of free seizure can be most easily observed. According to Raymond of Aguilers the attack on the city halted at dusk, but not before the Christians had breached the wall. While the knights of the army stood guard through the night to entrap any fleeing citizens, many poor and starving crusaders slipped in through the breach. The poor thereupon claimed for themselves most of the booty and houses, and when the knights entered the city on the following morning they found meagre rewards for their vigilance. Bohemond's knights, who, Raymond of Aguilers grumbles, were 'only half-hearted in pressing the siege', also managed to obtain a larger share of the property in the city than the Provençal chronicler thought they deserved.[50] While omitting the details about the nocturnal activities of the poor, the *Gesta* corroborates Raymond's statement that the Christians retained whatever they could capture in the chaos of the sack.[51] Peter Tudebode makes the significant comment: 'There were many of our people who found whatever they needed in the city, and many who found nothing to capture.'[52] This succinctly points up the fact that an unrestricted scramble for booty could be distinctly inequitable.

It was not only in captured strongholds, however, that the free seizure of booty took place. It also occurred when the Franks operated in the field. One searches in vain for an explicit statement comparable to that made by Fulcher about the sack of Jerusalem, or an incident like the capture of Ma'arrat-an-Nu'mān, that provides an unequivocal illustration of the crusaders' practices. Nevertheless, there is no evidence for any centralised collection and division of spoils gained in the field, and there are a number of indications that crusaders were able to retain what they seized. The *Gesta Francorum*, for instance, relates that when the foragers who had accompanied Bohemond into Syria in December 1097 returned, 'some, to be sure, had found provisions, but others had returned empty-handed'.[53] Such an observation shows that no division of spoils had taken place before their return and the implication certainly is that none was to occur thereafter. Raymond of Aguilers' description of the jubilant warriors returning laden with booty after a victory over the defenders of Antioch in March 1098 also suggests that free seizure rather than formal division had been the basis for the disposition of the plunder.[54]

Further persuasive evidence for the free seizure of booty in the field is furnished by the crusaders' efforts to stop men from turning aside to take plunder before battles were decided.[55] If riches were to be acquired simply by stopping to plunder, the temptations for the poorer soldiers must have been great, and even the wealthiest would not have been entirely immune. The leaders of the expedition tried to counter those temptations by issuing strict orders to abstain from pillaging until victory was certain. At Antioch, before the crusaders marched out to engage Kerbogha of Mosul, this command was given other-worldly authority when St Andrew, in one of Peter Bartholomew's visions, forbade the Christians to 'turn aside to the enemy tents for gold or silver'.[56] The eye-witness sources assert that 'the knights of Christ' were more eager to pursue Kerbogha's vanquished forces than to plunder the Muslim camp, but Albert of Aachen accuses the Provençals of turning to looting and inciting avarice in many others who then abandoned the pursuit. Albert may have been misinformed about these events, but he did not doubt that the crusaders could seize booty freely.[57] Guibert of Nogent, in fact, declares that the spoils were so abundant that rich and poor alike plundered the Muslim camp without altercations and that the Franks became satiated with the booty.[58]

Before the battle of Ascalon in August 1099, a similar prohibition – against taking booty until the Egyptian army was defeated – was issued by the newly-created patriarch of Jerusalem, Arnulf of Chocques, who threatened violators with excommunication. In spite of the anathema, many of the crusaders turned aside from the pursuit to loot the Muslim tents. The letter addressed to the pope in September of the same year by Daimbert of Pisa, Godfrey of Bouillon and Raymond of Toulouse recounts that great numbers of Muslims perished on the field, but more would have been slain had not 'many of our men been occupied with the spoils of the camp'.[59] The *Gesta Francorum* emphasises the freedom the Franks enjoyed in looting the Egyptian camp: 'Our men returned to the tents of the enemy, and took innumerable spoils of gold, silver and goods of every kind, herds of all the animals, and stocks of all types of arms. They carried off what they wished, and burned the remainder.'[60]

The danger that the unrestrained taking of plunder could pose to a force is well illustrated by the events that took place at Ḥiṣn al-Akrād in 1099. The crusading army, advancing under Raymond of Toulouse, Robert of Normandy and Tancred, assaulted the strong castle there. Near the fortress, the Christian army found herds of cattle, horses and sheep, which soon distracted many of the attackers. Raymond of Aguilers recounts that:

While the count and certain knights were engaged in battle, one after another our poor began to retire with the booty they had seized. The poor foot-soldiers then took the way and after them the common knights. Our tents lay some ten miles from the castle.

When the Muslim defenders observed that the crusader forces were melting away, they made a sudden foray and almost succeeded in overwhelming Raymond of Toulouse and the few troops, perhaps members of his military household, who had remained with him. When he had extricated himself from danger the count severely upbraided his men for deserting him in the midst of battle.[61] Yet, while Raymond could thunder at his knights for imperilling his life, he could do little to discipline the poor who had precipitated the situation by so eagerly availing themselves of the booty.[62]

When the lack of evidence for any organised division of plunder after major crusader engagements is considered in conjunction with the material presented above, there can be no question that the principle of free seizure was applied to booty taken in the field as well as in captured localities. Given that free seizure of spoils could result in the uneven distribution of captured property within the host and cause fighting men prematurely to abandon the pursuit of their enemies, one must attempt to explain why the crusaders were willing not only to accept it, but even to approve it as the rule for the disposition of moveable property in conquered strongholds. The answer undoubtedly lies in the composition of the crusading host and the nature of command on the expedition. Although the army of the First Crusade could act as a unified force, it remained a volatile assemblage of a number of reasonably well-defined contingents under the command of the crusading princes, smaller forces under lesser leaders, and a large crowd of fighting men, poor and non-combatants whose allegiance fluctuated according to their fortunes and those of the leaders.[63] Any attempt to divide captured moveables, in a situation where these various groups could assert rights, would probably have raised the spectre of rivalry between contingents, caused quarrels over the principles and fairness of division,[64] and led to countless other disputes – quite apart from the organisational problems created by the need to collect and then redistribute the spoils.

It might have been possible to deal with all of those difficulties had there been a single commander who exercised a universally respected authority over the army. He would have been able to act as an impartial judge in the challenging task of disposition and to silence any complaints about the equitability of the apportionment. The crusade, however, never had such a leader. Adhémar of Le Puy, while he lived, definitely enjoyed an authority respected by all, but there is no hint that he could have acted in the capacity just described.[65] Perhaps Stephen of Blois was expected to fill just such a role when he was elected *dominus* of the army at some time before 29 March 1098. If so, the sources fail to record that the count of Blois ever performed that function, and one may doubt whether Stephen, or any of the other princes, would have been equal to the task.[66] The crusaders probably realised that free seizure, in spite of its drawbacks, was the only realistic option they had for the disposition of spoils when the army or a large part of it operated in the field or in the reduction of a city. Nevertheless, as the actions of Raymond Pilet and Galdemar Carpinel on the road to Jaffa and those of Tancred in the *Templum Domini* clearly show, the policy of free seizure did not necessarily prevent a commander from maintaining discipline within his own force and apportioning any booty that it won.

It is important to note that both formal division and free seizure would have worked to concentrate captured moveables in the hands of the active combatants in the crusader army. If booty was apportioned within a contingent, once the lord had reserved his share, the remainder would have been returned into the hands of the fighting men who had seized it. Perhaps some portions would have been given to infirm members of the group and to the clerics who attended to the soldiers' spiritual needs, but organised allotment would have spread spoils no further among the pilgrims of floating allegiance and the non-combatants who accompanied the host. Free seizure clearly did not suffer from the same inherent limitation; if the opportunity arose, a non-combatant would have been able to seize property and to retain it just like any other crusader. When spoils were abundant, as they were after the defeat of Kerbogha at Antioch in June 1098 or after the capture of Jerusalem in July 1099, this, in fact, seems to have been the case.

However, when provisions were in short supply – the ordinary state of affairs for much of the crusade[67] – competition for booty would have been intense, and active fighting men would have been best placed to take what fortune offered. The weak, the ill, the lesser clergy, and even able-bodied crusaders who, for one reason or another, were unassociated with one of the military contingents would have found it difficult to obtain captured property, even though they could, in theory, freely seize it. Those who were able might undertake a foraging foray, but any entry into enemy territory was fraught with danger. The anonymous author of the *Gesta Francorum*, writing of the famine that gripped the Christian host late in 1097, mentions that: 'No one dared to enter the land of the Saracens, unless with a great force'.[68] The crusader princes, as noted earlier, sometimes tried to protect the foragers by furnishing escorts, but need often drove the hungry and impoverished to risk their lives in the hope of gaining some loot.

Albert of Aachen furnishes an interesting insight into the response of those non-combatants and leaderless crusaders to the imperative need to take plunder in time of famine. After describing the virtual failure of the foraging expedition of Bohemond and Robert of Flanders and the resulting famine in early 1098, Albert continues:

> With this very serious scarcity afflicting the people of the living God, many wandered into every region of Antioch to look for food. Three hundred or two hundred banded together for defence against Turkish attacks, and for the equal division of all they managed to find or capture.[69]

Shortly after this statement, he reports that Ludwig, archdeacon of Toul, joined just such a group of three hundred 'clerics and laypeople' for a raid into Muslim territory. Ludwig, however, perished in a Turkish attack on the party.[70]

The chronicler's use of the word *conspirati* – which has here been translated as 'banded together' – suggests that these were more than loose associations of convenience. William of Tyre, who drew on this earlier account of the groups in drafting his own, understood that the foragers were bound together by oaths.[71] Such descriptions call to mind the martial confraternities of a later age in which fighting men swore as equals to aid and to defend one another.[72] The evidence is too insubstantial for any firm conclusion but, in light of the fact that a knightly confraternity of uncertain character existed in the Provençal force, one can at least entertain the possibility that other crusaders resorted to similar means to protect their wellbeing.[73] Although the members of these bands intended to divide their gains, the emphasis on equality of shares and the apparent lack of commanders in their ranks suggest that the motivating principle was not the organised allotment of European practice, but the common need of men in adversity.

Because regulated division and free seizure generally left captured moveables in the hands of the fighting men in the crusader host, other mechanisms had to operate to sustain those who either could not obtain vital supplies directly as spoils, or could not obtain enough by their own efforts to survive. Several important channels of distribution need only be considered in passing here, since one can confidently assume that they served to spread captured property in the army even though definite evidence is wanting. Surplus spoils must often have been offered for sale in the crusader host. However, during times of dearth, the purchase of provisions that had been secured as booty, like the purchase of any other foodstuffs, would have been beyond the means of the poor.[74] At all times, some captured property must have reached the poor and the non-combatants in the form of alms. The papal legate, Adhémar of Le Puy, is said to have constantly reminded the knights of their obligation to succour the poor,[75] and figures like Raymond of Toulouse and Godfrey of Bouillon certainly showed great solicitude for the sufferings of the needy.[76] If, as is likely, the princes and lesser leaders regularly received fractions from the booty taken by their followers, they could have diverted some of that income into almsgiving.[77] A leader in receipt of spoils from his men could also have redistributed the property as rewards to his own followers or employed it to entice others into his service.[78]

All of these actions would have redistributed booty within the host, but doubtless in a haphazard and inefficient fashion. Two efforts were made during the journey to the Holy City to institute a more regular system for the distribution of property that had been obtained as booty. The first such initiative is reported by Albert of Aachen who claims that it was made after the battle of Dorylaeum in July 1097. According to Albert, after the Franks had enriched themselves with the belongings of their foes, the crusading princes met in council and decreed that from 'that day, rations and all necessary supplies should be pooled, and everything should be held in common'.[79] The chronicler adds that this was done. None of the eye-witness authorities confirm this testimony, but Albert's claim is not implausible. This was not an attempt to impose a general disposition of booty, only to institute a system for the communal enjoyment of the necessary provisions and supplies.[80] This may have been prompted by the recent sufferings of the poor during the siege of Nicaea, but one must conclude that the princes' scheme was short-lived. Certainly by the end of 1097, six months after the battle of Dorylaeum, crusaders were dying of starvation before Antioch and there were gross inequalities in the distribution of food within the besieging army.[81]

The next attempt to tap the booty seized by the crusaders to provide for the indigent pilgrims occurred during the siege of 'Arqah in the spring of 1099. Peter Tudebode records that at Ma'arrat-an-Nu'mān in late 1098, the crusaders instituted a tithe 'on all things which are possessed' with three-quarters going to the church and one-quarter to the poor.[82] This use of a fraction of a tithe to relieve the suffering of the poor was developed at 'Arqah and expressly tied to the spoils of war. Raymond of Aguilers reports its institution: 'Indeed, at that time it was proclaimed that the people should give a tithe of everything they had seized, since there were many poor and infirm in the army'.[83] The tithe was divided as at Ma'arrat-an-Nu'mān, but one-half was entrusted to Peter the Hermit for the clergy and the people. According to Raymond of Aguilers, the establishment of the tithe brought immediate prosperity to the army. It is not clear if this tithe continued to be levied throughout the rest of the march to Jerusalem, but widespread and lasting shortages among the Franks disappeared after the siege of 'Arqah. That may have been due, however, to the handsome payments that the crusaders received from local Muslim rulers during that part of the expedition.

The general departure from the organised division of booty familiar to them from eleventh-century Europe underscores the exceptional situation in which the participants in the First Crusade found themselves. They were members of a huge force waging war in a foreign land under the command of a committee rather than a single lord. Under such circumstances, the crusading princes abandoned any attempt to control the division of captured moveables within the host at large. Indeed, the simple logistical problems of collecting and distributing booty were probably beyond the capabilities of the leaders.[84] The acceptance, perhaps at the outset only passively, of a general rule of free seizure in the army did not, however, entail a ban on the division of captured moveables. Those crusaders in the households of the princes or lords like Tancred probably continued to divide booty and deliver up portions of their spoils to their lords.

The speedy return to the organised apportionment of booty by the settlers in the Latin East unquestionably bears witness to the clear military advantages of that method for the disposition of booty. Yet the free seizure of booty that had such a marked influence on the course of the First Crusade was not entirely forgotten in the Frankish principalities. William of Tyre, writing in the 1170s, had occasion to observe that 'even to this day, a custom stands among us for a law that, in cities violently stormed, anyone entering shall possess for himself and his heirs by perpetual right whatever he seizes'.[85] When all the disorder and division in the army of the First Crusade was only a distant memory, the 'mutually approved right of possession' of the crusaders still shaped the conduct of fighting men in the East. There is no clearer testimony for the powerful force of custom in medieval military affairs.

Notes

1 Although, strictly speaking, non-Christians taken captive by the crusaders were enslaved and thus reduced to the status of captured moveables, the Franks' willingness to ransom high-status prisoners reveals a more complex situation. Limitations of space preclude an examination of the crusaders' treatment of captives here, but the author hopes to deal with that subject in a future publication.

2 J.S.C. Riley-Smith, *The First Crusade and the Idea of Crusading* (London, Athlone Press, 1986), p. 63.

3 W. Porges, 'The clergy, the poor and the noncombatants on the First Crusade', *Speculum*, 21 (1946), 9–13; Riley-Smith, *First Crusade*, pp. 63–71; A.V. Murray, 'The army of Godfrey of Bouillon, 1096–1099: structure and dynamics of a contingent on the First Crusade' *Revue Belge de Philologie et d'Histoire*, 70 (1992), 324–8; R. Rogers, 'Peter Bartholomew and the role of "the poor" in the First Crusade', in T. Reuter (ed.), *Warriors and Churchmen in the High Middle Ages: Essays Presented to Karl Leyser* (London, Hambledon Press, 1992), pp. 116–20; K. Leyser, 'Money and supplies on the First Crusade', in K. Leyser, *Communications and Power in Medieval Europe: The Gregorian Revolution and Beyond*, ed. T. Reuter (London, Hambledon Press, 1994), pp. 86–90.

4 For instance: J. Prawer, *Histoire du royaume latin de Jérusalem*, trans. G. Nahon, 2 vols (Paris, Centre national de la recherche scientifique,

1975), vol. 1, pp. 231–2; C. Cahen, *Orient et occident au temps des croisades* (Paris, Aubier Montaigne, 1983), p. 74; Rogers, 'Peter Bartholomew', pp. 117–18.

5 J.S.C. Riley-Smith, 'The motives of the earliest crusaders and the settlement of Latin Palestine, 1095–1100', *EHR*, 98 (1983), 723; Murray, 'Army of Godfrey', 327–8; France, *Victory*, p. 22.

6 On the importance of ravaging in medieval warfare, see: J. Gillingham, 'Richard I and the science of war in the Middle Ages', in J. Gillingham and J.C. Holt (eds), *War and Government in the Middle Ages: Essays in Honour of J.O. Prestwick* (Woodbridge, Boydell and Brewer, 1984), pp. 83–5; M.J. Strickland, *War and Chivalry: The Conduct and Perception of War in England and Normandy, 1066–1217* (Cambridge, Cambridge University Press, 1996), pp. 258–90. For the logistical capabilities and limitations of medieval armies, also consult: J. Gillingham, 'William the Bastard at War', in C. Harper-Bill *et al.* (eds), *Studies in Medieval History presented to R. Allen Brown* (Woodbridge, Boydell Press, 1989), pp. 148–9, 155–8; H.J. Hewitt, *The Organisation of War under Edward III, 1338–62* (Manchester, Manchester University Press, 1966), pp. 100–4.

7 For the text of the indulgence, see R. Somerville, *The Councils of Urban II: I Decreta Claramontensia* Annuarium Historiae Conciliorum, Supplementum I (Amsterdam, 1972), p. 74. According to the accounts of Urban II's crusade sermon at Clermont by Baldric of Bourgueil (BB, p. 15) and Robert the Monk (RM, p. 728), the pontiff actually made reference to the temporal rewards awaiting the crusaders. He can never have expected the crusaders to refrain from taking plunder, and he undoubtedly considered the possibility that the Franks might conquer lands in the East. The reference to 'honour and money' must surely be understood as an effort to ensure that those who took the Cross did so with *intentio recta*, not as a ban on enjoying the worldly gains that the holy war might incidentally bring. France, *Victory*, pp. 13–16; R. Somerville, 'The Council of Clermont and the First Crusade', *Studia Gratiana*, 19–20 (1976), 334–7.

8 GF, pp. 19–20.

9 D. Hay, 'Booty in border warfare', *Transactions of the Dumfriesshire and Galloway Natural History and Antiquarian Society*, Third Series, 31 (1954), 145.

10 OV, 2.144–5.

11 See, for instance, Orderic Vitalis' account of the activities of Hubert of Sainte-Suzanne, *c.* 1085: OV, 4.46–9.

12 Both the attraction of booty for soldiers and the threat it posed to military discipline are clearly reflected in the titles concerning the disposition of captured property in *Las Siete Partidas*, the legal code which

Alfonso X of Castile (1252–84) produced but was unable to promulgate during his lifetime. *Las Siete Partidas* provides a comprehensive treatment of the disposition of captured property that is unparalleled north of the Pyrenees for another century. *Las Siete Partidas del Rey Don Alfonso el Sabio*, ed. Real Academia de la Historia, 3 vols (Madrid, Imprenta Real, 1807; reprinted Madrid, Atlas, 1972), vol. 2, pp. 272–5, 310–14; *Las Siete Partidas*, trans. S.P. Scott (Chicago, Commerce Clearing House, 1931), pp. 474–6, 502–5. For a recent discussion of *Las Siete Partidas* and its place in the Alfonsine legal *corpus* (with references to further literature), see J.R. Craddock, 'The legislative works of Alfonso el Sabio', in R.I. Burns (ed.), *Emperor of Culture: Alfonso X the Learned of Castile and his Thirteenth-Century Renaissance* (Philadelphia, University of Pennsylvania Press, 1990), pp. 186–93.

13 See, for example, the celebrated episode of Clovis and the 'vase of Soissons' in Gregory of Tours, *Libri Historiarum X*, eds B. Krusch and W. Levison, *Monumenta Germaniae Historica, Scriptores rerum Merovingicarum*, 1.1 (Hannover, Hahnsche Buchhandlung, 1951), pp. 72–3. Short discussions of the Merovingians' treatment of booty may be found in: J.P. Bodmer, *Der Krieger der Merowingerzeit und seine Welt: Eine Studie über Kriegertum als Form der menschlichen Existenz in Frühmittelalter*, Geist und Werk der Zeiten, 2 (Zürich, Fretz und Wasmuth, 1957), pp. 100–1; T. Reuter, 'Plunder and tribute in the Carolingian Empire', *TRHS*, Fifth Series, 35 (1985), 79–81.

14 For the disposition of the gains of war in the fourteenth and the fifteenth centuries, see the following works and the references contained therein: D. Hay, 'The division of the spoils of war in fourteenth-century England', *TRHS*, Fifth Series, 4 (1954), 91–109; Hay, 'Booty in border warfare', 145–66; M. Keen, *The Laws of War in the Late Middle Ages* (London, Routledge and Kegan Paul, 1965), pp. 137–55; P. Contamine, *Guerre, état et société à la fin du moyen âge: Études sur les armées des rois de France, 1337–1494* (Paris, Mouton, 1972), pp. 522–6; P. Contamine, 'Rançons et butins dans la Normandie anglaise (1424–1444); in *La guerre et la paix: Frontières et violences au Moyen Age*, Actes du 101ᵉ congrès national des sociétés savantes (Paris, Bibliothèque Nationale, 1978), pp. 241–70.

15 On the disposition of booty before the fourteenth century, see the studies cited in note 13 above and Hay, 'Division of spoils', 107–9 and the works cited therein.

Hispanists have been able to draw upon the detailed regulations concerning captured property that were embodied in municipal *fueros* and other legal texts produced between 1050 and 1300. C. Pescador, 'La caballeria popular en León y Castilla', *Cuadernos de Historia de*

España, 35–6 (1962), 172–89; J. Powers, 'Frontier competition and legal creativity: a Castilian–Aragonese case study based on twelfth-century municipal military law', *Speculum*, 52 (1977), 478–81: J. Powers: *A Society Organized for War: The Iberian Municipal Militias in the Central Middle Ages, 1000–1284* (Berkeley, University of California Press, 1988), pp. 162–87.

16 Since the crusaders' treatment of their prisoners of war has been excluded from this study (see note 1 above), the Western conventions relating to captivity and ransom will not be considered in what follows. An excellent discussion of the subject may be found in Strickland, *War and Chivalry*, pp. 183–203.

17 On the Spanish laws, see Powers, 'Frontier competition', 478–9. For the Welsh laws: D. Jenkins (trans. and ed.), *The Law of Hywel Dda: Law Texts from Medieval Wales* (Llandysul, Dyfed, Gomer Press, 1986), pp. xi–xxvi, 10, 14, 17–20, 29, 35. Keen, *Laws of War*, pp. 15–17 emphasises the continuing importance of customary usage even in the late medieval law of arms.

18 William of Malmesbury, for example, asserts that many of Harold Godwinson's forces deserted him before the battle of Hastings in 1066 because he had refused to distribute the booty taken at the earlier battle of Stamford Bridge. *De gestis regum Anglorum*, ed. W. Stubbs, 2 vols, *RS*, 90 (London, HMSO, 1887–9), vol. 1, pp. 281–2, vol. 2, p. 300. Similarly, some of the historians of the Normans in southern Italy relate that the Byzantine general, George Maniakes, alienated his Norman soldiers by refusing to accord them a share of the spoils after a victory in Sicily in 1038. William of Apulia, *La Geste de Robert Guiscard*, ed. and trans. M. Mathieu, Istituto Siciliano di Studi Bizantini et Neoellenici, Testi 4 (Palermo, Bruno Lavagnini, 1961), p. 110: Geoffrey Malaterra, *De rebus gestis Rogerii Calabriae et Siciliae Comitis et Roberti Guiscardi ducis fratris eius*, ed. E. Pontieri, *Rerum Italicarum Scriptores*, 5.1 (Bologna, Nicola Zanichelli, 1928), pp. 11–12.

19 Isidore of Seville, writing in the early seventh century, had already come to regard the allotment of plunder as the martial norm, for he identified 'the treatment of spoils, their just division according to the rank of individuals and their labour, and the prince's portion' as matters governed by the *ius militare*. See *Etymologiarum sive originum libri XX*, ed. W.M. Lindsay, 2 vols (Oxford, Oxford University Press, 1911), vol. 1, 5.7.1–2 (not paginated).

20 William of Apulia, *Geste de Robert Guiscard*, p. 148. For other instances of commanders supervising the division of booty, see: Widukind of Corvey, *Rerum gestarum Saxonicarum libri tres*, eds H.-E. Lohmann and P. Kirsch, *Scriptores rerum Germanicarum in usum scholarum ex Monumentis Germaniae Historicis separatim editi*

(Hannover, Hahnsche Buchhandlung, 1935), pp. 115, 121; Thietmar of Merseburg, *Chronicon*, ed. R. Holtzmann, *Monumenta Germaniae Historica, Scriptores Rerum Germanicarum*, New Series, 9 (Berlin, Weidmannsche Verlagsbuchhandlung, 1955), pp. 258–9; 'Historia Roderici vel gesta Roderici campidocti', in E. Falque *et al.* (eds), *Chronica Hispana Saeculi XII*, part 1, Corpus Christianorum, Continuatio mediaevalis, 71 (Turnhout, Belgium, Brepols, 1990), p. 89.

21 Although no clue is given to the make up of the force involved, another reference to the use of equal shares in the division of spoils may be found in the late tenth-century life of Maiolus of Cluny by Syrus Monachus. 'Vita Sancti Maioli', *PL*, 137, cols. 768–9.

22 Thus, the Genoese chronicler, Caffaro, remarks that, in the partition of the riches gained while the commune's fleet assisted Baldwin I of Jerusalem in the reduction of Arsuf and Caesarea in 1101, not only did 8,000 men each receive forty-eight Poitevin solidi and two pounds of pepper, but a large 'award' (*honorem*) was also made to 'the consuls, the ship-masters and the better men'. 'Annales Ianuenses', in L.T. Belgrano and C. Imperiale di Sant'Angelo (eds), *Annali Genovesi di Caffaro e de' suoi Continuatori dal MXCIX al MCCXCII*, 5 vols, Fonti per la storia d'Italia, 10–15 (Rome, Istituto Storico Italiano, 1890–1929), vol. 1, p. 13. On Caffaro and his historical works, see R.D. Face, 'Secular history in twelfth-century Italy: Caffaro of Genoa', *JMH*, 6 (1980), 169–84.

23 This is evident in the provisions made by the fourth crusaders for the apportionment of the property taken in Constantinople in 1204: Geoffrey of Villehardouin, *La Conquête de Constantinople*, ed. and trans. E. Faral, 2 vols, Les classiques de l'histoire de France au moyen âge, 18–19 (Paris, Société d'édition 'les Belles Lettres', 1938–9). vol. 2, pp. 58–60; Robert of Clari, *La Conquéte de Constantinople*, ed. P. Lauer, Les classiques Français du moyen âge, 40 (Paris, Édouard Champion, 1924), pp. 95–6. Also see: Ambroise, *L'Estoire de la guerre sainte: Histoire en verse de la troisième croisade (1190–1192)*, ed. G. Paris, Collection de documents inédits sur l'histoire de France (Paris, Imprimerie Nationale, 1897), p. 283; *Las Siete Partidas*, ed. Real Academia, pp. 298–9; *Las Siete Partidas*, trans. Scott, p. 493.

24 The seventh-century author, Isidore of Seville, mentions the 'prince's portion'; see note 19 above.

25 Powers, 'Frontier competition', 478–9; Powers, *Society Organized for War*, p. 173; Jenkins, *Law of Hywel Dda*, p. 10. The levying of the *quinta* was evidently not solely a royal prerogative. The early twelfth-century bishop/archbishop of Compostela, Diego Gelmirez, is reported to have taken a fifth of the booty captured by his men on a number of occasions. E.F. Rey (ed.), *Historia Compostellana*, Corpus

Christianorum, Continuatio Mediaevalis, 70 (Turnhout, Belgium, Brepols, 1987), pp. 119, 176, 264.

26 William of Poitiers, *Histoire de Guillaume le Conquérant*, ed. and trans. R. Foreville, Les Classiques de l'histoire de France au moyen âge, 23 (Paris, Société d'édition 'les Belles Lettres', 1952), p. 98.

27 Thietmar of Merseburg remarks that the soldiers of the early eleventh-century Polish ruler, Boleslav Chrobry, assigned the 'best' of their spoils 'to God and their lord'. The same author also records that Pope Benedict VIII, who had organised a successful expedition against a Muslim force harassing the region of Luna in 1016, claimed, 'before the others', a bejewelled golden crown as his share of the spoils. *Chronicon*, pp. 262–3, 452–5.

Strickland, *War and Chivalry*, pp. 188–91, persuasively argues that Anglo-Norman rulers had a prescriptive right to noble and knightly prisoners-of-war.

28 On the privileges enjoyed by captains and leaders of independent forces at the time of the Hundred Years War, consult: Hay, 'Division of spoils', 94–107; Keen, *Laws of War*, pp. 147–9.

29 FC, pp. 364–5; Caffaro, 'Annales Ianuenses', pp. 6–7. Also see WT, p. 460.

30 FC, pp. 501, 689–90, 772–3; AA, IX.47, X.47, XII.8; WT, pp. 468, 474, 534, 573, 575. For portions taken by rulers, see: AA, X.31; Walter the Chancellor, *Bella Antiochena*, ed. H. Hagenmeyer (Wagner'schen Universitäts-Buchhandlung, 1896), p. 76. Further evidence for these usages in the Latin East can be found in a variety of sources from the late twelfth and thirteenth centuries, but it cannot be reviewed within the compass of this study; for brief references to this later material, see: G. Dodu, *Histoire des institutions monarchiques dans le royaume latin de Jérusalem, 1099–1291* (Paris, Hachette, 1894), pp. 246–7; J.L. LaMonte, *Feudal Monarchy in the Latin Kingdom of Jerusalem, 1100 to 1291* (Cambridge, Mass., Medieval Academy of America, 1932), pp. 117, 119–21, 163; R.C. Smail, *Crusading Warfare, 1097–1193* (Cambridge, Cambridge University Press, 1956), p. 103.

31 See, for example, Galbert of Bruges' description of the orgy of looting in the castle of Bruges that followed the expulsion of the murderers of Charles the Good in 1127. Galbert expressly mentions that while some of the besiegers entered the castle to fight, many were seeking plunder. *De multro, traditione, et occisione gloriosi Karoli comitis Flandriarum*, ed. J. Ryder, Corpus Christianorum, Continuatio mediaevalis, 131 (Turnhout, Belgium, Brepols, 1994), pp. 90–2.

32 Bruno, *Buch vom Sachsenkrieg*, ed. H.-E. Lohmann, Deutsches Mittelalter: Kritische Studientexte des Reichsinstitut für ältere deutsche

Geschichtskunde, 2 (Leipzig, Karl W. Hiersmann, 1937), pp. 116–17.

33 Geoffrey Malaterra, *De rebus gestis*, p. 74 (cited in n. 18). Also see Malaterra's report of the seizure of the contents of the Muslim camp after Count Roger's victory at Cerami in 1063: *De rebus gestis*, p. 44.

34 On the small size of medieval armies, see J. Beeler, *Warfare in Medieval Europe, 730–1200* (Ithaca, Cornell University Press, 1971), pp. 249–50.

35 France, *Victory*, pp. 121–42, provides the most recent discussion of the size of the crusader force.

36 For instance: Hagenmeyer, *Epistulae*, pp. 145, 158; GF, pp. 33, 35, 89; RA, pp. 49, 105, 140; FC, p. 222; AA, III.40, III.43, III.46–8, III.53, V.30, VI.4, VI.6.

37 Hagenmeyer, *Epistulae*, p. 158; GF, p. 30; RA, pp. 50, 89, 101–2; AA, III.50, V.30.

38 FC, p. 212. Raymond of Aguilers also observes that the Turks habitually dropped their arms and possessions when in flight from their foes. RA, p. 142.

39 The meagre spoils carried back by Bohemond and Robert of Flanders after driving off the relieving force led by Dukak of Damascus in December 1097 show that victory was not inevitably accompanied by rich gains. RA, p. 53; France, *Victory*, pp. 237–41.

40 See, for example, Raymond of Aguilers' account of the plundering of Ma'arrat-an-Nu'mān. RA, p. 98.

41 On Raymond Pilet and Galdemar Carpinel, see: Riley-Smith, 'Motives', 728; Riley-Smith, *First Crusade*, p. 71; France, *Victory*, p. 21.

42 RA, pp. 141–2. William Sabran's role in these events is unclear. France suggests that he accompanied Raymond Pilet's force; his presence would in no way alter the interpretation of the events. The other accounts of the engagement make no mention of the division of the spoils, but the *Gesta Francorum* and Peter Tudebode remark that the Franks captured 103 horses. GF, pp. 88–9; PT, pp. 135–6; AA, VI.4; France, *Victory*, pp. 336–7.

43 On the plundering of the Dome of the Rock, see: AA, VI.23; RC, pp. 129–130; FC, pp. 302–3; R.L. Nicholson, *Tancred: A Study of his Career and Work in their Relation to the First Crusade and the Establishment of the Latin States in Syria and Palestine* (Chicago, University of Chicago Libraries, 1940), pp. 93, 96–7.

Albert also portrays Tancred distributing booty to his followers after the violent capture of Mamistra in 1097, but the account must be regarded with reservation since other well-informed sources assert that the Armenian inhabitants surrendered the city to the crusaders. William of Tyre's account is manifestly based on Albert's. AA, III.15;

RC, pp. 634–6; GF, p. 25; WT, p. 225. For other references in Albert's chronicle to the division of spoils, though not by crusaders, see: AA, I.7, I.12, III.14–15.

The *Chronicon Monasterii Casinensis* states that all of the booty 'in gold and silver, clothes and animals' taken from the Turks after the battle of Dorylaeum was divided amongst the crusaders, but this is not supported by the eye-witness sources. H. Hoffman (ed.), *Die Chronik von Montecassino*, *MGHSS*, 34, 480.

44 FC, p. 304. This passage shows that the rule of free seizure was also applied to real property. This 'law of conquest' deserves further investigation, but see the comments in J. Prawer, 'Burgage-tenure', in J. Prawer, *Crusader Institutions* (Oxford, Oxford University Press, 1980), pp. 253–4.

45 FC, pp. 215, 331–2, 368–9.

46 AA. VI.23; RC. p. 701; GN, p. 228; OV, 5, p. 172; WT, pp. 412–13. Although they do not expressly report the 'right of possession', the following accounts also attest to the free seizure of property in Jerusalem: GF, pp. 91–2; RM, p. 868; Bartolf of Nangis, 'Gesta Francorum Iherusalem expugnantium', *RHC, Oc.* III, p. 516; 'Historia peregrinorum euntium Jerusolymam ad liberandum sanctum sepulcrum de potestate ethnicorum', *RHC, Oc.* III, p. 222.

47 RC, pp. 699–703.

48 GF, pp. 24–5.

49 FC, pp. 234–5; RC, p. 655. William of Tyre states that all the possessions of the inhabitants of Antioch fell to whoever first took them, but he then adds that some Franks who had banded together to loot the richer houses cast lots for the contents. The casting of lots would have been a perfectly reasonable method for fellow soldiers to employ for the division of plunder amongst themselves if they had all entered a house together. The source of William's information, however, is uncertain. Caffaro rather curiously reports that the Christians 'took and held the houses of the city and all the things that were in them in common (*communiter*)'. The correct interpretation of this passage is unclear. WT, pp. 301–2; Caffaro, 'De liberatione civitatum orientis', in L.T. Belgrano and C. Imperiale di Sant'Angelo (eds), *Annali Genovesi di Caffaro e de' suoi Continuatori dal MXCIX al MCCXCII*, 5 vols, Fonti per la storia d'Italia, 10–15 (Rome, Istituto Storico Italiano, 1890–1929), vol. 1, pp. 104–5.

50 RA, pp. 97–8.

51 GF, p. 79.

52 PT, p. 124.

53 GF, p. 32. Peter Tudebode adds that the foragers who had found no plunder hastened to return to the Frankish camp. PT, p. 67.

54 RA, p. 61.

55 However, this is not conclusive in itself. Roger of Antioch divided the plunder taken after his defeat of Bursuk ibn-Bursuk in 1115; but, before the battle, corporal and spiritual penalties had been announced for anyone who turned aside to plunder before victory had been achieved. Walter the Chancellor, *Bella Antiochena*, p. 73.

56 RA, p. 78.

57 GF, p. 70; RA, p. 82; FC, p. 256; AA, IV.56.

58 GN, p. 208.

59 Except for Fulcher of Chartres, all of the chronicles written by first crusaders mention the patriarch's prohibition against taking booty before the battle was won. It is also mentioned by Albert of Aachen and some other later sources: GF, pp. 94–5; PT, p. 145; RA, p. 157; AA, VI.42; GN, p. 235; BB, p. 107, OV, V. 178. For the letter from Daimbert, Godfrey and Raymond to the pope, see Hagenmeyer, *Epistulae*, p. 172.

60 GF, p. 97. Peter Tudebode's account adds more detail about the spoils taken, but otherwise differs little from that in the *Gesta Francorum*. Other sources stress the large quantities of booty taken by the Franks. PT, p. 149; RA, p. 158; FC, pp. 315–18; BB, p. 110.

61 RA, p. 106. The *Gesta Francorum* states that the castle garrison, in fact, released the animals to divert the attention of the crusaders. GF, p. 82.

62 Porges' assertion that this episode represents a case of looting 'conducted in accordance with the wealth of the participants' has no foundation. 'The clergy, the poor and the noncombatants', 11.

63 Riley-Smith, *First Crusade*, pp. 73–9, 86–90.

64 Ralph of Caen relates that Tancred and Baldwin quarrelled over the division of booty between their two contingents before Tarsus; RC, p. 633.

65 J. Brundage, 'Adhemar of Puy: the bishop and his critics', *Speculum*, 34 (1959), 201–8, 211–12; Riley-Smith, *First Crusade*, pp. 86–9.

66 Hagenmeyer, *Epistulae*, p. 149; GF, p. 63; RA, p. 77; Riley-Smith, *First Crusade*, p. 74.

67 Riley-Smith, *First Crusade*, pp. 64–6.

68 GF, p. 30.

69 AA, III.52.

70 AA, III.53.

71 WT, p. 258.

72 J.S.C. Riley-Smith, 'A note on confraternities in the Latin kingdom of Jerusalem', *Bulletin of the Institute of Historical Research*, 44 (1971), 304–7; M. Keen, 'Brotherhood in arms', *History*, 47 (1962), 5–9.

73 Raymond of Aguilers (RA, pp. 54–5) describes the role played by the

Provençal confraternity in providing funds so its members could replace horses lost in the fighting before Antioch in early 1098. See J. Richard, 'La confrérie de la croisade: à propos d'un épisode de la première croisade', in *Études de civilisation médiévale (IXᵉ–XIIᵉ siècles): Mélanges offerts à Edmond-René Labande* (Poitiers, CESCM, 1974), pp. 617–22.

74 GF, pp. 33, 62; RA, pp. 53, 76–7; AA, III.52, IV.34, IV.36.

75 GF, p. 74.

76 RA, pp. 88–9, 101–2; AA, IV.55.

77 On almsgiving during the expedition, see Riley-Smith, *First Crusade*, p. 68.

78 Ralph of Caen, for instance, relates that during the famine before the capture of Antioch, Tancred not only never excluded any of his household from his table, but even received and fed men who had been excluded by other leaders. In an act that shows similarities to the division of booty, Tancred also distributed among his men 70 marks that he had received as a gift from Adhémar after sending the bishop 70 Turkish heads. RC, p. 644; RC, p. 650; AA, IV.54. On the importance of such lordly largesse during the crusade, see: Riley-Smith, *First Crusade*, pp. 68–70; Leyser, 'Money and Supplies', pp. 88–93.

79 AA, II.43.

80 However, Baldric of Bourgueil's claim that among the Franks at Nicaea 'just as in the primitive Church, nearly all things were shared between them' smacks too much of the monastic chronicler's attempt 'to see the crusaders as lay pilgrims adopting a kind of monastic life'. BB, p. 28; Riley-Smith, *First Crusade*, p. 150.

81 GF, pp. 30–3; RA, pp. 50–5.

82 PT, p. 122.

83 RA, p. 91.

84 One may note that the orderly collection of booty for division posed problems for the second crusaders who assisted in the siege of Lisbon and the fourth crusaders in Constantinople. C.W. David (ed. and trans.), *De Expugnatione Lyxbonensi*, Columbia University Records of Civilization, 24 (New York, Columbia University Press, 1936), pp. 173–7; Geoffrey of Villehardouin, *La Conquête de Constantinople*, vol. 2, pp. 56–60.

85 WT, p. 798. For another reference, see WT, p. 922.

Postscript

Jonathan Phillips

The armies of the First Crusade faced almost insurmountable odds in their attempt to conquer the Holy Land. Many crusaders deserted during the campaign and the slow progress of the remainder of the expedition must have signalled that the enterprise was struggling, but on 15 July 1099 Jerusalem fell to the Christians. When the capture of the Holy City became known in Europe, it caused an enormous stir – people were convinced that God had wished the crusade to succeed. The majority of the crusaders returned home as heroes, leaving only a small number of their coreligionists in the Levant. There was, however, the prospect of support because from the autumn of 1100 several contingents of crusaders set out for the East led by men such as Duke William IX of Aquitaine and Count William I of Nevers. This campaign is known as the 1101 crusade, although it should really be seen as the final stage of the First Crusade, because it was initially preached before the fall of Jerusalem and was intended to provide new impetus to the ongoing campaign in the East.

In fact, the expedition foundered during the march across Asia Minor and, as a coda to Jonathan Shepard's chapter concerning the difficult relationship between Alexius Comnenus and the leaders of the First Crusade, managed to sour Latin–Byzantine feelings even further.[1] The losses suffered in the course of the march meant this expedition offered little useful help to the Franks in the East. Nonetheless, the settlers managed to hold on to the territory they had captured and began to establish their rule more thoroughly. As Carole Hillenbrand's chapter demonstrates, the Muslims of the eastern Mediterranean were a divided force and the Latins exploited this to mop up the pockets of resistance they had bypassed in their enthusiasm to reach Jerusalem. Attention has been drawn to the chronicle of Albert of Aachen and it is worth indicating that his work provides information on the activities of the Franks in the East down to April 1119. When, therefore, Susan Edgington's edition and translation are completed they will complement the existing translation of Fulcher of Chartres (whose chronicle ends in 1127) and enable a wider audience to assess the progress and impact of the first two decades of Frankish rule.[2] Two further Latin chronicles that remain to be translated are also important in studying this period. First, the work of Ralph of Caen, which covers the crusade and the period down to 1105. Secondly, that of Walter the Chancellor, who wrote about events in northern Syria between 1114 and 1122.[3] The latter in particular will continue the history of the principality of Antioch discussed here by Thomas Asbridge.

Only a few hundred knights stayed in Jerusalem in 1099. Other Latin forces remained in the Levant – with Bohemond in Antioch for example, but in essence there were not enough westerners to settle the conquered territory properly. We know of the later existence of Frankish villages and so the first decades of the twelfth century must have seen some emigration from Europe although hardly any information on this subject survives.[4] Larger numbers of westerners chose to visit the Holy Land as pilgrims.[5] Latin Christian custodianship of the holy places meant that the contemporary enthusiasm for pilgrimage could be satisfied more safely and every spring thousands of people embarked on sailings from Europe to the eastern Mediterranean. Transport on such a scale was only possible through the involvement of the Italian city–states. Important trade routes to the Levant already existed, but the advent of Frankish rule, the need to provide men and supplies to the settlers, as well as the rise in pilgrim traffic, combined to increase the Italians' level of interest dramatically and was also to provide another arena for their commercial rivalry.[6]

The Franks in the Levant had close bonds with the people of Europe on account of shared faith, the presence of relatives in the West and the powerful badge of honour conferred by participation in the First Crusade, and the settlers laid emphasis on all of these factors in their efforts to secure support for the defence of the holy places. The leading men of western Europe found themselves, therefore, on the receiving end of a series of appeals for help – both military and financial – designed to sustain the Crusader states. If they agreed to these requests, of course, they would be required to absent themselves from their lands for at least two years and to undertake a highly dangerous, albeit prestigious, expedition to the Levant. Some leading men in the West had specially close ties with the settlers and this, in combination with favourable political and economic circumstances, enabled particular rulers to undertake a series of crusades – the counts of Flanders for example, visited the Holy Land seven times in the course of the twelfth century.[7]

Perhaps one of the most interesting points to emerge from the current studies on the First Crusade is to consider how this work will impact upon our treatment of the subsequent phase in the history of the crusades, particularly down to, and including the Second Crusade (1145–9).[8] Relatively little work has been conducted on this period and while we have seen that much remains to be done with regard to the history of the First Crusade, it should be worth capitalising on recent progress to start to reassess the events of the following decades too. We now recognise that a series of crusades to the Holy Land took place between what we know as the First Crusade and the Second Crusade. The traditional numbering system failed to take into account a series of smaller crusading expeditions. Yet because of limited evidence, and the fact that the idea of crusading itself was evolving, it is often difficult to distinguish between early crusades and large-scale armed pilgrimages.[9] It now appears, however, that Bohemond of Antioch's expedition of 1107–8 (which attacked the Byzantine empire), the Venetian-led fleet that helped to capture Tyre in 1124 and Count Fulk V of Anjou's campaign against Damascus in 1129 should certainly be regarded as crusades.[10]

Close scrutiny is required of the papal attitude towards crusading in the period 1095 to 1145. This may also affect our understanding of the papacy's approach to the preaching of the Second Crusade. Paschal II endorsed Bohemond's expedition and a papal legate proclaimed the crusade. Yet two decades later we know that the papacy was aware of Fulk's forthcoming crusade to Damascus, but there is no evidence of a bull being issued or a formal preaching tour being set in train to raise support for the campaign.[11] By the time of the Second Crusade, however, Pope Eugenius III and his principal representative, Bernard of Clairvaux, were determined to direct all aspects of preaching and issued stern warnings against any unauthorised recruitment.[12] Another notable development during the early years of crusading was Paschal II's decision c. 1114–16 to accord participants in the conflict with the Muslims of the Iberian peninsula and the Balearics the same spiritual rewards as those fighting in the Holy Land.[13]

The relationship between participation in the First and Second Crusades (and those in between), and the influence of traditions of crusading on recruitment for subsequent expeditions, is an important subject. Jonathan Riley-Smith has examined traditions of crusading and the French involvement in the crusade and the Latin East down to 1131 and clearly this idea can be extended to the Second Crusade and beyond.[14] But, as the chapters here by Susan Edgington and Alan Murray have shown, we must not overlook the German contribution to the First Crusade. A similar point applies to the German interest in the Second Crusade. In part this topic has received relatively little attention because the only continuous narrative of the crusade to the Latin East was written by King Louis VII's chaplain, Odo of Deuil, and quite naturally it presents a largely French perspective.[15] While some information survives on the progress of Conrad III's army we need to look elsewhere to enhance our understanding of German involvement in the crusade. Marcus Bull's paper indicates why studies of the First Crusade have benefited from the use of charter material and by employing this form of evidence for the 1147–9 expedition it should be possible to gain a clearer picture of German participation in the Second Crusade and to identify any traditions of crusading that may have existed in the empire.

The First Crusade had many, many consequences. Amongst other things it influenced the treatment of Jews in the West, cultural and economic contacts with the Mediterranean, developments in warfare and the emergence of the chivalric ethos.[16] The Byzantine empire had to reassess its position with the establishment of a new Christian power in the eastern Mediterranean and again, cultural and political interaction can be noted. The crusade also opened up a new stage in the conflict between Christians and Muslims in the Mediterranean and with the development of the crusade the struggle acquired a more overt and institutionalised religious focus than had been the case before. The longer-term consequences of the crusade are outside the scope of this book, but it is hoped that this collection has provided new insights into the forces in medieval society that shaped the crusade, the information that we can use to understand the events of 1095–9, and the immediate impact of the expedition in the eastern Mediterranean.

Notes

1   For information on the 1101 expedition see J.S.C. Riley-Smith, *The First Crusade and the Idea of Crusading* (London, Athlone Press, 1986), pp. 120–34; Runciman, *Crusades*, 2, pp. 18–31. Alec Mullender of Swansea University has completed a Ph.D. on the 1101 crusade and his work should enhance our understanding of the expedition.

2   Fulcher of Chartres, *A History of the Expedition to Jerusalem, 1095–1127*, trans. F.R. Ryan, ed. H.S. Fink (Knoxville, University of Tennessee Press, 1969).

3   Thomas Asbridge and Susan Edgington are collaborating to produce a translation of Walter the Chancellor's work.

4   R. Ellenblum, 'Colonization activities in the Frankish East: the example of Castellum Regis (Mi'ilya)', *EHR* 111 (1996), 104–22.

5   See the pilgrims' accounts of their visits in *Jerusalem Pilgrimage 1099–1185*, ed. J. Wilkinson, Hakluyt Society Second Series No. 167 (London, 1988).

6   D. Abulafia, 'Trade and Crusade, 1050–1250'. *Cross-Cultural Convergences in the Crusader Period. Essays presented to Aryeh Grabois on his 65th birthday*, eds M. Goodich, S. Menache and S. Schein (New York, Peter Lang, 1995), pp. 3–20; M.-L. Favreau-Lilie, *Die Italiener im Heiligen Land vom Ersten Kreuzzug bis zum Tode Heinrichs von Champagne (1098–1197)* (Amsterdam, Adolf M. Hakkert, 1989).

7   J.P. Phillips, *Defenders of the Holy Land: Relations between the Latin East and the West, 1119–87* (Oxford, Oxford University Press, 1996), pp. 271–81.

8   The most important recent studies on the Second Crusade are: G. Constable, 'The Second Crusade as seen by contemporaries', *Traditio* 9 (1953), 213–79, and the collection of essays *The Second Crusade and the Cistercians*, ed. M. Gervers (New York, St. Martin's Press, 1992).

9   For example, King Sigurd of Norway was accompanied by a large military force on his visit to the Levant in 1107–10, but because he was not responding to a papal appeal this can be regarded as a pilgrimage, rather than a crusade. For details of Sigurd's journey see Snorri Sturluson, *Heimskringla: The History of the Kings of Norway*, trans. L.M. Hollander (Austin, University of Texas, 1964), pp. 689–99.

10 Phillips, *Defenders*, pp. 14–43; J.S.C. Riley-Smith, *The Crusades: A Short History* (London, Athlone Press, 1987), pp. 88–93.

11 Phillips, *Defenders*, pp. 38–9.

12 Saint Bernard of Clairvaux, *Opera*, eds J. Leclerq and H. Rochais, 8 vols (Rome, Editiones Cisterciences, 1955–77), 8, no. 365, pp. 320–2.

13 Bull, *Knightly Piety and the Lay Response to the First Crusade: The Limousin and Gascony c. 970–1130* (Oxford, Clarendon Press, 1993), pp. 107–10.

14 J.S.C. Riley-Smith, *The First Crusaders, 1095–1131* (Cambridge, Cambridge University Press, 1997).

15 Odo of Deuil, *De profectione Ludovici VII*, ed. and trans. V.G. Berry, Columbia Records of Civilization Series No. 42 (New York, Columbia University Press, 1948).

16 R. Chazan, *European Jewry and the First Crusade* (Berkeley, University of California Press, 1987); R.C. Smail, *Crusading Warfare, 1097–1193* (Cambridge, Cambridge University Press, 1956); M. Keen, *Chivalry* (New Haven, Connecticut, Yale University Press, 1984).

Chronology of key events

1095

1–7 March	Council of Piacenza – envoys arrived from Alexius Comnenus
27 November	Pope Urban II proclaimed First Crusade
December	Peter the Hermit preached the cross
	Urban toured France and preached the cross

1096

January–July	Urban continued tour of France
8 March	Peter the Hermit set out for the Holy Land
May–June	Jewish communities of the Rhineland attacked by Emicho of Leiningen's forces
6–7 August	Peter the Hermit's contingent crossed the Bosphorus
c. 15 August	Godfrey of Bouillon left for the East
September	Bohemond took the cross
September–October	Robert of Normandy, Robert of Flanders and Stephen of Blois left for the East
	Defeat and destruction of first wave of crusaders, including forces of Emicho of Leiningen, in Asia Minor
23 December	Godfrey of Bouillon reached Constantinople

1097

April	Forces of Bohemond and Raymond of Saint Gilles

	reached Constantinople
May–June	Crusade armies assembled and besieged Nicaea
19 June	Nicaea surrendered to forces of Emperor Alexius
1 July	Battle of Dorylaeum
c. 15 August	Crusaders at Konya
September–October	Baldwin of Boulogne and Tancred split from main army and headed into Armenia, taking Tarsus and Adana
20–22 October	Crusaders arrived at Antioch and began siege of the city

1098

20 February	Baldwin of Boulogne reached Edessa
10 March	Baldwin took power in Edessa
2 June	Stephen of Blois deserted army at Antioch
3 June	Antioch taken by the crusaders
14 June	Holy Lance discovered
c. 20 June	Alexius decided to turn back from relief of Antioch on hearing erroneous reports of impending crusader defeat
28 June	Battle of Antioch
1 August	Death of Adhémar of Le Puy
11–12 December	Sack of Ma'arrat-an-Nu'mān

1099

January	Raymond of Saint Gilles and Robert of Normandy began to march south to Jerusalem
February–May	Siege of Arqah; Raymond joined by Godfrey of Bouillon and Robert of Flanders
7 June	Crusaders arrived before Jerusalem
15 July	Fall of Jerusalem
22 July	Godfrey of Bouillon elected as ruler of Jerusalem
29 July	Death of Pope Urban II
12 August	Battle of Ascalon
Late August	Many crusaders returned home

Select bibliography

Editor's note: This is not intended to be an exhaustive list of all the primary sources referred to in this volume. The emphasis here is on narrative sources and attention is drawn to translations into English. Three important collections of translated material are Gabrieli's *Arab Historians*, the Riley-Smiths' *Crusades: Idea and Reality* and Peters' *First Crusade*. Similarly the list of secondary materials is not concerned to include all the works used here and is simply a reflection of the most important and accessible studies relevant to this collection. The reader is referred to the bibliography in volume 6 of *A History of the Crusades*, eds K.M. Setton and M.W. Baldwin (Madison, University of Wisconsin Press, 1989) for a more complete listing of works on the First Crusade.

Primary sources

Albert of Aachen, 'Historia Hierosolymitana', *RHC Oc.* IV, pp. 265–713. A new edition and translation of this work is being prepared by Susan Edgington.

Anna Comnena, *Alexiad*, ed. and trans. B. Leib, 3 vols (Paris, Société d'édition les belles lettres, 1937–45). Trans. E.R.A. Sewter (Harmondsworth, Middlesex, Penguin, 1969).

Anonymi Auctoris Chronicon ad Annum Christi 1234 Pertinens, ed. J.-B. Chabot, trans. A. Abouna, 2 vols (Louvain, Belgium, L. Durbecq, 1952–74). Partially trans. A.S. Tritton as 'The First and Second Crusades from an Anonymous Syriac Chronicle', *Journal of the Royal Asiatic Society* (1933), 69–101, 273–305.

Arab Historians of the Crusades, ed. and trans. F. Gabrieli (London, Routledge and Kegan Paul, 1969).

Baldric of Bourgueil, 'Historia Jerosolimitana', *RHC Oc.* IV, pp. 9–111.

La Chanson d'Antioche, ed. S. Duparc-Quioc, 2 vols (Paris, Librairie Orientaliste Paul Geuthner, 1977–8).

The Crusades: Idea and Reality, 1095–1274, eds and trans. L. and J.S.C. Riley-Smith (London, Edward Arnold, 1981).

Ekkehard of Aura, 'Hierosolymita', *RHC Oc.* V, pp. 1–40.

Epistulae et chartae ad historiam primi belli sacri spectantes quae supersunt aevo aequales ac genvinae, ed. H. Hagenmeyer (Innsbruck, Verlag der Wagner'schen Universitätsbuchhandlung, 1901).

The First Crusade: The Chronicle of Fulcher of Chartres and Other Source Materials, ed. E. Peters (Philadelphia, University of Pennsylvania Press, 1971).

Fulcher of Chartres, *Historia Hierosolymitana (1095–1127)*, ed. H. Hagenmeyer (Heidelberg, Carl Winters Universtätbuchhandlung, 1913), Trans. F.R. Ryan, ed. H.S. Fink as *A History of the Expedition to Jerusalem, 1095–1127* (Knoxville, University of Tennessee Press, 1969).

Gesta Francorum et aliorum Hierosolimitanorum, ed. and trans. R.M.T. Hill (Oxford, Clarendon Press, 1962).

Guibert of Nogent, 'Gesta Dei per Francos', *RHC Oc.* IV, pp. 117–263.

'The Hebrew First Crusade chronicles', trans. in R. Chazan, *European Jewry and the First Crusade* (Berkeley, University of California Press, 1987).

Ibn al-Qalānisī, *The Damascus Chronicles of the Crusades*, ed. and trans. H.A.R. Gibb (London, Luzac and Co., 1932).

Matthew of Edessa, 'Chronicle', in *Armenia and the Crusades: Tenth to Twelfth Centuries*, trans. A.E. Dostourian (Lanham, Maryland, University Press of America, 1993).

Michael the Syrian, *Chronique de Michel le Syrien, Patriarche Jacobite d'Antioche (1166–99)*, ed. and trans. J.B. Chabot, 4 vols (Paris, Ernest Leroux, 1899–1924).

Orderic Vitalis, *The Ecclesiastical History*, ed. and trans. M. Chibnall, 6 vols (Oxford, Clarendon Press, 1969–80).

Peter Tudebode, *Historia de Hierosolymitano Itinere*, eds J.H. and L.L. Hill (Paris, Librairie Orientaliste Paul Geuthner, 1977). Trans. J.H. and L.L. Hill (Philadelphia, American Philosophical Society, 1974).

Raymond of Aguilers, *Liber*, eds J.H. and L.L. Hill (Paris, Librairie Orientaliste Paul Geuthner, 1969). Trans. J.H. and L.L. Hill with the title *Historia Francorum qui ceperunt Iherusalem* (Philadelphia, American Philosophical Society, 1968).

Ralph of Caen, 'Gesta Tancredi', *RHC Oc.* III, pp. 603–716.

Robert the Monk, 'Historia Iherosolimitana', *RHC Oc.* III, pp. 721–882.

William of Tyre, *Chronicon*, ed. R.B.C. Huygens, Corpus Christianorum, Continuatio Mediaevalis, 63/63A, 2 vols [continuous pagination] (Turnhout, Belgium, Brepols, 1986). Trans. as *A History of Deeds done beyond the Sea*, E.A. Babcock and A.C. Krey, 2 vols (New York, Columbia Records of Civilization Series No. 35, Columbia University Press, 1943).

Secondary works

Alexios I Komnenos, eds M. Mullett and D. Smythe, Belfast Texts and Translations 4.1 (Belfast, Belfast Byzantine Enterprises, 1996). An important collection of essays covering many aspects of Alexius's reign.

E.O. Blake and C. Morris, 'A hermit goes to war: Peter and the origins of the First Crusade', in *Monks, Hermits and the Ascetic Tradition*, ed. W.J. Shiels, Studies in Church History 22 (Oxford, Blackwell, 1985), pp. 79–109.

M.G. Bull, *Knightly Piety and the Lay Response to the First Crusade: The Limousin and Gascony c. 970–1130* (Oxford, Clarendon Press, 1993).

R. Chazan, *European Jewry and the First Crusade* (Berkeley, University of California Press, 1987).

P.J. Cole, *The Preaching of the Crusades to the Holy Land, 1095–1270* (Cambridge, Massachusetts, Medieval Academy of America, 1991).

G. Constable, 'Medieval charters as a source for the history of the crusades', in *Crusade and Settlement: Papers read at the First Conference of the Society for the Study of the Crusades and the Latin East and presented to R.C. Smail*, ed. P.W. Edbury (Cardiff, University College of Cardiff Press, 1985), pp. 73–89.

H.E.J. Cowdrey, 'Pope Urban II's preaching of the First Crusade', *History* 55 (1970), 177–88.

—, 'Pope Urban II and the idea of the crusade', *Studi Medievali* 37 (1995), 721–42.

V. Epp, *Fulcher von Chartres: Studien zur Geschichtsschreibung des Ersten Kreuzzugs*, (Düsseldorf, Droste, 1990).

J. France, *Victory in the East: A Military History of the First Crusade* (Cambridge, Cambridge University Press, 1994).

J.J. and L.L. Hill, *Raymond IV Count of Toulouse* (New York, Syracuse University Press, 1962).

C. Hillenbrand, *The Crusades: The Islamic Perspective* (Edinburgh, Edinburgh University Press, 1997).

R.-J. Lilie, *Byzantium and the Crusader States, 1096–1204*, trans. J.C. Morris and J.E. Ridings (Oxford, Clarendon Press, 1993).

C. Morris, 'The aims and spirituality of the First Crusade as seen through the eyes of Albert of Aix', *Reading Medieval Studies*, 16 (1990), 99–117.

—, 'The *Gesta Francorum* as narrative history', *Reading Medieval Studies*, 19 (1993), 55–71.

A.V. Murray, 'The origins of the Frankish nobility of the Kingdom of Jerusalem 1100–1118', *Mediterranean Historical Review*, 4 (1989), 281–95.

—, 'The army of Godfrey of Bouillon: the structure and dynamics of a contingent on the First Crusade', *Revue Belge de Philologie et d'Histoire*, 70 (1992), 301–29.

J.P. Phillips, *Defenders of the Holy Land: Relations between the Latin East and the West, 1119–87* (Oxford, Oxford University Press, 1996).

J.S.C. Riley-Smith, *The First Crusade and the Idea of Crusading* (London, Athlone Press, 1986).

—, *The Crusades: A Short History* (London, Athlone Press, 1987).

—, *The First Crusaders, 1095–1131* (Cambridge, Cambridge University Press, 1997).

— (ed.), *Atlas of the Crusades* (London, Times Books, 1991).

— (ed.), *The Oxford Illustrated History of the Crusades* (Oxford, Oxford University Press, 1995).

S. Runciman, *A History of the Crusades*, 3 vols (Cambridge, Cambridge University Press, 1951–4).

K.M. Setton and M.W. Baldwin (eds), *A History of the Crusades*, 6 vols (Madison, University of Wisconsin Press, 1969–89).

J. Shepard, 'Aspects of Byzantine attitudes and policy towards the West in the 10th and 11th centuries', in *Byzantium and the West c. 850–1200*, ed. J.D. Howard-Johnston (Amsterdam, Adolf M. Hakkert, 1988), pp. 67–118.

—, 'When Greek meets Greek: Alexius Comnenus and Bohemond in 1097–8', *Byzantine and Modern Greek Studies*, 12 (1988), 185–277.

—, '"Father" or "Scorpion"? Style and substance in Alexios's diplomacy', *Alexios I Komnenos*, M. Mullett and D. Smythe (eds), Belfast Texts and Translations 4.1 (Belfast, Belfast Byzantine Enterprises, 1996), pp. 68–132.

E. Sivan, *L'Islam et la Croisade* (Paris, Librairie d'Amérique et d'Orient, 1968).

R.C. Smail, *Crusading Warfare (1097–1193)* (Cambridge, Cambridge University Press, 1956).

K.B. Wolf, 'Crusade and narrative: Bohemond and the *Gesta Francorum*', *JMH* 17 (1991), 207–16.

Index

Note: 'n' after a page reference indicates the number of a note on that page.